Scale of map: one inch to 33.2 miles

N

©1958, JEPPESEN & CO. DENVER, COLO., U.S.A. REVISED 9-67

The Middle
Atlantic States

LIFE WORLD LIBRARY
LIFE NATURE LIBRARY
TIME READING PROGRAM
THE LIFE HISTORY OF THE UNITED STATES
LIFE SCIENCE LIBRARY
INTERNATIONAL BOOK SOCIETY
GREAT AGES OF MAN
TIME-LIFE LIBRARY OF ART
TIME-LIFE LIBRARY OF AMERICA
FOODS OF THE WORLD

TIME-LIFE Library of America

The Middle Atlantic States

Delaware Maryland Pennsylvania

By Ezra Bowen
and the Editors of
TIME-LIFE BOOKS

TIME-LIFE BOOKS, New York

The Author: Ezra Bowen is a staff writer for TIME-LIFE BOOKS. A native Pennsylvanian, he grew up in Philadelphia, where, according to a family tradition, a direct ancestor, one Joseph Drinker, went down to the Delaware riverbank one day to mark the arrival of a new proprietary governor named William Penn. Mr. Bowen began his writing career as a reporter for *Newsweek*. He later served for 10 years as a writer and senior editor for SPORTS ILLUSTRATED. He joined TIME-LIFE BOOKS as Director of Educational Research and Development in 1964, then resumed his writing in late 1965. Since then he has co-authored the LIFE Science Library's *Wheels* and written on many topics for various publications. He lives with his wife (a novelist who writes under the name Joan Williams) and two sons in Westport, Connecticut.

The Consulting Editor: Oscar Handlin, Charles Warren Professor of American History at Harvard University and director of the university's Charles Warren Center for Studies in American History, is one of America's foremost social historians. His work on U.S. immigrants, *The Uprooted*, won the Pulitzer Prize in 1952.

Middle Atlantic States Consultant: Alfred D. Chandler Jr., a native of Delaware and editor of the papers of Dwight Eisenhower, is Chairman of the Department of History at Johns Hopkins University.

The Cover: Colorful "hex" symbols, a popular Pennsylvania Dutch decoration, brighten the side of a barn in the heart of the Middle Atlantic States' richest farmland.

TIME-LIFE BOOKS

Editor
Maitland A. Edey
Executive Editor
Jerry Korn
Text Director
Martin Mann
Art Director
Sheldon Cotler
Chief of Research
Beatrice T. Dobie
Picture Editor
Robert G. Mason
Assistant Text Directors:
Harold C. Field, Ogden Tanner
Assistant Art Director:
Arnold C. Holeywell
Assistant Chief of Research:
Martha Turner

Publisher
Rhett Austell
General Manager: Joseph C. Hazen Jr.
Planning Director: John P. Sousa III
Circulation Director: Joan D. Manley
Marketing Director: Carter Smith
Business Manager: John D. McSweeney
Publishing Board: Nicholas Benton,
Louis Bronzo, James Wendell Forbes

TIME-LIFE Library of America

Series Editor: Oliver E. Allen
Editorial Staff for *The Middle Atlantic States:*
Assistant Editor: David S. Thomson
Picture Editor: Sheila Osmundsen
Designer: John Newcomb
Assistant Designer: Jean Lindsay
Staff Writers: Tony Chiu, Frank Kendig,
Victor Waldrop, Peter Wood
Chief Researcher: Clara E. Nicolai
Text Research: Sondra Albert, Evelyn Hauptman,
Clare Mead, Don Nelson, Victoria Winterer
Picture Research: Joan Gerard,
Rhea Finkelstein, Marcia Gillespie,
Gail Lowman, Margo Dryden
Art Assistant: Mervyn Clay

Editorial Production
Color Director: Robert L. Young
Assistant: James J. Cox
Copy Staff: Marian Gordon Goldman, Patricia Miller,
Florence Keith
Picture Department: Dolores A. Littles,
Marquita Jones
Traffic: Douglas B. Graham
Studio: Patricia Byrne, Jean Held

The text chapters of this book were written by Ezra Bowen, the picture essays by Mr. Bowen and by the editorial staff. Valuable aid was provided by these individuals and departments of Time Inc.: LIFE staff photographer Henry Groskinsky; the Chief of the LIFE Picture Library, Doris O'Neil; the Chief of the Bureau of Editorial Reference, Peter Draz; the Chief of the TIME-LIFE News Service, Richard M. Clurman; Correspondents Sherley Uhl (Pittsburgh), Daniel J. McKenna (Philadelphia), Timothy Tyler (Washington), James Bready (Baltimore); and FORTUNE Associate Editor A. James Reichley.

Contents

Introduction

"Too soon old and too late smart." That Pennsylvania Dutch saying described the states of the Middle Atlantic region precisely—until recently. Now, however, history and tradition are melding with a new age. The result is that my state, Pennsylvania, and Delaware and Maryland as well, have become interesting, exciting—yes, even fascinating—places to live and work.

All three states have long histories. Settled early, they were among the first to ratify the Constitution and help form the republic. Delaware can claim to be "The First State" and Pennsylvania the second, while Maryland came in not long after. Capitalizing on their early births and their great natural resources, they long were counted among the nation's leaders in wealth and influence. But early prosperity gave way, especially in Pennsylvania and Maryland, and especially in the earlier decades of this century, to decay and depression. "Too late smart" almost became their epitaph—but not quite. Now old Maryland has been jolted into action by burgeoning Washington suburbs and a new zing in Baltimore. Delaware is happy with Du Pont affluence, although it suddenly realizes it needs diversification. And Pennsylvania is rapidly emerging from the coal-rail-and-steel days to capitalize on other assets: great natural beauty, crossroads geography, astonishing variety and a people all the stronger for the fact that they are descended from about as many diverse backgrounds as Heinz (of Pittsburgh) has "varieties."

The term "crossroads geography" includes the four great river systems that cover Pennsylvania, Delaware and Maryland and remain of vital importance even in these days of rail and truck transportation. The Allegheny and the Monongahela, which join to form the Ohio at the "Golden Triangle" in Pittsburgh, moved the traffic of the 19th Century coal-and-steel empire and now serve a more diversified economy. The Delaware helps nourish Philadelphia and Wilmington. The Susquehanna not only serves all of central Pennsylvania—half the Commonwealth—but, joined by its bay, the Chesapeake, is the essence of Baltimore and eastern Maryland. And the Potomac helps invigorate western Maryland.

Then there is the marvelous and varied scenery. On a fresh sapphire day in the spring of the Presidential year of 1964 a cynical Washington newspaper reporter visited our home among the mountains of northeastern Pennsylvania. He walked through the house, out onto the terrace, eyed the panorama for a few minutes, then sighed and said, "Now I know why you don't want to run for President!" The Laurel Highlands and blue ridges of western Maryland and both central and northern Pennsylvania make for such allowances. "The wilds of Pennsylvania," my sister calls them, these magnificently forested mountains with spectacular views. And wild they are with deer and some of the most varied hunting that can be found anywhere in the United States.

Then, most important of all, there are the people. The region is populated by courageous citizens of more than 40 national origins who, in proportion to their numbers, have sent more than their share of sons to fight America's wars; people who even now, after thousands of their friends and members of their families have been forced to leave to find work elsewhere, are proving their strength of character in building a new life for themselves and their area. New industry, new highways, new schools and colleges, excellent recreation and conservation facilities—all of these have resulted from one of the nation's most successful "bootstrap"—or self-help—operations. Some credit belongs to the leadership, but most of it to a stouthearted people, firmly rooted, with strong ties to family and church.

The region got its start and then grew wealthy through the efforts of men who were remarkable in their ways, too. William Penn, surely the greatest of the colonial proprietors, was one of those rare men of history who, though way ahead of their time, have succeeded in their own eras. Penn's "Holy Experiment" outshone them all. Peace, tolerance and understanding were not just principles; they were practiced by Penn's Quakers. And the colony flourished, as it deserved to do. Philadelphia was the largest city in the 13 colonies and America's commercial and cultural center.

It was here that the United States was founded, both the Declaration of Independence and the Constitution being written and signed (not without the help of sage Ben Franklin) in Philadelphia. Gouverneur and Robert Morris helped, too; the latter almost singlehandedly guided the financing of the Revolution and the early republic. Then came America's industrial era. Iron, coal, steel, railroads and shipping took over—and in no place more so than in the Middle Atlantic States. Here a race of kings was bred: kings of business, kings of money and finance, kings of politics and government. This was the time of Carnegie, Frick and Schwab, of ornate Victorian and Edwardian architecture, of glorious mansions with mansard roofs and of powerful mills with spewing smokestacks. But the region paid a terrible price in human suffering for its often heedless and headlong progress. Violence came with the Homestead strike and the repeated outbreaks in the coal fields. "Whatsoever a man soweth, that shall he also reap," the Bible says, and the region found itself gathering a bitter harvest of management-labor disruption, stagnation and finally deep depression.

It was not this bad everywhere, of course. There were the affluent areas—the fox-and-hounds country of Maryland and the well-to-do parts of that state's Eastern Shore ruled by its squirearchy; the dogwooded suburbs of Philadelphia, Baltimore and Pittsburgh, where the wealthy lived in large numbers and lived surrounded by beauty. Then there were the thrifty, hard-working Pennsylvania Dutch in the Lancaster-Reading-Allentown triangle, many sticking faithfully to the "plain life" of their ancestors and thriving at it. Tiny Delaware had its fabulously successful Du Pont Company plus a comfortable Southern tinge that mellowed the fast pace of business.

Much of the region, however, was sinking into torpor and poverty—until this decade. But now change has come, and lots of it, and mostly for the good. "Power politics" are fast disappearing. The improvement in the state constitutions has been outstanding, notably in Maryland and Pennsylvania. The educational level is rising. There has been

a commendable growth in research facilities, and the region possesses more good small private colleges than any other part of the nation. The Ph.D.s so desperately needed by the "new businesses" that are springing up are being produced.

Perhaps the most dramatic change has been in the cities. "Renaissance" is the word, notably in central Philadelphia and in Pittsburgh's Golden Triangle. "I went to Philadelphia on Saturday night and it was closed" is still true to a degree, but the city is far more exciting than it once was, and it is culturally alive. The symphony has long been tops; the ballet, the museums and the universities are all making great strides forward. Pittsburgh, led by the extraordinary Mellons, has also made enormous advances, renewing itself, bringing in new businesses and revitalizing its old ones. Even the sports organizations of our region seem to have caught the fever, taking on more glamorous dimensions with the Eagles, the Colts, the Steelers, "Wilt the Stilt" Chamberlain's 76ers, the Orioles and the Pirates. Even the Phillies are doing better.

Overshadowed in business and finance by New York, and outglamored by it as well, this is a good place to *live*—more calmly and more slowly perhaps but in a new era of progress and opportunity. Here you can ski in the Poconos, fish in good streams, golf everywhere or hunt through vast miles of gorgeous country. You can eat oysters and terrapin, Philadelphia scrapple, shoofly or deep-dish huckleberry pie.

No, it isn't perfect. Though the pockets of despair in the coal and steel valleys are being erased, though a renaissance has come, and the living is good, and, as one national magazine notes, we enjoy "the most consistently beautiful part of the nation," still we have not solved "the urban problem." Far from it. Pittsburgh and Baltimore have been singularly free from major riots, so far, and are making progress. Philadelphia, which has experienced open violence, is trying new programs. But for far too many people, unfortunate conditions persist—lack of opportunity especially in education, employment and housing.

Ezra Bowen knows the area well and proves it in his text. His family is steeped in its traditions and has been a leader in researching and describing them. The TIME-LIFE Library of America is a welcome survey of modern America, more welcome perhaps in the Middle Atlantic States than elsewhere because these states deserve more attention than they get.

—WILLIAM W. SCRANTON
Former Governor of Pennsylvania

1

To Lead
the Nation

On a bleak night in the winter of 1946 Victor Diehm, radio-station manager and Chamber of Commerce president of Hazleton, Pennsylvania, settled his 200 pounds into a seat on a homebound railroad car and stared out at the monstrous rows of blast furnaces, rolling mills, coke ovens and coal breakers that formed the backbone of the mightiest industrial complex on earth. Aliquippa, Homestead, Pittsburgh, Latrobe, Duquesne, Johnstown—the soot-blackened stations of western Pennsylvania slid by, each depot built close beside a steel mill that alone could produce more of the metal than most countries in the world. But even at this late hour of the night and in this triumphal postwar year for U.S. industrial power, Diehm could see too many signs of a sickness that was spreading outward from the Pennsylvania ravines to infect the body and blood of the whole Middle Atlantic region. Through the gritty rain of coal dust and fly ash that swept past the window, he made out, here and there, the stark silhouette of an open-hearth furnace whose fires had grown cold in some bitter

labor dispute, dirty clumps of newly deserted houses in the mining settlements, empty freight cars beneath the unmoving machinery of shutdown coal breakers. And there was little comfort in a sudden comment from a cohort in the opposite seat: "All right, you fat idiot," said the manager of a Hazleton hotel, "you said we could do it, you do it!"

Specifically, Victor Diehm was being challenged to find a fast half a million dollars, a sum he had just promised an Ohio firm to finance construction of an auto-parts plant with as many as 2,400 new jobs for the worn-out mining town of Hazleton. However, to raise that much money around Hazleton, or in scores of rusted, down-at-the-heels communities—not only in Pennsylvania but in other parts of the region, too—was like trying to pull a quart of blood from a very sick man. More broadly, Victor Diehm, like a handful of other perceptive, deeply worried people in Delaware, Maryland and Pennsylvania, was trying to find out what was ailing the whole Middle Atlantic region, and to do something—anything—to put it right. For a drastic slump had taken hold of the region's economy, and its causes went far deeper than the normal strains of a postwar readjustment. Something was critically wrong in these three states, not only in the mining communities and manufacturing cities,

Buildings in Philadelphia's Penn Center, a rebuilt area symbolic of the region's reawakening, frame the ornate 19th Century City Hall. Atop the old tower is a statue of William Penn, while in the foreground is a sculpture by Seymour Lipton, on loan to the city.

9

but in the outlying farm counties as well. And by all the signs, before things got better they were going to be much worse.

That year, thousands of GIs came home to Hazleton and the other towns in the anthracite fields of northeastern Pennsylvania—Scranton, Wilkes-Barre, Shenandoah, Mauch Chunk. Here men had made their living for more than a century on the veins of hard coal crosshatching the deep earth beneath the city streets. But when the veterans got home they found there was little work in the mines any more. The railroads were changing from coal-fired steam engines to diesels, homeowners switching from coal heat to gas and oil. No one was buying anthracite any longer. By and large, they never would; and until men like Victor Diehm showed these towns new ways to make a living, the people would be in deep trouble.

The same year, other war veterans came back to the farmland that stretches from the Delaware River near Easton, Pennsylvania, across to the Susquehanna basin and down into the tidewater flats of Maryland and Delaware. In some sections, notably southeastern Pennsylvania, the living was still good, thanks to the closehanded industry of the Pennsylvania Dutch farmers who worked the land. But in too many other places the countryside had a worn-out look, and the old ways suddenly seemed like very tired ways.

Along the shores of Chesapeake Bay, for example, at a spot like Cambridge, Maryland, the young soldiers saw with fresh eyes the tumble-down oyster- and crab-packing plants and the weathered truck farms where a man might live out his life on $1,600 a year—average for the county. In town, there was nothing to do, no good college nearby for an ex-soldier on the GI Bill, no decent school, either, for a baby born of a wartime marriage and almost ready now to enter first grade. For the next 10, 15 or even 20 years, the Middle Atlantic's many Cambridges would stay this way, before time and the higher aspirations of the young people and of people like Victor Diehm took hold to give these conservative communities a sharp push into the mainstream of the 20th Century.

In Pittsburgh Richard King Mellon came home with his wife, Constance, to resume command of the family's three-billion-dollar financial-industrial domain of oil, aluminum, coal, banking concerns and other interests. The old town should have looked good to them; after all, they owned a fair piece of it. But Constance Mellon, peering into an industrial smog so thick that from the William Penn Hotel she could not even see the lights of the

Mellon National Bank half a block away, is reputed to have said, "I had almost forgotten how bad it is." In the Pittsburgh of 1946, 5,600 tons of soot fell each month on the city. Almost every year the Allegheny and Monongahela Rivers, which join to form the Ohio at the city's western tip, rose into flood, drowning the downtown streets, drowning people, drowning, too, some of Pittsburgh's hope. For many years Pittsburgh had been losing more and more of its share of the nation's business to mill towns set closer to the lucrative young markets of the Midwest, California and Texas. And though Pittsburgh still turned out some 20 per cent of America's steel, nevertheless it was a bad place to look for work, since thousands of laborers per year would be laid off as machines took the place of men in the mills and in the surrounding bituminous mines that turned out coking coal for the blast furnaces.

"You have a lot of ideas about how to make things better," said Mrs. Mellon that night. And indeed Mellon had begun to search, even before the war, for ways to reshape the life of the grimy, soot-ridden city.

"Will [those things] ever get done?" asked Mrs. Mellon.

"They *must* get done," said Richard King Mellon; and in Pittsburgh, whenever a Mellon says "must," the city has been wont to move.

Finally, too, a couple of Philadelphia lawyers named Richardson Dilworth and Joseph S. Clark Jr. came back home from the Pacific to the mansions of Philadelphia and its suburbs—Chestnut Hill and the lush towns along the Main Line of the Pennsylvania Railroad. On the surface everything here still looked fine, just as it had for 100 years, and just as it does today. Along the wooded byways of Bryn Mawr, Haverford and Paoli, cupolaed gate-houses guarded the sprawling estates, whose great halls had been built many years ago on shipping profits, banking profits, petroleum, textiles, and, of course, railroads, coal and steel. This was, and is, a land of old money.

The heirs to these old fortunes—here and around Baltimore, Wilmington and Pittsburgh, too—used them to create enclaves of privilege within which the social and economic distress of the region was rarely permitted to penetrate. Nor was this mercantile-industrial nobility very interested in searching out any kinds of trouble; rather, they kept to themselves and invested their time and money in the pursuit of their own private interests.

On the Main Line, particularly, good living was cherished—and refined—to a high degree. Here the wherewithal of original capital was lovingly nurtured (in Philadelphia it is bad form to take a flier) and rarely displayed with flash—a Bentley, perhaps, for local shopping, or better yet, a four-year-old Chevrolet, but never a cream-colored Cadillac. The land had always been tended with equal care, producing an almost smothering richness of green growth, boxwood and oak and maple and forsythia, in spring great explosions of purple rhododendron, and everywhere the white and pink mottlings of dogwood. Beside the winding suburban roads, yellow highway signs said HORSE CROSSING, to warn a motorist that the gentry of the Radnor Hunt might be cantering across.

About four in the afternoon, handsome, bony, straight-eyed ladies in quiet tweeds and sensible shoes were out walking the quieter lanes, swiping with their briarwood canes at an occasional mannerless dog, then turning through an iron arch and up a gravel way to settle on a terrace for tea. And in the evening, in town, on the polished floors of the Hotel Barclay and the Bellevue-Stratford, gawky young Rushes and McKeans, names written on the Declaration of Independence at Carpenter's Hall a dozen blocks to the east, danced at coming-out parties with golden princesses named Toland and Pew. Together they spoke cheerfully and endlessly the same cheerful, endless nothings that their mothers and fathers once spoke in these rooms decades before.

But in the lean days of the late 1940s Dick Dilworth and Joe Clark and a small platoon of other rebels within the Establishment were neither talking nonsense nor seeing only lush greenery within the islands of privilege. Their eyes, like those of the other young veterans, had been washed clear in four years of war. And they saw, beneath the prosperity, the fundamental sickness of the region's ancient overcommitment to an economy of big industry, weighted too heavily by steel and coal and rails. They saw the crumbling mill towns of Manyunk and Conshohocken, where laid-off workers could stand in the dirty streets and look—across a valley or up toward a bluff—at the big estates of the industrial barons whose fortunes had come out of those very mills. They saw and smelled the stinking Schuylkill River, so full of silt that most marine life had long since died and so sewage-fouled as it entered the center of Philadelphia that in summer motorists had to roll up the windows of their cars before driving across its bridges. Downtown they saw the impossibly narrow brick and cobblestone streets trying to carry the millrace of modern automobile traffic and saw, too, the bloated corpus of a

political machine that had fed off both the city and the state for 80 years. And they heard the bankers and the Philadelphia lawyers talking the same stodgy, narrow nothings that their fathers had spoken decades before.

They saw it, and they heard it, and—as did a number of other farsighted people in other parts of the region—they began to move. Clark and Dilworth themselves, joining hands to run for office against the political machine, went out onto street corners to shout for a brand-new charter to govern the city; before they were through they had been elected mayor and district attorney, and they and their allies found themselves shouting for a whole new city, to be rebuilt from the Delaware on the east all the way across to a sparkling, reclaimed Schuylkill. The dreary downtown, which had been the despair of anyone who came near it, has since bloomed into an urban model, not just for the region, but for the entire world. Today, city planners from as many as a dozen foreign countries have come in a single month to the office of Edmund Bacon, longtime Executive Director of Philadelphia's Planning Commission, to look out at the new Penn Center with its sunken gardens and high-rise offices where a jungle of rail-passenger tracks used to split the city in two; to see the meticulous restoration of Philadelphia's historic eastern section from Independence Hall all the way down to Penn's Landing on the Delaware; and to study the design for the transportation-shipping complex known as Market East, in which glass-enclosed pedestrian malls are subtly woven together with bus depots, subways, commuter rail lines, stores, hotels and offices, all in one immense, air-conditioned structure.

Two hundred and ninety miles away, Richard K. Mellon, no shouter, started moving in his own quiet, potent way. At the war's end, Mellon had pulled together the czars of Pittsburgh's crumbling industrial empire into a citizens' action group called the Allegheny Conference, which laid down a series of bold plans to revive the town. These plans were quickly taken up by tough, hard-eyed David Leo Lawrence, for many years the most powerful political figure in Pennsylvania and, in 1946, Pittsburgh's mayor. Lawrence as a Democratic politician had no more desire to preside over the death of his city than did Mellon's Republican business allies. And so the two men formed a working partnership that in many ways saved Pittsburgh as a major urban center.

Thanks to this partnership and the reform zeal of the Allegheny Conference, today little more than random puffs of legally clean smoke drift over a fresh-scrubbed city. At the point of land where the rivers join, the floodwaters have been permanently checked by an upstream system of dams. Where the stinking slums once bred 5,730 cases of typhoid in a single year and one of three babies born to impoverished millworkers died before the age of five, the city now has half a billion dollars' worth of gleaming new office buildings, grassy walkways, hotels and plazas.

As the two great cities at either end of the Middle Atlantic region emerged from the rust and sludge of the 19th Century, a flood tide of fresh spirit began to rise through all three states and form into currents of renewed achievement that have started to sweep away the worst of the region's industrial flotsam. Up in the coal country Victor Diehm did succeed in getting his half a million, some of it through such bareknuckle, coal-country methods as issuing subpoenas for reluctant contributors to the town's new-industry fund and calling out the strike-hardened wives of the unemployed coal miners to throw picket lines around stores whose owners would not contribute. In the years since 1950, putting local money together with state matching funds from the Pennsylvania Industrial Development Authority, Diehm's town of Hazleton has brought in 47 new plants with 5,510 jobs. Other towns have done the same: Scranton, where mining jobs had plummeted from 35,000 before World War II to less than 300 in 1967, put some 40,000 people back to work in community-financed light industry. Wilkes-Barre created new jobs for 16,400. And in the steel and soft-coal towns around Pittsburgh, electronics and chemical plants are beginning to sprout among the obsolescent mills, bringing total state employment in new industry up to 150,000 at the end of 1966.

In a broad effort to insure its future, Pennsylvania has also poured $3.4 billion into a highway program (vital for providing the flexible truck service the new industries require) and has more than doubled the investment in its lagging public-education institutions—the wellspring of talent for a continuing business resurgence.

Maryland is also moving with the renaissance. On the Eastern Shore, educational institutions such as Salisbury State and Chesapeake Community College have pooled resources with local businessmen to find ways both to wake up the economy and to improve the procedures of town and state government. Baltimore, too, has begun to recast its rather stodgy image, in a project less spectacular than those in Pennsylvania but perhaps more difficult to achieve. For this fence-straddling city, still half

Rebel and half Yankee from its days as a Civil War border town, has a ruling class of moss-grown aristocrats and contented branch-plant managers who do not leap at fresh notions, but much prefer to sip a bourbon while looking down at the weathered fences at the Maryland Hunt, to motor quietly to a Chesapeake duckblind, or at best to give a lusty cheer for Johnny Unitas, the cavalier quarterback of Baltimore's beloved pro football team, the Colts. "One thing Baltimore never wants to be called is 'hep,'" says a solidified citizen, fending off a faint danger.

Nevertheless, since 1961 the center of Baltimore has been largely rebuilt, and a member of the city's tight little group of new reformers says boldly, "We're dragging this city, kicking and screaming, into the Twentieth Century." Indeed he is, joined each month by more defectors from the unrocking boat of the old-line families.

The battle is by no means ended. In fact, it has only half begun. But at least the twin enemies of outmoded industry and old-line thinking have been fought to a standstill at certain critical points. Even in politics, renewal has become an important fact of life. At the Statehouses in Annapolis (Maryland), Dover (Delaware) and Harrisburg, and at the city halls of the bigger cities, the traditional machine bosses and a fair number of the more rascally officeholders have long since been turned out (Pennsylvania, particularly, with 50,000 patronage jobs, had a whole houseful of rascals). During June of 1967, Maryland voted to recast its weedy old constitution. And in Pennsylvania, after six false starts dating back to 1891, the voters finally put through a mandate for revision of their own constitution, a preposterous anachronism that had frustrated coherent government for the 90-odd years of its unnatural life. So bullish have the people become about the region-wide renaissance that when Raymond Shafer began running for the governor's seat at Harrisburg in 1966, he discarded the "get things moving again" slogan of his very able predecessor, William Scranton, and put forth an even bolder notion that people hereabout had not heard for many years: "To lead the nation" was his rallying cry, and he repeated it over and over again.

To lead the nation. How long had it been since the people of these three states had truly led the nation? Too long. Yet here the nation itself had been born. Even before that, and at many times since, the Middle Atlantic States had led the country and the world, too, in all manner of critical endeavor, ranging from colonial trade to industrial research. This was the region that, historically, had played the pivotal role in changing the U.S. from a slow-moving agrarian society to a worldwide industrial power. It was, in fact, Pennsylvania iron—cannon and rails—that powered the Northern victory over the South in the Civil War; two out of three tons of Union metal were forged here for a conflict that turned at a Pennsylvania town called Gettysburg. Soon after, Pennsylvania-built locomotives rolling on Pittsburgh steel track sped the nation's pell-mell expansion to the Pacific Coast.

In the course of this victory and the booming progress that ensued, the region prospered so mightily that "Pittsburgh millionaire" became a label for any faceless man who made a million dollars overnight; and Philadelphia's Main Line became synonymous with the best of the Good Life, as did, at a later date, Maryland's lush Eastern Shore and Delaware's Greenville. Furthermore, from the early 18th Century right up to the dark days that began here in the mid-1920s, it had been relatively easy for a citizen—particularly a white Anglo-Saxon Protestant citizen of the caste that quickly grabbed the reins in the region—to carve a comfortable niche for himself in these three states. Because wherever a man put down his feet, and almost anywhere he turned, he could find the natural means for prosperity right at hand—or just over the next ridge.

From the beginning of colonial settlement, the land itself was bursting with riches, of soil, of timber, of minerals and—perhaps most important—of deep natural waterways. The whole region is nurtured by four great river systems, three east-flowing, the Susquehanna, the Delaware and the Potomac, and the other west, the Ohio. Along the east-flowing rivers the nation grew and harvested the first fruits of its colonial birth—grain, commerce and the American government itself. Some Indians of the east-central sector named the longest of these rivers the Tree of Life (Susquehanna). Small wonder. Its thousand branches drain a basin so fertile ("Fast fat earth," wrote William Penn, "like our best vales in England") that it quickly became the prime food source for the whole nation. And even today, when farming elsewhere is typically a mass-produced 1,000-acre proposition, Lancaster County, on the lower section of the river, with an average farm size of only 110 acres, is one of the most prosperous agricultural counties in America. York County, right across the river, is so rich and happy among its ordered green plots that in 1966 it dispatched a delegation to Harrisburg to ask the governor *not* to send any more new industry to York since everyone was working and more plants would merely create labor problems.

By a happy accident of ancient geology, the easterly rivers scoured out deep, protected estuaries, Delaware Bay and the Chesapeake, where ocean-going vessels could fetch goods to and from world markets. Between 1800 and 1860 these waters became the womb of the graceful Baltimore clippers, which cleared the Virginia Capes with wheat and flour for the West Indies trade, and of the work-horse Liverpool packets, outbound from Philadelphia under God-fearing skippers like Sandwith Drinker, who bade his crew and passengers gather on the oaken deck every Sunday to pray for deliverance from their sins while the waters splashed over the scuppers and swirled around the hull of the ship. Today the packets are gone, but the bustle of international trade continues, concentrated around the imports and exports of heavy industry. Along the banks of the Delaware, 800-foot ore boats stand into the docks of the sprawling Fairless steelworks—almost as impressive as Baltimore's huge Sparrows Point complex on the Chesapeake—where they unload the red iron ore while other freighters take out thousands of tons of raw steel.

Not far from these steel plants, 750-foot tankers deliver Venezuelan and Middle Eastern crude oil into a redolent forest of cracking plants and storage tanks. Painted with the company seals of Sun, Gulf, American and Atlantic Richfield, these oil refineries have given parts of the region a fair measure of prosperity—though they have given it, too, an occasional share of economic dismay.

By another happy physiographic circumstance, the head of tidewater here reaches into the coastal Fall Zone, where the rivers make their last plunge down a row of steep hills to the ocean. Thus, seagoing ships could sail right into the heart of the colonial mill villages, which drew their energy from the last falls of the tumbling streams. Virtually every major town here—Trenton, Philadelphia, Wilmington, Baltimore and on south—built much of its basic economy around a cluster of mills. Today, in the cleft of Philadelphia's Wissahickon Creek, the ruined foundations of a few old mills remain.

In fact, down in Delaware, along the Brandywine, there not only remains but flourishes what may well be the least-ruined mill operation in all the world: here in 1802 Eleuthère-Irénée du Pont put up a powderworks that prompted his father, Pierre-Samuel, to write to a friend that the gunpowder made there would hopefully "not be used for war but for those deeds which prevent war. . . ."

A decade after this peacefully paternal comment, the company was prosperously filling U.S. government orders for more than 750,000 pounds of black powder to shoot at the British in the War of 1812. A hundred years later, from 1914 to 1918, four of every 10 shells fired by all the Allied armies were propelled toward the Central Powers by Du Pont smokeless powder. Even before the war's end the company farsightedly began to diversify out of the explosives business into a broad new venture in chemical products for the civilian market.

But the heirs of Pierre-Samuel du Pont had not begun their reformation soon enough to avoid being branded as "merchants of death" by a Senate investigating committee. And, smarting under the grim label, the Du Pont Company bent every sinew to create a fresh image of a firm dedicated to discovering "Better Things for Better Living . . . Through Chemistry." The company was so successful in re-creating itself that both Du Pont and large segments of the home state of Delaware were able to avoid the region's postwar economic collapse. By the mid-1960s Du Pont employees comprised about 10 per cent of the whole state of Delaware, and they made some 1,200 diverse Better Things, from nylon to influenza pills. The company's annual sales of two and a half to three billion dollars led those of all other chemical firms. And at the end of each money-making day the Du Pont scientists and technicians went home to well-planned, well-scrubbed suburbs like Westover Hills and Wawassett Park, which are, by many standards, splendid examples of Better Living.

While the easterly rivers bred a culture of farming and commerce, something else was beginning to happen along the western streams. The Allegheny and the Monongahela, converging at Pittsburgh to form the Ohio, became arteries for pumping people and products into the booming heartland of the old Northwest Territory. Pittsburgh was the natural jumping-off point to these open territories. And here the first emigrants trundled their wagons onto flatboats, festooned with plows and pots and other iron goods made in the Pittsburgh area. For even in that early day, Pittsburgh and its environs had begun to forge metal from the local iron deposits with such gusto that a visitor described the town as "being a great manufacturing place and kept in so much smoke and dust, as to effect the skin of the inhabitants."

Ever since those first years as supplier and departure point for the westward migration, it has been the reflex of Pittsburgh to keep one eye cocked to the West, on the markets beyond the Ohio border. It was a reflex doubly easy to develop. For Pittsburgh was separated—almost blocked off— from the mother cities of the East by the millions

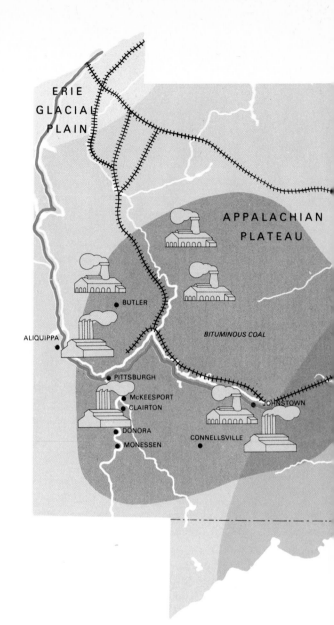

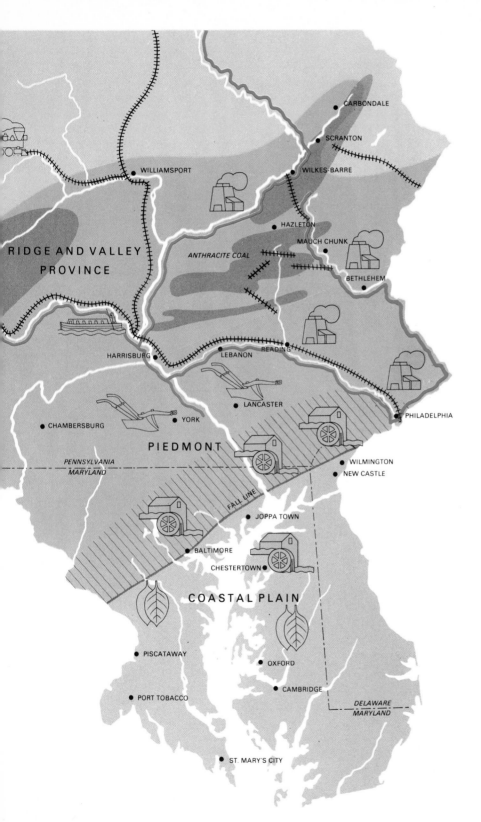

CARBONDALE

SCRANTON

WILLIAMSPORT

WILKES-BARRE

HAZLETON

RIDGE AND VALLEY
PROVINCE

MAUCH CHUNK

ANTHRACITE COAL

BETHLEHEM

HARRISBURG

LEBANON

READING

CHAMBERSBURG

YORK

LANCASTER

PHILADELPHIA

PIEDMONT

WILMINGTON

PENNSYLVANIA
MARYLAND

NEW CASTLE

FALL LINE

JOPPA TOWN

BALTIMORE

CHESTERTOWN

COASTAL PLAIN

PISCATAWAY

OXFORD

CAMBRIDGE

DELAWARE
MARYLAND

PORT TOBACCO

ST. MARY'S CITY

Patterns of the region's growth

The principal geographic divisions of the Middle Atlantic States, and the industries that were historically significant in each area's growth, are illustrated on this map. Until about 1785 the major development was along the low, flat Coastal Plain, where the first settlers had landed. There the people found the soil ideal for growing tobacco, which they shipped from nearby tidewater ports to Europe and to other colonial cities. Long before 1785, however, people had begun to move into the Piedmont, a rich farming area of rolling hills that extends westward to the Blue Ridge Mountains. The Piedmont was separated from the Coastal Plain by the Fall Zone *(crosshatched area)*, where waterfalls and rapids marked the inland limit of river navigability. There mills were built, which used the water power of the falls to grind the grains produced by Piedmont farms. This led to the rapid expansion of shipping and milling centers such as Baltimore, Wilmington and Philadelphia, which were ideal ports, being close to inland markets yet easily accessible to the ocean. This development was overlapped by the boom in the Ridge and Valley Province that lasted a full century, from about 1730 to 1830. In the eastern part of this area, deposits of anthracite coal *(shaded areas in east)* provided fuel for the smelters of early iron furnaces in the Lehigh and Schuylkill Valleys; here some of the cannon used by George Washington's army were forged. Toward the end of the Ridge and Valley Province's century of growth, a number of canals were dug, which, along with the region's rivers, provided a network of inland waterways that facilitated the flow of goods between the growing West and the bustling towns and ports of the East. The canals were quickly supplanted by railroads, however, first by short lines that were built to carry coal from the mines to the smelters and to nearby rivers and canals, then by a vast rail network that came to cover the state. This railroad building speeded the development of the Appalachian Plateau, which by the 1850s had begun to mine intensively its enormous deposits of bituminous coal *(shaded western areas)* and to build ironmaking mills. By the time of the Civil War it had supplanted the Ridge and Valley Province as the nation's largest coal- and iron-producing area. As the mills grew in the Pittsburgh area—the greatest expansion occurred between 1860 and 1910—they increasingly looked to the Great Lakes for their iron ore and limestone. This ensured the extension of the transportation network across the Erie Glacial Plain, which takes in the northwestern tip of Pennsylvania.

and millions of timbered acres of the Middle Atlantic hinterland. Here, between the Ohio headwaters and the Eastern farmland, the tall Appalachian hills and ridges march across the land for hundreds of miles, the ridge crests aligned in such long, even rows that the first pioneers, despairing of the steep sameness, called them the "Endless Mountains," and often settled right there to live rather than struggle farther across them. Today this folded ridgeland remains a major barrier. Fully 50 per cent of Pennsylvania is still in forest, a land where black bears roam in astonishing numbers (Richardson Dilworth recently infuriated everyone in the northern part of the state by saying, of its wooded half, "Nobody lives up there but bears"), and where each fall hunters kill the awesome total of 100,000 white-tailed deer. Only one major east-west road, the venerable Pennsylvania Turnpike, cuts through the ridges, though one more superhighway went into construction in the 1960s.

"We aren't really part of Pennsylvania," says a Pittsburgh business executive. "We're part of the Cleveland-Youngstown complex, the new American Ruhr which we're building out here. These present political divisions don't make sense. If I were running things I'd do like Napoleon did with France and redivide things into logical Departments." Pittsburgh people always talk this way.

This executive was talking some truth. But it is equally true that below the soil of William Penn's "fast fat earth," under the very streets of Pittsburgh and the other ravine towns east to the Delaware, lie the ravaged remains of the mineral resources that tied together the whole Middle Atlantic region in a bond of common industry almost 150 years ago, even before the Pennsylvania and Baltimore and Ohio Railroads tied it together in fact by linking Baltimore and Philadelphia to the Pittsburgh area in the decade just before the Civil War.

These minerals, iron and coal, and the heavy steel instruments fabricated from them, were the central facts of life for the region from 1860 right through World War II and beyond. The cities of the Middle Atlantic States existed on a diet of coal and iron. In fact, the economy of the whole region was overcommitted to these industries. A superb network of railroads had been laid down to serve them; at one point not long before the Civil War there were more miles of track in Pennsylvania than in any other state. Before 1920 the railroad employed 19,000 men in just one of its maintenance yards, at Altoona in central Pennsylvania. And as late as the 1930s the Pennsy alone carried 20 per cent of all American land-passenger traffic.

Today, in some parts of the region, perhaps half the people are third- or fourth-generation descendants of immigrants—Slavs, Irish and Italians —who came here specifically to work on the railroads or in the mines or mills. These immigrants literally lived coal and steel, even though for most of them that living was frequently very bad. The early arrivals were hustled onto westbound trains by dockside flesh peddlers who delivered them to the industrial barons at fees of up to $1,500 a head. On the job, they worked 12 and 14 hours a day often for six and seven days a week, lived in squalid company houses in grim company towns and made one or two dollars a day, with most of it going back —with interest—to the company store. Their children cut their teeth on coal and steel, working as slate pickers on the mine dumps or as sweepers in the mills at 25 cents a day. And when the people tried to protest these wretched exploitations, the answer frequently came back in the form of bullets. As late as 1928 Richard Mellon, the elder, was asked during a U.S. Senate investigation why so many of the coal-mine police carried machine guns. "Oh," said the father of Pittsburgh's current civic leader, "it is necessary. You cannot run [the mines] without them."

In a series of often bloody labor wars that lasted right into the 1940s, the workers showed that the mines, mills and railroads not only could but would be run without either guns or starvation wages. These wars, fought first by the United Mine Workers, then by the United Steelworkers and finally by the consolidated power of the Congress of Industrial Organizations (the CIO), were much more than local battles between labor and management. They were the violent manifestations of a basic social protest by industrial workers, and particularly by immigrant workers, a protest as vital and bitter as the Negro upheaval today. They spoke to such fundamental questions as equal opportunity in a society that made its money from a worker's muscle; equal education for the worker's children; and perhaps most of all, to the question of a place in the sun, where nobody called an immigrant a bohunk, or treated him like one.

In time, the labor wars were won. But even after some of the underlying social questions were resolved at the bargaining tables and, ultimately, by labor's new strength at the voting booth, the coal-and-iron mentality continued to permeate the thinking and, in some cases, the living habits of the people. For a miner might now have decent wages and hours, but he was still trapped by his circumstances, living where he had always lived and caught in the long, dismal downslide of the region's heavy-industry economy.

Just outside Hazleton, for example, there stands the village of Audenried, with its dirty weather-board houses still clustered forlornly around a rusty string of Lehigh Valley and Pennsylvania railroad cars that carry a trickle of anthracite from the Honeybrook Mines. Audenried has looked like this since the early 1860s, when the Molly Maguires, a group of labor vigilantes, killed their first company man here and left a hardfisted mine operator bleeding to death in his own front parlor.

A half-hour's drive away, in a cleft between two green ridges, lies the disaster area of Shenandoah, slowly expiring in a ghastly swale of strip mining. From McAdoo, 15 miles northeast of Shenandoah, to Mount Carmel, 15 miles to the west, there is nothing but ruined earth, yawning pits filled with foul green water, and mountains of coal waste, many of them burning with a nauseating sulfur stench that drifts across the town. The valley here is too narrow and ruined to seem attractive to new industrial complexes—which probably could not be put up here anyway, since the deep mines beneath the streets keep caving in.

In Shenandoah itself, the sidewalks are cracking and wavering crazily, the houses tipping out of plumb, tipping until the doors will not open and the owners have to leave. Half the streets are alleys wide enough for only one car, lined with houses, some abandoned, some still occupied by heavy-set, old Slavic women with weathered faces, sitting in pairs on the outside stairs to talk. On the main street old men of 60 and 70 rest on benches, hard-core unemployables with miner's asthma and perhaps a driblet of social security. Past them walks a slow procession of healthy, astonishingly pretty Polish-American girls with good strong bodies, some of them with young babies. And around the vacant lots there are scurrying clots of towheaded boys, quiet, obedient children trained by parents with Old World ideas. But many of the young men have left for other towns, where there are easier, cleaner ways to make a living. The few miners left are growing old—most are in their late fifties. And Shenandoah is dying of the habit-forming old disease called digging coal.

This death grip of outmoded industry, overlaid upon the even older living patterns of the truck farmers of Maryland, rural Pennsylvania and the Delaware counties, has hung on right through the current renaissance; and it still exists today in too many places and in too many different shapes. For old wounds are often slow to heal, whether they be physical scars like an abandoned strip mine or emotional ones like the attitude of an old-line industrialist or farmer who still believes that the familiar profits are eternal. These feelings have been particularly difficult for the Middle Atlantic States to excise, not only because this is an old region that established its ways of doing things long ago, but also because the people here happen to be, most of them, of a conservative, sometimes stubborn turn of mind. They have been known to make haste with interminable caution. In fact, they often prefer to keep—or at least tolerate—things as they have always been. They possess powerful loyalties, within their families, within their churches and within their towns. And they have an occasionally heavy-footed habit of going their own individualistic way.

Under certain circumstances these tendencies have been a source of the region's strength, and of its considerable charm as well. It was, for example, pride in the old hometown that started Pittsburgh on its renaissance. "We were getting to the point that if we didn't do something, everything we'd had here was just going to wash right down the river," said one Pittsburgher. Another added, "That whole renewal project down at the Point, what we call the Golden Triangle—one hundred and thirty-five million dollars to start and a lot more —that's all private money down there; we didn't go to the government for a cent."

It was this same pride, mingled with the powerful heritage of the Quaker conscience of William Penn and spiced with a touch of *noblesse oblige*, that prodded Philadelphia's conservative bankers and lawyers to join up with Joe Clark and Dick Dilworth and help pull their degenerated city back toward the image of Penn's intended "greene countrie towne." The same spirit is prodding them now to get moving on the critical problem of the city's Negro jungle. "It's initially and primarily a moral issue and that's the reason for doing it," said a businessman who is helping underwrite the redevelopment, adding, "although I'm sure in the long run that it's going to be good business."

It was family solidarity that put food into the bellies of the children, kept the juvenile crime rate close to zero, and held homes together when a fourth of the men were out of work in any given town because of a depression and when relief payments were the biggest single source of income even in good-sized cities like Scranton. "The old man runs the house," explained a local businessman, in the blunt accents handed down by his Slavic father, "and the rest look up to him. They even did when he was home out of work and the mother scratching for pennies in some fly-by-night garment factory.

"The church is the other thing that held people together," he added. And indeed the church is still a powerful force throughout the region. A hard-drinking town like Hazleton, with 105 bars, has no less than 60 churches where a man can get straight with God on Sunday morning after getting thoroughly bent with booze on Saturday night. In Wilkes-Barre a group of bankers coming together to underwrite a bond issue for an intercity sewage project begin their meeting with half a minute of silence to invoke the blessings of almighty God on the water-processing plant. And in Maryland a restaurant owner who does not want to integrate his place is called in by a priest and told, "Look, you *got* to do this." And he does.

Out in the countryside the perpetuation of the old ways is even more evident. On the Eastern Shore of Maryland a miasma of arrested time still pervades the anachronistic world of the oystermen (average age: 53), crabbers and rock fishermen who harvest the Chesapeake in their old-fashioned sailing craft, the clipper-bowed skipjacks whose swept-back masts were the fashion here in 1814 when the British sailed up the bay to bombard Fort Mc-Henry. On the bay shore, in a quilted pattern of hedgerows and brown rail fences, some of the working farms and great houses still bear the names given them by the families that settled here back in the 17th Century. And some of the farms still retain the crumbling signs of that ancient economy: graying, abandoned Negro cabins; the decimated remnant of an alley of maples marking the no-longer-used entry road of a once-prosperous tobacco plantation.

Up in the Pennsylvania Dutch countryside the plump, friendly farmers tend the land in much the manner of their fathers. In the evening, on a by-road between Shenandoah and Harrisburg, a farm woman in a green 19th Century sunbonnet and a faded pink cotton dress, her big pale legs disappearing into white cotton anklets, walks down a row of beet sprouts, sprinkling them with a galvanized watering can. Down the road fat cattle with bulging milkbags graze the side of a green hill, while below them three men, big in T-shirts, lean on the after end of a tractor, talking quietly, smiling, in the easy way of neighbors.

Through the quiet of the late day comes the neigh of a Shetland pony who shares his paddock with a spraddle-legged brown colt. Behind the paddock is a clean-painted barn, sturdily built on a fieldstone foundation, its upper walls splashed with the bright-colored star-in-circle hex signs that the people still put up for decoration or good fortune. "Red is love," explains the farm lady, answering a stranger's doorbell ring, "yellow is sunshine and warmth. And blue is purity." Near the roof peak of the barn, above the hex signs, is the proud, 18-inch-high legend of the owner, ART W. BEIBELHEIMER— a good Pennsylvania Dutchman. Things have been all right here, for the Art Beibelheimers, for a span of more than two centuries. And it is easy to think that they will never change. In fact, why would anyone want to change?

The answer is that the world has already changed, and so have some parts of the Middle Atlantic region. But throughout the three states there is still some urgent catching up to do. Art Beibelheimer runs a good farm and his neighbors have always been good, solid farmers. But it was their solid, conservative farm instincts that caused them to vote down a new state constitution year after year and to stubbornly oppose tax rises aimed at upgrading their local school systems. The Eastern Shore has long been a pleasant place for a tourist to visit; but to the people who live there, it has been a place where half the incomes are less than $3,000 a year and in some towns a Negro has an even chance of finding no work at all. There has been a patina of charm about the people of the Main Line and suburban Baltimore, who play string quartets and ride to the hounds and bring out their daughters at glittering cotillions; but there is nothing charming about the white noose they have drawn around their cities, leaving big portions of the urban core as down-and-out Negro ghettos. The coal and steel towns have made exciting progress in the renaissance, but 60 per cent of manufacturing employment in the Pittsburgh area is still in steel and related industries, whose frantic production cycles make the region prosper in certain years (wars and auto booms) and decline terribly in others.

For the whole region, these pockets of slow-footed sameness, and the cyclical slumps of heavy industry, are the sooty heritage of an older day, when Andrew Carnegie coined the phrase that became a regional *modus operandi:* "Pioneering don't pay." But today the leaders of the Middle Atlantic renaissance have shown how richly the right kind of pioneering does pay. They have moved parts of the region ahead into a position "to lead the nation," as Governor Shafer has urged, in such vital pursuits as the rebuilding of cities and the recasting of state governments. But there remains the even longer labor of keeping the region moving and of showing the laggards the futility of living off the overripe fruits of a prosperous past.

Like a giant's finger tipping a teacup, a huge crane hook spills a ladle of fiery pig iron into an open-hearth furnace to be made into steel.

A great industry's murky beauty

From the roaring furnaces of American mills pours the world's largest river of molten steel, the prime determinant of a modern nation's industrial might. Centered in the Middle Atlantic States, the steel industry is a rugged colossus with a voracious appetite for minerals, water, hydroelectric energy and raw manpower, a colossus that works with huge tools and intense heat. Much of steelmaking is violent and crude. To get raw materials, the earth is often robbed of its riches and the landscape made as barren as the surface of a dead planet. Without modern treatment, smoke from the furnaces would poison the air, and water, used by the mills, would pollute the streams. Yet there is a murky beauty, too, in the glow of fire pits, the sensuous flow of liquid metal and the efficiency of skillful men working under harsh conditions.

Photographs by Richard Noble

Blast furnaces in Rankin, Pennsylvania, tower about 200 feet above the ground amid clouds of steam generated by the ironmaking process.

Amid a furious splattering of metal, molten pig iron is added to scrap metal and limestone in an open-hearth furnace.

Sam Latherow, a veteran steelworker, reflects the strength, competence and cumulative weariness of decades in the mills.

Outlined against a bleak autumn sky and dwarfing the men *(lower left)* who operate the controls, a gargantuan dragline prepares to take

an 85-cubic-yard scoop from a strip mine in a coal field near Hazleton, Pennsylvania.

A worker, clad in armor evoking a medieval knight, prepares to face intense heat.

A forging press shapes a huge steel ingot in a blinding glare that creates surrealistic silhouettes of man and machine.

With weird patterns of light, billowing smoke and steam, and the flow of molten metal creating a scene reminiscent of Dante's "Inferno,"

workers direct a flood of pig iron from a blast furnace.

The 39 signers of the Constitution of the United States appear, along with the Convention Secretary, in the stylized portrait at right. A total of 62 delegates from 12 states labored for four months to frame an acceptable Constitution at the historic Philadelphia Convention of 1787; only Rhode Island, which was fearful that the document would damage its economic interests, sent no delegates.

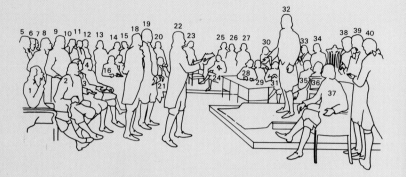

1. James Madison, Virginia
2. Charles Pinckney, South Carolina
3. Jacob Broom, Delaware
4. Rufus King, Massachusetts
5. John Langdon, New Hampshire
6. John Blair, Virginia
7. Richard D. Spaight, North Carolina
8. Pierce Butler, South Carolina
9. Benjamin Franklin, Pennsylvania
10. Jonathan Dayton, New Jersey
11. William Blount, North Carolina
12. Richard Bassett, Delaware
13. Abraham Baldwin, Georgia
14. Nicholas Gilman, New Hampshire
15. William Paterson, New Jersey
16. Gouverneur Morris, Pennsylvania
17. Jared Ingersoll, Pennsylvania
18. James Wilson, Pennsylvania
19. Nathaniel Gorham, Massachusetts
20. William Livingston, New Jersey
21. Robert Morris, Pennsylvania

22. John Rutledge, South Carolina
23. William Few, Georgia
24. William S. Johnson, Connecticut
25. Thomas Mifflin, Pennsylvania
26. James McHenry, Maryland
27. C. C. Pinckney, South Carolina
28. William Jackson (Convention Secretary)
29. George Clymer, Pennsylvania
30. David Brearley, New Jersey
31. Daniel of St. Thomas Jenifer, Maryland
32. George Washington, Virginia
33. Daniel Carroll, Maryland
34. George Read, Delaware
35. Hugh Williamson, North Carolina
36. Gunning Bedford Jr., Delaware
37. Alexander Hamilton, New York
38. Roger Sherman, Connecticut
39. John Dickinson, Delaware
40. Thomas Fitzsimmons, Pennsylvania

2

The Seeds of Government

It was a fine May morning, that Thursday in 1787, and the city of Philadelphia was bursting with a happy sense of its own importance. "Perhaps this city affords the most striking picture that has been exhibited for ages," crowed the *Pennsylvania Packet* in a lyric story. "Here, at the same moment, the collective wisdom of the Continent deliberates upon the extensive politics of the confederate empire." There was in town, noted the *Packet*, a "Grand Convention," called with some urgency by the bickering, disaffected confederation of the 13 states for the "sole and express purpose," as a preliminary gathering had put it, "of revising the Articles of Confederation." But before the Convention finished the following fall, its delegates would go much beyond any sole and express revision. They would fashion a new frame of government called the Constitution of the United States of America. Upon this new government would grow a nation, sang the *Packet*, in a final, giddy burst of poesy, wherein:

> *Faction shall cease, Industry smile*
> *Nor next-door neighbors each revile . . .*
> *The powerful league will all unite,*
> *Destroy invidious smiles and spite. . . .*

And that was not all that was happening in Philadelphia during May of 1787, not by a long measure. The Presbyterian Church was holding its own convention, too; and of course its leaders had chosen Philadelphia, a town whose church steeples poked upward like channel markers to guide the lost sinner, and whose bluenosed Quaker merchants, still influential in city affairs, had once passed a succession of laws forbidding, among other things, "rude or riotous" sports, fireworks, gambling and "being Maskt, or Disgis'd in Women's apparell." In the same week, too, the Society of the Cincinnati, a glittering association of Revolutionary War officers, had arrived for its own get-together (from whose inner chambers, thought a few nervous citizens, there seemed to emerge the faint aroma of a budding junta).

And as a kind of comic relief from all this pomp and circumstance, there labored down by the banks of the Delaware River an ugly, ill-mannered sort of fellow, "one Fitch," as a townsman reported of the inventor John Fitch, who had rigged up a 45-foot skiff with a set of 12 paddles driven by a steam engine. The device actually moved forward at about three miles per hour to the accompaniment of much hissing and clanking, mingled with derisive hoots from the riverbank. And though the wild-tempered Fitch insisted that a steamboat would "be the mode of crossing the Atlantic in time, whether I shall bring it to perfection or not," any right-thinking businessman could see that Fitch's invention had no real future.

Though Philadelphia was proud to be the host for all these diverse and arresting people, the city was by no means surprised that so many things were going on in its streets during the spring of 1787. For in that year, in fact for a dozen years on either side, this busy young port, perched as it was on the edge of a bursting green hinterland, was the place in America where things happened, the place where people came to make them happen. Geographically, its situation was perfect, at the keystone of the coastal arc of 13 states, as far north as a Georgia or Virginia man would come, as far south as Boston men would go to sign a Declaration of Independence, sit in a Continental Congress or meet in a Grand Convention to remold the instruments of government.

Philadelphia was, in fact, the first capital of the confederation, the biggest city in the New World, with a population of 40,000—it had been one of the largest cities in the whole British Empire. In recent years the town had grown so fast that the elderly Benjamin Franklin, long since retired from his lucrative printing business into the service of his country, had been forced to move from his old midtown residence on High Street because "the din of the Market increases upon me; and that,

with frequent interruptions, has, I find, made me say some things twice over."

In commerce, too, Philadelphia had grown until it rivaled London: along three miles of wharves and piers on the Delaware several thousand vessels a year nosed in and out with their cargoes, whose annual return was well above three quarters of a million pounds sterling and whose variety was well-nigh infinite. "To the West India Islands," wrote the Reverend Israel Acrelius, "are sent wheat flour, bread, Indian corn, beef, bacon, cheese, butter, staves, bar-iron," and, he might have added, other Pennsylvania products such as lumber, furs, pork, and a generous tonnage of tar, pitch and turpentine. Philadelphia ships also carried goods direct to ports in the Old World, even to China, but especially, at this time, to France and to the old enemy, England. There were plenty of customers also in South Carolina and particularly in New England.

Massachusetts merchants were not pleased that the annual trade balance was more than £50,000 in favor of Pennsylvania. But that was just fine with Philadelphia, whose very life was built upon commerce, and whose profits from it were enormous: a legitimate cargo worth £50,000 at loading could net an eventual return of £430,000—almost 900 per cent. On an illegitimate cargo the rewards might be even better; for example, one privateer brought in prizes worth £135,000 from a single excursion. Others did handsomely in the illegal convict trade, operating out of a Chesapeake port called Charlestown.

So fat were these various returns that a merchant like Joseph Galloway, Speaker of Pennsylvania's colonial Assembly in the 1770s, piled up a fortune reputed to be one of the greatest in America. And John MacPherson, a hard-nosed old privateer who had invested his plundered profits in more genteel enterprises, could establish a dazzling, 31-acre estate along the Schuylkill and send his son Jack to the College of New Jersey at Prince Town to learn the ways of a gentleman.

Such prosperity had come early to Philadelphia. The people here, and in the fertile hinterland to the west, had learned to regard the rich flow of commerce as an eternal blessing, justly bestowed upon them for their industrious ways. Therefore, Philadelphia was deeply disturbed in the years following the Revolution—and lately the city had felt outright alarm—at a rising tide of nationwide political chaos that threatened to drown the profits of both the farmers and the merchants. For the fact was that in 1787, despite the grandeur of the capital city and the confidence that lay on the surface, there were spiteful factions abroad in the land so strong that they threatened not only the economy but the very existence of the young country.

Under the Articles of Confederation there had been only a weak semblance of national authority. As a result, each of the several states tended to go its own way, jerry-building its own private policies on money, trade and control of any troops within its borders. During the recent War for Independence from Britain, the confederation of the 13 states had nearly collapsed from the disunion of its parts. New Jersey troops refused to take the oath of allegiance to the confederation, claiming instead that "New Jersey is our country"; and hostile Pennsylvania farmers had done little to help Washington's ragtag Continental Army at Valley Forge.

In the four years since the shooting stopped, the attitudes of the states, and the general effectiveness of the Continental Congress in controlling them, could hardly be said to have improved. The nation's commerce was stumbling along in a mire of conflicting tariffs and other trade regulations. The federal government—such as it was—had gone bankrupt and could only beg the states for revenue. Paper currency, issued with equal enthusiasm by the Congress and seven of the states, degenerated in value until, as Thomas Paine wrote, it was worth less in the open market than hobnails and wampum; and a band of Pennsylvania infantrymen, not wishing to be paid in either, at one point surrounded the Continental Congress where it sat in the State House in Philadelphia, forcing an ad hoc adjournment that left the Congress with a reduced measure of its dignity and its shaky authority.

Such chaos sat poorly in the minds of the lawyers and merchants and gentlemen-farmers who had created the nation here at Philadelphia in 1776. And it was particularly upsetting to Philadelphia's own powerful merchant-politicians, who saw their lush local commerce sinking in the tangle of contentious trade laws that the federal government was powerless to unravel. Then, as now, Philadelphia's ruling class had a passion for order. And so the city's mercantile grandees were preparing to sit in a Grand Convention with their colleagues from other parts of the country to establish a stable climate in which trade could flourish. Their meeting would have a fundamental significance not only for the new nation but, in a very special sense, for the region in which they lived. Over the short run they would succeed in creating the hoped-for political stability in which both the country and its commerce could survive. In the long run, however, they

would create a document so flexible and so full of compromises that while on the one hand it would be able to survive the massive stresses of a changing society, on the other hand its broad, often ambiguous provisions would give rise to a succession of formidable crises throughout the U.S.—and particularly in the Middle Atlantic States themselves.

It was natural that such a document as the new Constitution, full of compromises and flexibility, should be brought forth in Pennsylvania. For the state was the keystone of the nation in politics—as well as geography and commerce. With its powerful farming and commercial factions, Pennsylvania long ago had had to learn the art of compromise to keep peace within its own borders. Thus in the Convention the Pennsylvania delegation occupied the middle ground between the shipping-manufacturing interests of New England and the predominantly farm-oriented Southern states. Furthermore, since its founding as a colony, Pennsylvania had maintained a popular, even liberal, frame of government, one in which each freeman's voice was by law permitted to be heard. Pennsylvania, and particularly Philadelphia, provided a perfect stage —and some of the key actors—for the drama of the Constitutional Convention.

The building of this stage had been made possible, in large measure, by the foresight of the colony's remarkably enlightened founder, William Penn. By dint of an immense and rather vague grant from King Charles, Penn had been made the biggest landowner in the western part of the British Empire. But he was, first and foremost, a Quaker. As such, he believed that free Englishmen, in direct touch with God through their own conscience, could handle their political and religious affairs with no help from the lords of the realm or of the pulpit. Hence King Charles, among others, had probably been only too glad to see Penn depart for the remote forests of the New World—anything to rid England of this man who was forever stirring people up with outrageous writings such as *No Cross, No Crown*. And indeed, even before Penn landed on the site of Philadelphia in 1682, he sent to his colonists a message that contained words unlike those of any other British proprietor.

"You are now fixt at the mercy of no Governor that comes to make his fortune great," he wrote. "You shall be governed by laws of your own making, and live a free, and if you will, a sober and industrious people. . . . I shall not usurp the right of any or oppress his person." In another communication, he promised, "I shall have a tender care of the government, that it will be well laid. . . . My God

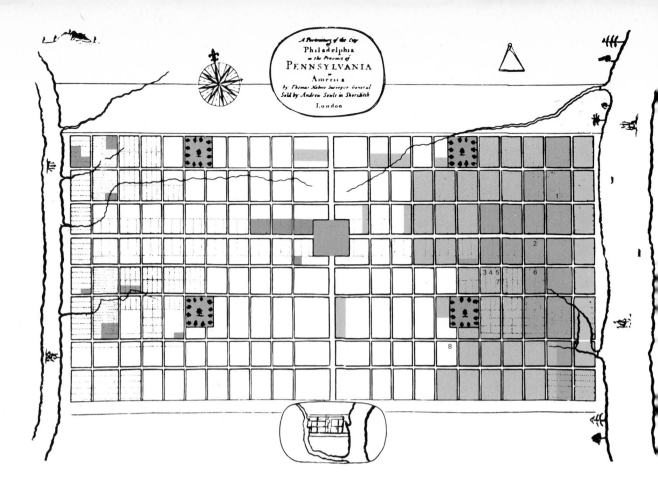

that has given me [this land] through many difficultys will, I believe bless and make it the seed of a nation. . . ."

The well-laid system envisioned by Penn began with a "frame of government" that he brought over with him. When the people began asking for changes in it, Penn consented: "If . . . there be any thing that jarrs—alter it." By the time the free, sober and industrious people had finished with their alterations, the revised constitution had become an exemplar for the other colonies and the wellspring of present-day Pennsylvania law. More than that, it was to be an important source of many doctrines the Convention would write into the Constitution of the United States in 1787. No less an authority than Thomas Jefferson would one day call Penn "the greatest lawgiver the world has produced."

Of principal importance, Penn's amended document, formally adopted in 1701, included sweeping provisions for religious freedom and provided that the colony's laws were to be made "*with the Consent and Approbation of the Freemen in General Assembly met.* . . ." This clear mandate for a permissive, popular government was one of the pillars upon which, in time, the U.S. Constitution would rest. There were other guideposts to future republican government written into the young colony's

pioneering frame of laws. For example, the Pennsylvania Assembly, to be chosen by an annual popular election, was to have its own powers to initiate legislation, set up membership qualifications and conditions of election, and to adjourn only when it got good and ready.

Besides his trail-breaking in the wilderness of popular government, Penn had a Quaker's quick eye for potential commerce. He laid out the site of Philadelphia at the confluence of the Delaware River and the tributary Schuylkill, a pair of inland-trade avenues that joined at tidewater. And in so doing, he also laid down the foundation of the city's wealth. Along the upper reaches of these rivers, and westward to the Ohio, lay 30 million acres of forest, with pine and hemlock 120 feet high—perfect for the masts of seagoing vessels—and massive white oak, a seemingly inexhaustible supply of wood for hull frames and planking. In the scattered clearings on the Schuylkill and on out to the Susquehanna, there was rich soil that, under the right hands, would give up 25 to 30 bushels of wheat per acre and 60 bushels of corn—a far greater yield than that given up by the tired farms of Europe.

Those hands arrived quickly; as early as the 1720s thousands of immigrants a year were pouring through the funnel of Philadelphia. The first

William Penn planned better than he could have imagined when he guided the design of Philadelphia, as the map at left indicates. It shows the original 1682 scheme *(black grid system)* and the city's development within that plan as of 1776 (areas that are devoted to specific uses are keyed by color, landmarks by number). Penn selected the site for his city at the narrowest point between the Delaware and Schuylkill Rivers, as shown in the tiny map at bottom, and he ordered his Surveyor General, Thomas Holme, to lay out streets providing for orderly growth. Two wide avenues, Broad and High (now Market) Streets, served as axes that divided the city into quadrants. Each quadrant had its own park, and Centre Square, where Broad and High intersected, was set aside for public buildings. Through the years this farsighted basic plan was adhered to; and today, with downtown Philadelphia undergoing extensive redevelopment, the city planners are using Penn's original scheme, almost three centuries old, as a guideline.

were Welsh (most of them Quakers), then Scotch-Irish (Presbyterians whose Scottish forebears had been brought over to Northern Ireland by the British), and floods of Lutheran, Quaker and Pietist Germans, drawn not only by Penn's own advertisement of fertile soil and "fat deer, which sells here for two shillings, sixpence," but by the promise of freedom of worship.

By 1750 half the people of Pennsylvania were immigrant Germans. And though they provided the early farming-and-commerce economy with a critical share of manpower, nevertheless the Germans were no more accepted than the later waves of Slavs and Italians would be in Pennsylvania's upcoming era of coal and steel. And even a liberal like Franklin was worried by the influx. "The signs in our streets have inscriptions in [Dutch and English]," he complained, "and in some places only German. . . . In short, unless the stream of their importation could be turned . . . they will soon outnumber us." Nevertheless, the shrewd old commercial printer briefly experimented with a German-language newspaper for them, the *Philadelphische Zeitung.*

These Pennsylvania Germans—more familiarly called Pennsylvania Deutsch or "Dutch"—were deeply attached to the ways of the old country and

of their religions. They gave their towns names like Nazareth, Bethlehem, New Jerusalem and Old Zionsville, or, alternately, Manheim, Seisholtzville and Friedensburg. They built stout German houses and beautiful barns, often carving symbols in the wood that were thought to bring good weather and keep out the evil spirits. They were standoffish from their neighbors and suspicious of the wicked, spendthrift ways of Philadelphia, whose petitions they voted down in the legislature. From the first, they resisted any change in their lives and customs.

But they were superb farmers, and together with the Welsh and Scotch-Irish they made Pennsylvania's central valley bloom as few pieces of earth had ever bloomed before. On the eve of the Revolution, Pennsylvania wheat was in such surplus that flour and bread made from it had become the leading trade items in the American colonies, the principal sustenance of the British West Indies, and an unfailing source of profit for Philadelphia's flour millers and shipping merchants. "[Everyone] sends his annual surplus to [Philadelphia] to be sold there," noted one European visitor. Without this Pennsylvania wheat and flour, admitted the British, the Indies might not even subsist.

In the course of their prosperous farming, and in addition to it, the central Pennsylvanians gave their colony the initial push toward an industrial future. They manufactured fine plows and sophisticated cultivating machinery. They built in quantity a new type of freight wagon called the Conestoga, covered with an arching canopy of canvas, that would become a fixture of the pioneering American West. The finest rifle of its day was made there, four feet long in the barrel and renowned for its accuracy. A Pennsylvania boy named Daniel Boone carried one such across the mountains, where it became known as the Kentucky long rifle. Most important of all, a few perceptive landholders found iron-ore deposits in low-lying bogs, refined that ore in charcoal furnaces and shipped the resulting iron downriver to Philadelphia. By 1775 sixty furnaces and forges were turning out one seventh of the world's pig and bar iron and selling the finished articles so successfully that jealous British iron interests persuaded their government to impose restrictions on colonial manufacturing—which had no effect whatever on the production of the stubborn Pennsylvania ironmasters.

As they developed their new industries and their farms, these tough, energetic back-country men kept edging westward, across the folded ridges, through the deep ravines, on out to the forks of the Ohio. "I have learned from experience," wrote one British observer, "[that] the Americans . . . forever imagine the Lands further off are still better than those upon which they are already settled." Around the old site of Fort Duquesne, a trading post grew up to be called Pittsburgh, a brawling frontier log town whose morals the strait-laced eastern counties found difficult to approve. A diary of 1759 carried this entry—"August 20th: Croghan has a black eye this morning, and I have been informed that he was drunk and fought with ye Indians." Thirty years later a shocked newcomer was still complaining that "all sort of wickedness were carried on to excess, and there was no morality or regular order."

But Pittsburgh, in its backwoods way, had a surly disregard for outland opinions. Even at this early date its people were showing a marked hostility toward the moneyed interests of Philadelphia, particularly toward land speculators like the rather quick-footed Robert Morris, who was forever trying to claim title to property already settled by grouchy, sharpshooting frontier farmers. This hostility toward the city, its merchant leaders and their rent collectors was heartily concurred in by the central valley farmers, who joined their western brothers in a political alliance against Philadelphia.

"I dread the cold and sower temper of the back counties," said the urbane lawyer Gouverneur Morris (no kin to Robert) in 1787. One hundred and eighty years later, Philadelphians would still dread that temper, as the renewal-minded leaders of the city battled—often futilely—in the state legislature for fresh industrial and urban development funds.

"Sower" or not, the west in 1787 was a good place to do business. The two-fisted Croghan was one of the premier traders in America, and there were others in Pittsburgh who prospered just as well: a single fur depot there handled 15,000 skins in one year, before sending them on to urban markets. Philadelphians, too, found ways to turn a neat profit even in this surly and remote outpost, which had not yet turned to manufacturing and hence could use the products of the big city. In 1766 one Philadelphia mercantile combine sent a train of 600 pack horses and many wagons out to Pittsburgh, carrying £50,000 sterling in goods.

On this broad base of thriving enterprise, and under the guidance of a relatively permissive government, Pennsylvania by the time of the Revolution had come very close to realizing Penn's vision of it as "the seed of a nation." And its queen city of Philadelphia was, in the eyes of at least one bedazzled visitor, a place of "grandeur and perfection. . . . Its fine appearance, good regulations, agreeable situation, natural advantages, trade, riches and power, are by no means inferior to any, even the most ancient towns of Europe." The houses of Philadelphia were elegant, ". . . built of Brick . . . three Stories high, and well Sashed." Other visitors remarked on the streets: "well paved in the middle for carriages," which at night were "illumined with lamps . . . of the best sort." Beyond the city limits the first evidence of today's lush suburbs were already beginning to appear. In the choice sections of land there were perhaps a hundred magnificent country houses, the most imposing being Fairhill, seat of the lawyer John Dickinson, a man envied for "the antique look of his house, his gardens . . . grotto . . . fish-pond, fields . . . vista, through which is a distant prospect of the Delaware River. . . ."

Once their income had been assured, men like Dickinson and Franklin tended to invest their excess time—and even money—in working for the good of the commonwealth. With their guidance and backing, the young University of the State of Pennsylvania had been able to turn out 274 graduates since its establishment as the Charity School in 1740; the city's circulating library, first in America, had grown to 8,000 volumes. The Pennsylvania Hospital, also America's first, boasted that in the 25 years of its existence, out of 8,831 admissions, 4,440 complete cures had been achieved as against only 852 deaths. "The Pennsylvania Hospital is as perfect as the wisdom and benevolence of man can make it," wrote Dr. Benjamin Rush, one of the men who made it so. There was much local pride, too, in the American Philosophical Society, meeting place for men like John Bartram, the celebrated botanist, and Dr. Thomas Bond, a physician and educator of no mean rank. The "public Spirit, of the Good People of this Province," commented Dr. Bond, "will shortly make Philadelphia the Athens of America and Render the Sons of Pennsylvania, reputable amongst the most celebrated Europeans. . . ."

By all odds the most reputable of these sons was Dr. Franklin, scientist, author, diplomat, politician, soldier, inventor, an enormously successful publisher and commercial printer, a living symbol of the city's achievements and himself prime mover behind many of them. His fame was international: in Europe, wrote John Adams, Franklin's reputation was "more universal than that of Leibnitz or Newton, Frederick [the Great] or Voltaire." And indeed Franklin had been honored on both sides of the water for his various works, including some inspired—and totally original—observations on the fundamental concepts of polarity and of the fluid

The "hex signs" that appear on many Pennsylvania Dutch barns like the one at right are actually misnamed, for they have no connection with hexes, or magic spells. Although it is commonly thought that these signs are painted on structures to keep evil spirits out, they are, in fact, purely decorative or, as one Pennsylvania Dutchman has remarked, "for fancy." But hexes did exist in the culture of these people. In the 18th and 19th Centuries the Pennsylvania Dutch were known to place amulets—often rolled-up pieces of paper with prayers written on them —in their barns to protect the livestock and other possessions. The myth about "hex signs"—they are usually a star within a circle painted in bright colors—originated in the 1920s when little was known of Pennsylvania Dutch culture. It was not commonly known then, for example, that similar ornaments adorned such items as dishes, towels and baptismal certificates in the region's households.

OAKWOOD ACRES

characteristics of electricity. (In a less inspired moment, Dr. Franklin once promised some friends that he would execute for them a fat turkey by the power of electricity. Before doing so, however, the eminent scientist, who had accidentally caught hold of some bare wires, was very nearly executed himself. "I am ashamed to have been guilty of so notorious a blunder," he wrote, after he had recovered from the adventure, "a match for the Irishman . . . who, being about to steal powder, made a hole in the cask with a hot iron!")

In the late 1780s, however, Franklin, like everyone else in town, had been caught up in the bustling urgency of the Grand Convention. For quite apart from the damaging confusion of the nation's internal turmoil, Philadelphia and the other major ports were suffering badly from a particularly vicious kind of foreign competition. British merchants, in a hurry to regain their prewar markets, were dumping floods of goods in America, sending prices so low that U.S. manufacturers were left with little or no profits. And the British government, in a vengeful mood for the loss of its richest colonies, closed the West Indian islands to American ships and shut its own home ports to a long list of U.S. commodities. Nor were France and Spain, although erstwhile friends of the U.S., willing to relax their

normal trade restrictions in order to benefit the young country.

Worse yet, under the existing frame of government, there was no way that the mercantile politicians could get things moving again in proper fashion. It was no good appealing to the Continental Congress, for that bland and disunited body had no real power to control imports and exports and thus was helpless to retaliate against the restrictive measures of European countries. As for reasoning with the separate states, those contentious bodies, far from agreeing on solutions to these urgent problems, had instead been busy creating new ones.

Massachusetts, New York, Pennsylvania and Virginia, to name just four, established their own tariff regulations, and each of these big, powerful states was busy sucking the juice from the commerce of its small neighbor states. "New Jersey," wrote James Madison, "placed between Philadelphia and New York, was likened to a cask tapped at both ends." Maryland was fighting with Virginia over navigation rights to the Potomac; earlier it had quarreled with Pennsylvania over property rights in the lower Susquehanna Valley. At various times this latter squabble had degenerated into shooting matches. And although two surveyors named Mason and Dixon helped clarify some of the

Products of an inquisitive mind

Benjamin Franklin, besides being an author, philosopher, printer, publisher and diplomat, was also a gifted inventor. Among the inventions credited to him are the lightning rod, bifocals—he is shown wearing a pair of these double-duty glasses in the portrait above —the glass harmonica and the Franklin stove. Franklin's ingenious inventions were nurtured by his intense interest in many areas of science, from meteorology to agriculture. This led to such other achievements as his charting of the Gulf Stream, his proof that lightning is electricity and his introduction of the concept of daylight saving time.

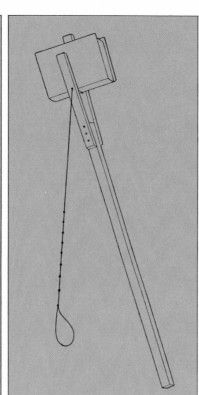

One of Franklin's most practical inventions was the Long Arm, designed to take books off high shelves. It consists of a pole tipped with a pair of "fingers" that, when pulled together by a string, grip the desired book. A modern adaptation is used by grocers to fetch cans off hard-to-reach shelves.

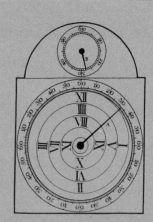

The one-handed Franklin clock, Franklin's attempt to design a timepiece with the simplest possible works, had the drawback of being unable to clearly indicate the hour.

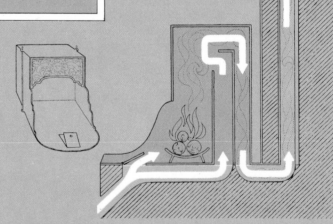

The Franklin stove, one of the inventor's most celebrated achievements, burned less wood and spread heat more efficiently than the ordinary fireplaces of the time. The stove consisted of an iron box *(above left)*, which was placed inside a conventional fireplace. A flue dug in the base of the fireplace fed air *(arrows)* into the box, thus fanning the flames. Air also passed behind the fire, helping to draw the smoke through a U-shaped channel and into the chimney. The stove had many advantages—Franklin listed 14 of them—but the chief one was that the box, surrounding the flames almost completely, prevented the fire's warmth from being lost up the chimney. Many manufacturers adapted and modified this stove; their products have been widely, if erroneously, known ever since as Franklin stoves.

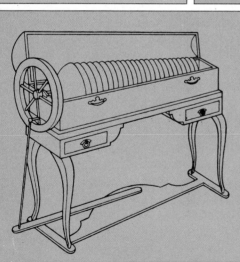

Franklin's glass harmonica, invented by Franklin in 1762, consisted of a series of shallow glass bells mounted on an axle attached to a foot pedal. When the axle was turned, the bells were made to revolve. By touching the bells with the fingers, a delicate, clear melody could be produced. The instrument achieved immediate if short-lived popularity, and both Mozart and Beethoven wrote music for it.

territorial questions by marking off a definitive border between the two states, the bad feeling was only temporarily assuaged.

One of the causes of the bad feeling was that Baltimore, once a muddy little backwater struggling along on the declining tobacco trade of southern Maryland, had some time ago discovered how profitable the flour-milling business could be. That would have been all right in itself, but the wheat that Maryland's entrepreneurs were grinding was wheat grown in Pennsylvania and floated down the Susquehanna straight into dockside storage bins on Chesapeake Bay. It was a cheap, easy way to tap the harvests of the whole Susquehanna Valley, and it hardly seemed fair to Philadelphians, who had to pay high wagon rates for overland haulage on any produce grown west of the Delaware River system. Then, too, Baltimore was a full sailing day closer than Philadelphia to the customers in the West Indies. And finally, Chesapeake shipbuilders had developed a superb cargo vessel called the Baltimore clipper. Sharp in the bow, with a light, shallow-draft hull, these sleek topsail schooners had a prideful habit of outrunning their Northern competitors to market (and of slipping past the lumbering British patrol frigates en route).

Thus Baltimore had quickly grown into a bustling commercial center of 10,000 people, with a volume of shipping dangerously close to that of Philadelphia—and with some strong ideas on who would shortly be No. 1 in the wheat trade. For their part, the Philadelphians were damned if they were going to see any more of their God-given grain drift off downstream to make money for somebody else.

A group of Philadelphia businessmen, including Benjamin Franklin, put forth a possible solution for their town: "We can devise no other means of saving ourselves [from the competition of Baltimore]," reported one of them, "but by a canal from the Susquehanna to the Schuylkill." However, two could play that game, and Maryland was already hatching plans of its own for canals up the Susquehanna, west to the Cumberland and perhaps all the way to the forks of the Ohio, where there were other kinds of Pennsylvania business to be siphoned off. In either case, canals took a long time to build; once built, they would hardly solve the snarled question of who had the right to ship what, and where. In the months leading up to the Convention, the farmers and merchant-politicians on both sides lost few opportunities to press their bitterly conflicting interests or to dream up contentious trade regulations that might embarrass the other's commerce.

Caught squarely in the middle of the furor, little Delaware could see not only its commerce but even its political identity sinking beneath the "enormous and monstrous influence" of the bigger states. "Will not these large states crush the small ones whenever [we] stand in the way of their ambitions or interested views?" asked stout, pugnacious Gunning Bedford, Delaware's Attorney General. Judging from the recent commercial sufferings of New Jersey, there was every indication that the big states would move in whenever they got the chance. Then (as now) Delaware wanted little more than an orderly, stable climate in which to carry out its private business. Along with most of the other small states, Delaware thought perhaps the Congress should regulate trade, so that everyone, big and little, could operate under the same laws.

The year before the Grand Convention of 1787, there had been a brief preliminary meeting convened at Annapolis principally (and unsuccessfully) to adjudicate the water-rights squabble between Maryland and Virginia, but also to see whether there might not be some solutions to the general tangle of trade interests that many delegates felt underlay the nation's distress. "Most of our political evils," said James Madison of Virginia, "may be traced to our commercial ones," a sentiment heartily echoed by the propertied politicians of Pennsylvania. That state's inclination to think in financial terms was, in fact, so powerful that at one point in the recent past Robert Morris had suggested that the real answer to America's problems was a national bank, which would "unite the several states more closely together in one general money connection and indissolubly to attach many powerful individuals to the cause of our country by the strong principle of self-love and the immediate sense of private interest."

This kind of thinking was typical of Morris, until recently the most powerful member of Philadelphia's ruling merchant class, a man, as a contemporary put it, "whose dictates none dare oppose, and from whose decisions lay no appeal." Big, energetic, not overly troubled by ethical questions, Morris would have been very much at home among Pennsylvania's latter-day industrial barons, in the high time of coal and steel. He was, in fact, a precursor of the 19th and 20th Century political bosses who would work in tandem with the barons to control the state. But during the final years of the confederation, Morris' colleagues had become wary of his aggressive schemes, and he had begun to lose some of his power.

Other people less hypnotized by their own private interests—among them many of the delegates who had attended the meeting at Annapolis—were beginning to see that the roots of the nation's trouble ran far deeper than trade and commerce. The trouble, simply stated, but fearsome in its real complexity, was, how would America be governed? Were the states to have supreme authority, supreme rights—*states' rights*—over trade and other matters, in a loosely knit federal republic? Or was there to be a truly national government, in which the Congress and/or some sort of executive had ultimate power over the states—power to keep order, to call out the troops, to enforce the laws? And whose troops? Whose laws? The people of the Middle Atlantic States, as much as any others in the confederation, wanted to find some answers before the government collapsed altogether.

Nowhere in history, however, were there any proper answers to fit these questions. It was no good talking about the cozy, face-to-face democracies, republics and confederations that had existed in places like ancient Greece, 17th Century Holland, or Switzerland. America measured 1,200 miles from top to bottom, 1,000 miles from the Atlantic on the east to the western border at the Mississippi River; more than 500 million acres of land—90 per cent of it still a howling wilderness—and heaven only knew how big and how powerful it would ultimately become. Stretched along the Atlantic fringe and scattered through the forest, there were already some 3.5 million people, most of them recent arrivals and very few in any agreement on how the country should be run.

As the Convention opened in the Pennsylvania State House at Philadelphia, the delegates, too, were in sharp disagreement over how the country should work. They disagreed not only from state to state but within the separate state delegations themselves. In fact, many of them disagreed on the fundamental nature of their mission to Philadelphia. Their charge was solely and expressly to revise the Articles of Confederation. But Edmund Randolph of Virginia quickly and boldly countered that bland notion by putting forth 15 resolves that added up to a plan for a new kind of government, "a *national* government," said Randolph, "consisting of a supreme legislative, executive, and judicial." From that moment on, any talk of simple revision slowly sank beneath Randolph's weighty—and highly contentious—proposal to recast the basic frame of government.

The proposal for a tripartite government was palatable; six states, including Maryland, already used the system. The loaded words were "supreme" and "national." They had a bitter flavor to many of these delegates, who had just shucked off a supreme national King and Parliament. And it would be a long, difficult summer in Philadelphia before a majority of the states could bring themselves to swallow any kind of supreme national government for a truly United States. During that summer, Pennsylvania, with its kaleidoscope of conflicting political views and commercial interests, in many ways represented the balance wheel among the purposeful, powerful notions generated at the Convention.

James Wilson of Pennsylvania, an erudite governmental theorist and sometime land speculator, challenged the delegates with a call for national solidarity: "Virginia is no more, Massachusetts is no more," he said, and finally, "Pennsylvania is no more. We are now one nation of brethren, we must bury all local interests and distinctions."

But Wilson and his friends were propertied gentlemen, "men of a mercantile cast." Most of them owned public securities (Pennsylvanians held a significant portion of America's outstanding Revolutionary War debts) or had plunged heavily into western lands. Naturally, thought the states' righters, such men leaned toward a strong national government that would pay face value in hard cash for their depreciated securities and honor their land claims against those of the states and the people.

In these and other matters there were plenty of delegates to speak out for the rights of the states. Dr. James McHenry of Maryland was among those wary of a national government; Maryland was doing quite well just now and would not welcome regulation of its commercial affairs by a central authority. Luther Martin of Maryland, a tiresome, bombastic man, talked interminably about "the rights of free men and free states." Here again, though, were men of means, speaking primarily for the states. Very few delegates at Philadelphia spoke in behalf of the common people. And this was odd. For the document that the delegates were beginning to hammer out would begin with the words, "*We, the people . . .*" Who were the people, anyway?

John Dickinson, late of Pennsylvania but now in the Delaware group, thought he knew, and he held them in bad odor. They were "those multitudes without property and without principle with which our country, like all others, will soon abound." They were, Dickinson said, "the most dangerous influence." George Washington, a good Virginia aristocrat, was equally wary of the people, particularly those of the region around Philadelphia. He wrote to a friend that the countryside here had "become the general receptacle of foreigners from all countries and of all descriptions, many of whom take an active part in the politics of the state; and coming over full of prejudice against their government—some against all governments—you will be [able] to draw your own inference of their conduct."

There were, however, a few delegates who thought the people a good deal more responsible. "The people at large are wrongly suspected of being averse to a general government," argued George Read of Delaware, a nationalist, who added, "The states must be swept away." The man closest to the common will was Dr. Franklin. At the Convention, Franklin, by now a mellow 81, functioned mainly as a genial host and peacemaker. But his politics were well known.

As President of the Pennsylvania Executive Council, Franklin had staunchly and successfully resisted the establishment of a state senate. He felt an upper house smacked too much of the House of Lords. For a long time Pennsylvania, originally under Penn's and later Franklin's guidance—and with the hearty assent of the independent farmers and frontiersmen—had maintained a relatively weak executive branch. For a time there had been no governor at all. Conservatives called Franklin "a dangerous man . . . an uneasy spirit . . . a sort of tribune of the people." Franklin did not argue the point, but rather "expressed his dislike of every thing that tended to debase the spirit of the common people."

With all these conflicting views, it was a miracle that the Grand Convention could ever agree on any form of government for the country. And the fact is that the delegates never did wholeheartedly agree. They compromised. The Pennsylvanians like Franklin and Wilson provided much of the basic structure for that compromise. And the document that came out of it, after 120 muggy, contentious days of debate, seemed mainly to provide means for the states and the people of America to disagree, henceforth, in a more orderly fashion.

The name of the document was the *Constitution of the United States*. It was of decidedly mixed parentage, though proud Pennsylvanians felt they could see in the new Constitution the heritage of old father Penn—his concepts of representative government, of the primacy of the law over the will of a single man, and of legislation contrived with "the consent and approbation of the free men assembled." Beyond this basic philosophy, even the men who directly framed the U.S. Constitution were not quite sure what it said or, for that matter, how good it was. At the signing, Franklin conceded, ambiguously, "I agree to this Constitution with all its faults, if they are such."

Delaware, delighted to be protected from the big states by a strong national government, hastened to ratify the new document. Maryland, wary of the implied national regulation of its commerce, indulged in a long, careful debate. But in the end the delegation voted for ratification (Maryland's own state constitution, after all, was quite similar in general form) with the protest that "the liberty and happiness of the people will be endangered if the system be not greatly changed and altered."

To the farm-dominated Pennsylvania legislature, the Constitution seemed to say that the city slickers, with their hard-money schemes and land claims, had won. The western farmers were furious, for they further suspected—quite rightly, as it turned out—that this central government represented a threat to the local, even personal, autonomy that they so cherished. In the course of Pennsylvania's debate on ratification, some nasty insinuations were made about the "lordly and profligate few." But on December 12, 1787, after much soothing by Franklin and some fast talking by Wilson (who later was beaten up by an antifederalist mob), Pennsylvania came aboard, where it was ultimately joined by the rest. To everyone's surprise Pennsylvania then recast its own constitution to provide for a single executive and a bicameral legislature, along the lines of the new national system. Again the farmers, together with the frontiersmen and the small artisans, were not pleased. For now the state itself loomed as a possible instrument of dominance by the powerful mercantile politicians of the cities.

Within two years, in response to a rising chorus of demands from radicals in general and states' righters in particular, the Bill of Rights was added as the first 10 amendments to the U.S. Constitution. Thus amended, the document now concluded with the provision that "the powers not delegated to the United States by the Constitution, nor prohibited by it to the States, are reserved to the States respectively, or to the people."

Now it seemed to say all things, good and bad, to all people and to all states. And indeed, there was in the document a basic soundness and flexibility that would enable it to hold up under a series of fundamental challenges that would plague it right down to the present day. In fact, the amended Constitution had hardly been put into effect when its permissive, sometimes ambiguous, framework was badly strained by the first of these challenges—right in Pennsylvania itself.

The frontiersmen around Pittsburgh, where one farmer in five owned a still, rebelled against an excise tax that the impecunious new Treasury Department, under the autocratic Alexander Hamilton, had begun to collect on the distilling of whiskey and other spirits. This is precisely what the farmers had feared: a government money grab engineered by friends of the big merchants, who were managing to keep their own enterprises tax-free. Loading their long rifles, the farmers applied a fast coat of tar and feathers to the local revenue collector and told the national government what it could do with its excise tax on an honest man's home-brewed liquor. Whereupon President George Washington ordered the farmers "to desist from all unlawful combinations." Later he directed the Secretary of War to call up 13,000 militiamen against the perpetrators of this Whiskey Rebellion. But the farmers had already capitulated. In their brief, bloodless war, however, they brought out two very prickly, very durable issues that the Constitution, apparently, had not truly solved. These were: Would the dominant will of the nation be that of the rural interests or of the urban financier and industrialist? And when should troops be called out, by whom, and for what purpose? For though the farmers had given in, the real questions had not been answered.

In time, these same questions of the dominant will and the use of troops would come up again and again, causing deep dislocations and even bitter conflict all over the country. A hundred years after the Whiskey Rebellion, scores of men would die in a series of uprisings by steel and railroad workers against their industrial overlords—who, like the 18th Century merchants, were in a position of influence and favor with the state or national government. In subsequent years the use of federal troops to put down strikes or riots in such places as Chicago and Detroit would arouse further controversy.

Nowhere would the conflicts be more severe, however, than in the region where the Constitution was born. For even during the 1780s, and continuing thereafter, things were happening in Pennsylvania and its neighbor states that would change the very nature of the country and put terrible stress on the documents by which it was governed. Near Pittsburgh, right in the middle of the Whiskey Rebellion, a daring businessman named George Anschutz was putting up the city's first iron foundry. Anschutz, a poor judge of costs, failed to make a go of it. But his successors decidedly did not. Within 20 years a "dark, dense smoke was rising from many parts" of Pittsburgh, smoke from many sources but most notably from iron furnaces whose annual production was already passing $750,000 in value. It would not be long before Pittsburgh's ironworks multiplied into America's most powerful business.

North of Allentown, Pennsylvania, Colonel Jacob Weiss in 1803 launched a small enterprise that he called the Lehigh Coal Mine Company and managed to send two bargeloads of anthracite down the rapids of the Lehigh River and the Delaware to Philadelphia. So started another giant industry, which would soon pervade the economy not only of the region but of the nation as well. And in February of 1827 a group of citizens in Baltimore met to "take under consideration the best means of restoring to the city of Baltimore that portion of the Western trade which has recently been diverted from it by the introduction of steam navigation and by other causes"—those other causes being, principally, canals in New York and Pennsylvania. The means they decided upon was a steam railway to the west, and in 1828 they began building one, chartered as the Baltimore and Ohio. As usual, Philadelphia, the old rival, replied in kind by chartering the Pennsylvania Railroad, whose clear course also was westward.

It was 1852 before either line reached the Ohio Valley. By that time Pittsburgh had 5,000 millworkers turning out six million dollars' worth of iron per year. By that time, too, the second great wave of immigration had started to flood into the region, drawn now by the promise not of rich farms but of jobs in the mines and mills. The cities had grown, too—Pittsburgh to 46,000, Baltimore to 169,000 and Philadelphia to 340,000. The region itself was tied together now by rails and was putting more and more of its energy into the production of coal, iron—and, ultimately, steel.

In all, the entire Middle Atlantic was changing from an agricultural-commercial community focused on one city, Philadelphia, into a vast industrial complex of a type that not even the most farsighted delegate at the Grand Convention could have foreseen. This industry would breed a kind of urban society whose welfare was by no means assured by the provisions of either the U.S. Constitution or the instruments of state government that developed under it. As this urban-industrial society grew, the conflicts between city and country, between farm and industry, between state and national interests would become more violent each year.

In 1861 they would all come to a flaming head along Mason and Dixon's old border line. But they would not be resolved there. For the conflicts had been built into the land and into the industries that grew out of the land. In many ways, too, they had been built into the Constitution itself. So that Pennsylvania and the surrounding region, which William Penn foresaw as the seed of a nation, and which had fulfilled that promise, had gone on to become, in a sense, the seed of the nation's troubles as well.

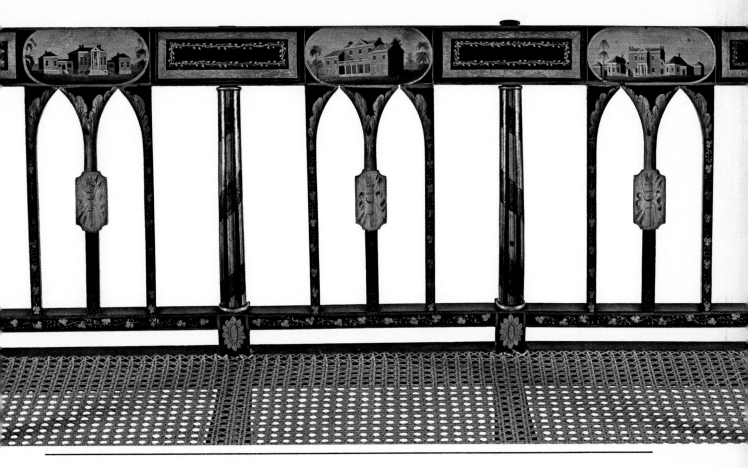

The elegant lines of this settee show one of the more sophisticated of the Federal styles in furniture. Decorated with views of Baltimore, the settee was made in the early 1800s by the Maryland craftsmen John and Hugh Finlay.

A new style
for a new country

In the years that followed the signing of the Constitution, from 1788 to about 1825, art and architecture in the United States flowered in a new and distinctive style now called Federal. The style was taken over from the English but modified and embellished by native Americans. Federal designs, which managed to be at once chaste and lavish, delicate and dignified, evolved from the English Georgian style, popular in America before the Revolution, making increased use of motifs borrowed from classical Greece and Rome plus American patriotic symbols. Although the style became the vogue in many parts of the U.S., nowhere were its practitioners more active —or more generously supported—than in Philadelphia, the largest and most influential city in the young nation, and in its rival in elegance, the thriving port of Baltimore.

Adapting the modes of Greece and Rome

Seeing themselves as inheritors of the classical ideals of democracy and freedom, Americans of the new republic eagerly adopted the fashions of ancient Rome and Greece. Their public buildings were often designed to look like Roman temples, their women's clothes were inspired by the flowing costumes of ancient Greece, and many details of their decorations reflected classical themes. The most influential architect of the time, the English-trained Benjamin Henry Latrobe, who lived and worked for a time in Philadelphia, was an outspoken advocate of the neoclassical styles. Through them, he argued, "the days of Greece may be revived in the woods of America, and Philadelphia become the Athens of the western world."

Classical styles in women's clothes, high fashion in Europe and in America, appear in an engraving *(near right)* and on a painted glass panel *(far right)* of the Federal period. The panel is set into a table made in Baltimore between 1795 and 1810 and shows a figure in a dress almost identical to those worn by the women on painted Greek vases. In the engraving (a detail of William Birch's *Back of the Statehouse, Philadelphia,* done in 1800) the flowing, high-waisted style is shown as it was adapted, with few changes, to American taste.

A mantel *(left)* from the Philadelphia home of Peter Breen includes busts of national heroes Washington and Franklin set atop Roman-style columns.

The columns of a Roman temple, supporting a magnificent pediment, frame the entrance to Philadelphia's Bank of the United States.

BENJAMIN HENRY LATROBE

Foremost among the architects of the Federal period was Benjamin Henry Latrobe, a designer and engineer who introduced the first pure Greek and Roman designs to American building. His Bank of Pennsylvania, built in Philadelphia about 1800, was faced with columns of the graceful Ionic design *(below)* that were nearly exact copies of those of the Erechtheum in Athens. Observing the spate of Greek designs that followed, he noted, "I have changed the taste of a whole city. My very follies and whims have been mimicked. . . ." Latrobe was a successful designer of houses, but he felt more at ease with public buildings. His Greek and Roman façades added a stateliness to such structures as the old Pennsylvania Academy of the Fine Arts, Baltimore's Bank of the United States, even the pump house of Philadelphia's waterworks *(pages 52-53)*. Perhaps his best-known contributions were the completion of the White House and the remodeling of the U.S. Capitol in Washington after the War of 1812.

A sculptured pediment at Homewood, built in Baltimore around 1802, has a window of shield design, a popular motif of the period.

Classically inspired cornices like this symmetrical one, drawn by English cabinetmaker George Hepplewhite, were emulated in the U.S.

Slender windows and a door with an elliptical fanlight—hallmarks of Federal architecture—form a façade of the Pennsylvania Hospital.

Elegance, simplicity and exquisite detail

Elegant detail, whether in the working of a piece of silver or in the construction of a doorway, was a striking characteristic of Federal design. These details played an important role in creating the Federal style in houses. In some homes the plain entrance was replaced by a columned portico, the door flanked by sidelights and topped by a fanlight window. The ideas for these details were often supplied by English professionals, such as George Hepplewhite and Robert Adam, but some of the finest American homes were planned and built by native amateurs. Thomas Jefferson designed his magnificent Monticello, and Charles Carroll, a well-to-do Baltimorean, was responsible for Homewood, seen in part at top left. In the best Federal-style homes, elegant simplicity and attention to detail produced structures of timeless beauty.

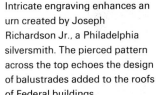

The large, curved bay of Lemon Hill, a mansion in Philadelphia, encloses an oval parlor and an upstairs bedroom. Repeated in the White House, the oval shape was used in many Federal homes.

Intricate engraving enhances an urn created by Joseph Richardson Jr., a Philadelphia silversmith. The pierced pattern across the top echoes the design of balustrades added to the roofs of Federal buildings.

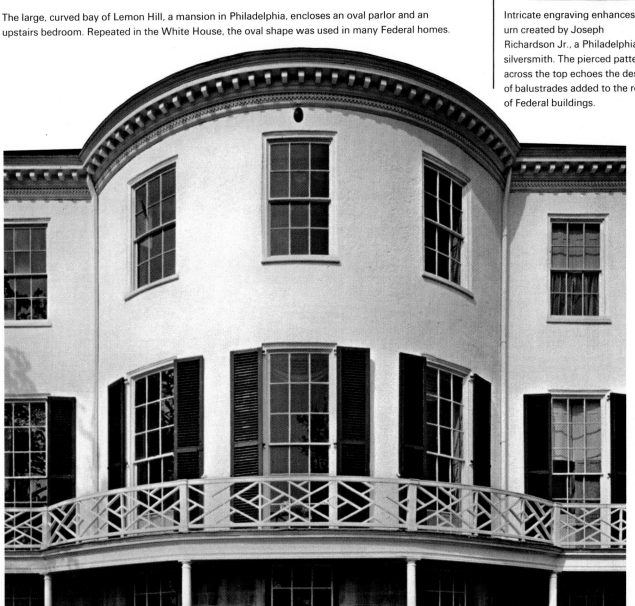

The Gentlemen Cabinet and Chair Makers are requested to meet in Church alley. *To-Morrow Morning*, the 4th of July, at 8 o'Clock, to proceed from thence to join the Federal Procession Every Master will inform his Journeymen that their Company is expected: likewise furnish their Appren tices with the Badges agreed on for the Day.
July 3.   JONATHAN GOSTELOWE, Chairman.

A notice to furniture makers in a Philadelphia newspaper of 1788 reveals that the craft was already organized there. Masters were usually shop owners. Journeymen worked in the shops for wages or on a piecework basis. Apprentices, aspiring craftsmen, trained from the age of 14 or 16 to 21.

The ornate but symmetrical design of Federal furniture

Some of the most dramatic changes from tradition in the Federal period occurred in furniture design. During the Revolution, the breaking of ties with England had served to strengthen American crafts. After the war, skilled workers again emigrated from Europe, bringing a host of new techniques. These forces for change were galvanized when, in 1788 and 1793, books by the London designers George Hepplewhite and Thomas Sheraton, illustrating the latest furniture fashions, were published. The result was an abrupt shift in style in America as the new designs were eagerly copied by local craftsmen. Despite the Revolution, London was still the fashion capital to Americans, and the new furniture's classically inspired details seemed a perfect match for the pride of the new republic in its growing wealth and in its democratic ideals.

The plan of a formal drawing room, designed by England's Thomas Sheraton and influential in the U.S., reflects his idea that "the drawing-room is to concentrate the elegance of the whole house, and is the highest display of richness of furniture." The room was devoid of such distractions as books so that nothing would divert the guest from the evening's objective— flowing and witty conversation.

A Plan & Section of a Drawing Room

SHERATON CHAIR   HEPPLEWHITE CHAIR

The impact of British furniture designs on America can be seen by comparing the original side chairs at left created by Thomas Sheraton and George Hepplewhite with the U.S.-made versions below. Although a few details have been altered, the overall designs are the same. The round-backed side chair and its copy below are both decorated in what Hepplewhite described as the "new and very elegant fashion" of finishing chairs "with paint or japanned work" to match the rooms he and Sheraton drew. The copy below of Sheraton's chair is one of a set of 24 made in 1797 for the banquet room at George Washington's Mount Vernon by the firm of John Aitkin, one of the best of Philadelphia's craft shops. At that time the chair cost some $10 and was one of the most expensive designs made. Of this price, some $3.30 went to the craftsman for three days' work. The basic price of chairs ranged from a little less than two dollars to about $12, and extra-cost details could be added. A price book of 1796 listed 27 extras, ranging from one penny for a scroll carved in a back rail and two pennies for veneering each rail to about 50 cents for adding a seat with a serpentine-shaped front instead of a plain, straight one.

A majestic American eagle glowers from an engraved glass goblet probably made in the early 1790s by the great glass blower John Frederick Amelung. Amelung, bringing along 68 expert glassmakers, arrived in America from Bremen, Germany, in 1784 and formed the glassmaking community called New Bremen in Maryland. Unhappily, problems of unfamiliar raw materials and the failure of the American public to buy enough of his wares doomed Amelung's firm, which lasted barely a decade before being declared bankrupt in 1795.

Patriotic designs adorn a Staffordshire plate, one of many with American themes made in England for sale in the U.S. Despite the American border, the view in the center is thought to be of an English mansion familiar to the designer.

Patriotic emblems to glorify the republic

Their patriotic spirit fired by the winning of independence, Americans were only too eager to see everything they owned emblazoned with symbols of the new nation. Likenesses of George Washington were painted on china, engraved on glassware, printed on curtains and bedspreads, and carved on mantelpieces *(page 44)*. Even pictures of Washington's home, Mount Vernon, appeared on many objects. But by far the most popular patriotic symbol was the eagle. Since ancient times eagles had been considered to be signs of power, and in 1782 an act of Congress made the American bald eagle the national emblem of the United States.

Even without its political connotation, the eagle made a powerful addition to Federal designs. Carved eagles, their wings grandly outstretched, appeared atop mirror frames, desks and the highly prized grandfather clocks that adorned the homes of the wealthy. The same motif also became popular for inlay work as American woodcraftsmen mastered that fine art.

Intricate inlay work, often used to add patriotic designs to Federal furniture, was the result of meticulous handiwork that reveals the origins of many pieces. Chests, tables and desks were richly patterned with eagles, flowers and other figures like those below, carefully fashioned of small pieces of wood, usually white holly. The delicate shading was created either by staining or by scorching the wood with hot sand until the right shade of brown or black appeared. Variations of these designs were used by craftsmen in nearly every major American city; the three shown here were probably made in Baltimore, the half oval and the full oval with the eagle insignia for a chest of drawers, the bottom oval for the desk at right. Sometimes experts can discover, through studying such designs and other decorations, where an item was produced. Certain combinations of woods were characteristically used in some areas and thus provide clues to the origin of a piece. On the legs of the desk at right, for example, the teardrop-shaped inlays of satinwood resemble forms used by Maryland craftsmen. The diagonal pattern of alternating light and dark woods in the narrow inlaid strip beneath the drawers is also typical of Marylanders' work.

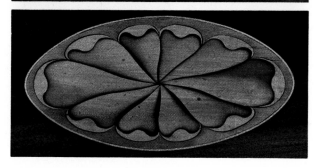

American eagles, inlaid and carved, add a note of authority to a mahogany desk made in Maryland about 1800. The piece is patterned after designs by English cabinetmakers.

51

The growing stature
of American arts

Artistic expression during the Federal period was not limited to craftsmen and architects. During this era, painting and sculpture were coming into their own in America, most brilliantly in Philadelphia. There, Gilbert Stuart and Charles Willson Peale were painting important figures of the day, while John Lewis Krimmel, one of whose works is at right, was pioneering in the portrayal of ordinary folk that critics call genre. His paintings represent a transitional stage, mixing dignified people with the comic figures that are genre's hallmark. The Federal period has also been called "sculpture's wooden age," and again Philadelphia led the nation, for it was home to the great wood carver William Rush *(below)*.

WILLIAM RUSH

William Rush was not only the first native sculptor in America but also one of its best. More than a century after his death, in 1833, some of his wooden anatomy models were still being used by the University of Pennsylvania Medical School. Among his first efforts were figureheads for ships. So well made were these works that one observer lauded them as being "superior to any . . . seen in any port of the world." It was his delightful *Water Nymph and Bittern,* however, that brought probably his greatest publicity, and near scandal. When carving the statue in 1809, Rush used a live model, Nancy Vanuxem, a Philadelphia debutante, posing her in what the era considered near nudity. The good burghers of the city were outraged and denounced Rush in the press, from the pulpit and even on the street. It mattered little that the girl was the daughter of a member of the City Council or that she was chaperoned throughout the sitting. The controversial statue, subsequently cast in bronze *(right),* stands today in the Philadelphia Museum of Art.

Fourth of July in Centre Square, painted about 1812 by the German-born Philadelphia artist John Lewis Krimmel, captures the spirit and fashions of the Federal era. Patriotic feeling then ran high, and crowds like these observed Independence Day with great merrymaking. In the left foreground a group of men celebrate in time-honored fashion by drinking. At the right, elegantly clad women show off the latest in clothes, the flowing robes patterned after the styles of ancient Greece *(page 44)*. In the middle, William Rush's famous wood sculpture, *Water Nymph and Bittern*, stands in the central fountain, still too daring a figure for some of the more conservative citizens. In front of it an austere Quaker turns brusquely away while his wife sneaks a glance back over his shoulder. In the background, like a temple to some ancient god, stands one of the city's most stylish Federal buildings, oddly enough a pump house for the Philadelphia waterworks, ennobled by Benjamin Henry Latrobe *(page 45)* with a Greek portal and Roman dome.

3

Might
and Right

During the decade of the 1920s, the officers of the Jones & Laughlin Steel Corporation reflected with pleasure upon the submissive mood in the company's captive mill town of Woodlawn—or Aliquippa, as it was later renamed—just outside of Pittsburgh. There had been an occasional attempt at union organizing around the town, fostered by outside agitators and political radicals who did not seem to understand that what was good for big business was good for little workers, too. And when the police dutifully clapped a few troublemakers in jail or ran them out of the district, the people of Aliquippa—though they may have felt resentment toward both the lawmen and the town government—had kept their feelings to themselves. Among the few people to speak out against the state of affairs was a local storekeeper who had the bad taste to complain out loud that the city council was being paid, in bald-faced violation of Pennsylvania state law, by Jones & Laughlin.

Officials of the steel company could see no reason why they should not oversee the welfare of

Aliquippa. "The company ought to have something to say about the way the town is run," said one executive. "The company owns pretty near everything in sight."

The company surely did. It owned the steel mill that provided jobs for 85 per cent of the labor force in town. It had built a fair portion of the workers' houses, and it owned the utility that sent water into those houses. Throughout the town the company's word was law. That law was enforced by the company's uniformed police, paid by Jones & Laughlin and legally deputized by the cooperative Pennsylvania government under a succession of state "coal and iron police" laws. Moreover, in an industrial fief like Aliquippa, the company held such powerful sway that no movie could be shown if it seemed critical of the cause of big industry, and even schoolteachers were selected with an eye toward their labor attitudes. Naturally that attitude was in tune with the company's. In one nearby mill town the schoolmarm caught a boy speaking up for the unions, whacked him with a yardstick and sent him home with the warning, "Next time, don't talk [like] that on the school grounds."

Finally, the steel company often controlled the stores where the families bought their food and

Rumbling through the slaty haze, a supply train enters the U.S. Steel plant in McKeesport, Pennsylvania. Steel's reliance on rail transportation and the railroads' dependence on steel for revenue and for its own equipment have kept the two industries close.

clothes; and by jacking up prices, then giving credit or loans against salary until workers were totally mired in debt, the company gradually came to own the very lives of the people. It was difficult for a right-thinking corporate servant to see why anyone should expect things otherwise. After all, in the roaring industrial era that climaxed in the 1920s, Aliquippa was no different from hundreds of other feudal enclaves where other companies owned pretty near everything in sight. Over in neighboring Johnstown, for example, 9,000 men from a town of 65,000 worked in a single operation just absorbed by Bethlehem Steel, and lived in a state of suitable vassalage beneath the company. These two companies, despite their power in these ravines, were only two cogs in a gigantic industrial machine whose long steel arms reached out from the manufacturing cities of Pennsylvania and the adjacent states to clamp a tight hold on the economy and, for a while, on even the government of the United States.

In 1920 some 260,000 U.S. millworkers turned out nearly three fifths of the world's supply of iron and steel, the most basic of all modern structural metals, and another 470,000 worked in fabricating, finishing and allied industries. The open-hearth and Bessemer furnaces of the Pittsburgh area alone made as much steel as France, Japan, Germany and Sweden combined, while the state of Pennsylvania accounted for nearly half of the total U.S. output. In the course of this triumph, the men who built the steel mills came to dominate the society as had no other special-interest group, even the propertied politicians of the Constitutional era. Their dominance had a critical effect not only on the Middle Atlantic States, which were the focus of productive power, but on the growth and future of the entire nation. Today, industry's dictatorial control has been broken: Jones & Laughlin and the other big companies must operate as closely within the scope of the law and public policy as any other institution, and must answer to the public for any jarring policies—as the steel companies discovered in 1962 when President Kennedy himself called in the industrialists to cut off a projected price rise. Nevertheless, the residue of the high time of steel still lies heavily upon Pennsylvania and its neighbor states, where leaders of the current renaissance are pulling hard to get both the economy and the mentality of the region out of the ravine towns where the steel is still made.

In the 1920s the hands pulling against Big Steel were few, and they got little effective support from either the government or the people at large. For this was a time when bigness in business tended to be equated with goodness, a time when sheer might seemed to make right. By this popular view, the mighty American steel industry, taking much of its strength from the mill towns of Pennsylvania, had about as much right on its side as any private undertaking in history.

During the 1920s, the reigning company in the industry was the United States Steel Corporation, which controlled as much as 46 per cent of the nation's steel production. The work force of U.S. Steel (averaging 240,000 men) was bigger than the standing army of the United States, and total sales for the company's first 19 years of life had exceeded $11.2 billion.

To the directors of U.S. Steel, the immensity of their enterprise was more than a monopolistic luxury. Bigness seemed a basic necessity in a business where the leading competitors all were giants. Furthermore, steelmaking was a business where it was physically and economically almost impossible to do things in a small way. A single change in technology at one plant, from old-fashioned Bessemer furnaces to a row of more modern open hearths, could cost millions of dollars; and a single customer—such as the U.S. Navy—might suddenly want enough steel to fight a war.

The production and sale of raw steel was only the root of power for the American steel industry in general and for U.S. Steel in particular, which was known more simply as *The Corporation* by deferential journalists and captains of industry. From its head office, U.S. Steel's pious, euphemizing board chairman, Judge Elbert Gary, held the reins of four Class I railroads and, through interlocking directorates, had a hand in running dozens of other lines. To assure a continuing supply of bituminous coal for its coking ovens and furnaces, The Corporation had become perhaps the biggest coal operator in the country—at a time when 734,000 men worked in the mines and coal made up three fourths of all the industrial and home-heating fuel in America. Across the country U.S. Steel owned or controlled scores of fabricating and finishing mills, where the raw metal was turned into steel products. In the normal course of its business, Judge Gary's Corporation, like the other steel producers, also became a front-ranking real-estate operator, with many millions invested in company houses, and at one point there were so many company stores in the empire that U.S. Steel inadvertently became one of the nation's larger wholesale grocers.

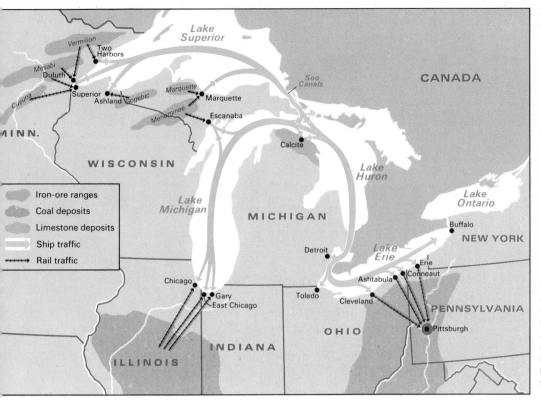

The Pittsburgh area has remained first in steelmaking despite an apparent geographical drawback —its remoteness *(shown on map)* from large present-day sources of two essential raw materials, iron ore and limestone. Although Pittsburgh once used Pennsylvania deposits of both raw materials, the area's mills now rely on the mines of Minnesota, Wisconsin and Michigan for their supplies. These bulky minerals can be shipped most cheaply on the enormous Great Lakes ore boats. It would seem, therefore, that port cities such as Gary and Toledo, with easier access to iron ore and limestone, should long since have outstripped Pittsburgh in steelmaking. But here Pittsburgh's counterbalancing advantages have come into play. One is that the city lies in the midst of a great coal-producing area. It can get this third essential raw material delivered cheaply via river, while other steel cities must get their coal by rail. Pittsburgh's second crucial advantage is historical: it has been a steelmaking center for so long and has so many huge mills that it has been able to withstand challenges from other areas.

Standing right next to The Corporation in size, if no longer in power, were its sometime friends, the railroads. At this time the Big Daddy of the rail lines was a massive, Philadelphia-based institution called the Pennsylvania Railroad, whose payroll in 1920 was larger by 12,000 than even The Corporation's, whose trackage carried one eighth of all American land passengers, and whose assets at one point would include 500 defunct corporations, a splendid source of tax loopholes.

As with Big Steel, the Pennsylvania Railroad's power only began with its original assets. Early in its history it had carefully absorbed, by one means or another, most of the small independent lines in its "territory" that either were useful as feeder or connecting roads or were susceptible to being grabbed by rivals. Later, the cutthroat competition that had characterized the railroads' expansionist era gave way to well-organized pools among the major lines. Around the turn of the century, through a series of bilateral stock purchases in which both the Pennsy and the New York Central were involved, some of the vital but financially shaky Eastern lines, like the Baltimore and Ohio, the Chesapeake and Ohio, and the Erie, were brought into a cooperative system. By this time, therefore, it had become either inconvenient or almost impossible for a shipper to move so much as a safety pin from the fabricating plants of Pennsylvania to the big markets and seaports of the East without going across the turf of the Pennsy and its friends. And he who crossed that turf rolled on the stock of the ruling roads. It was true that in the New York Central the Pennsy had one competitor—though a friendly one—for the major east-west traffic. However, ruinous rivalry with the Central had been averted before the turn of the century when in the middle of a bloody building and buying war, which, if continued, would have left both roads dangerously overextended, the financier J. Pierpont Morgan hauled the presidents of the feuding lines onto his yacht, *Corsair,* for enforced peace talks.

"I decided that something should be done," growled Morgan. And from his viewpoint it certainly should have, since he controlled a major block of stock in the Central and was anxious to continue as a financial agent of the Pennsy.

What the formidable banker did was hold the two rail tycoons, George Roberts of the Pennsy and Chauncey Depew of the Central, on board all day while they snarled at each other, and Morgan, slumped in a chair and puffing on a black cigar, glared at the combatants and occasionally

57

The making of a coal field

About 50 million years of geological history have gone into creating the rich seams of coal that stretch across much of Pennsylvania. The geological cross section of the state below shows the distinctive formations in which the major deposits are found—bituminous coal in the comparatively level strata of the plateau in the west, anthracite in the folded strata of the eastern ridges and valleys. At right is an idealized diagram showing, from left to right, the relationship between surface conditions and deposits, rocks and coal. The surface conditions varied over the ages, changing from dry land *(bottom of diagram)* to swamp and sea, and then sometimes reverting to dry land again. As swamps formed, ferns and other plant life flourished. When the water deepened, this organic material was covered by layers of clay eroded from the adjacent land and by layers of lime from the remains of sea creatures. As the seas retreated, swamps once again appeared with their teeming plant life. This cycle occurred again and again over hundreds of thousands of years, each time creating new layers of sediment. As the layers became more numerous, they compressed the deposits beneath them. The loose mineral sediments were transformed into layers of shale, limestone and other rocks. The partly decayed swamp vegetation first became peat, a forerunner of coal, and then, as increasing heat and pressure from overlying deposits drove water and gases from the peat, turned into a soft brown fuel known as lignite. More heat and pressure changed the lignite into the black soft coal called bituminous, which is found in large supply in western Pennsylvania in flat layers, reflecting the manner in which the original swamps were covered and compressed. But in eastern Pennsylvania the crust of the earth folded, subjecting the deposits to greater heat and pressure, and creating anthracite, a rare, hard coal with a very high carbon content.

ALLEGHENY PLATEAU

BITUMINOUS COAL DEPOSITS

LOCATION OF
CROSS SECTION

cut in with a curt remark. By evening the tumult and the shouting had substantially ceased. The principals had agreed to remove the galling competitive lines they had previously inserted—or planned to insert—in each other's flanks, and peace reigned once more along the pivotal railways of the Eastern U.S. No sleep was lost that night over the fact that the constitution of the state of Pennsylvania expressly forbade any railway to buy all or part of a competing line. Morgan simply made the transactions in his own name. Thus, in a typical, extralegal power play, the big men of big industry had hurdled right over the regulations of the civil government, as Roberts put it later, "with a view to securing remunerative rates of traffic and harmony along the lines."

A happy state of harmony came to exist between Big Rails and Big Steel. There were, after all, many reasons for harmony. Within Pennsylvania and nearby territories, the rail lines had grown up on a diet that was heavy on steel. The rails themselves and the locomotives that ran on them were made of steel. Between 1900 and 1919 alone, the Eddystone and Philadelphia works of the Baldwin locomotive company turned out 35,000 engines, each of which required many tons of steel. And perhaps most important of all, steel—including its raw materials and the finished goods made therefrom—was one of the railroads' most lucrative freight items.

Under such circumstances steel and rails saw no reason to fight. Rather, the railroads settled back to enjoy their income from the steel traffic. And the steel companies, in turn, protected their own incomes through such superb bits of profiteering as the Pittsburgh-plus pricing system, by which all steel made anywhere in America was delivered at a fixed wholesale cost plus a per-ton rail freight charge calculated as though the steel had been made in Pittsburgh. This imaginative policy enabled the old, established plants around Pittsburgh to compete all over the country on even terms with mills located closer to the growing Western and Southern markets. At the same time, it gave those other mills the chance to carry off piratical delights like the famous hole-in-the-wall caper, which a Chicago plant inflicted on a customer in an adjoining building. To deliver the steel, the Chicago mill simply cut a hole in the common wall between the buildings and wheeled the order through, pausing only to pocket the $7.60-per-ton phantom freight charge from Pittsburgh.

In order to maintain such profitable practices, it was necessary that the members of the steelmaking fraternity get along with one another. And, of course, they learned to be friends under the paternal guidance of The Corporation, which deeply disapproved of all forms of unseemly competition, especially price cutting. "We had come to regard each other as brothers," said The Corporation's first president, Charles Schwab, whose brotherly salary was $100,000 per annum. At intervals from

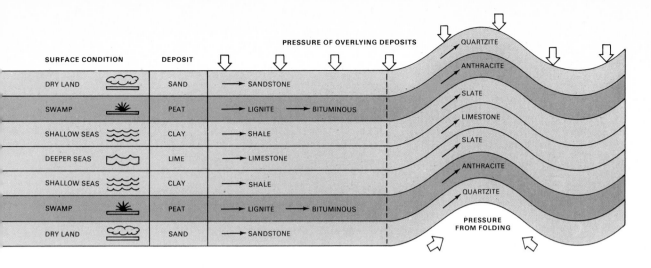

SURFACE CONDITION		DEPOSIT	PRESSURE OF OVERLYING DEPOSITS
DRY LAND		SAND	→ SANDSTONE
SWAMP		PEAT	→ LIGNITE → BITUMINOUS
SHALLOW SEAS		CLAY	→ SHALE
DEEPER SEAS		LIME	→ LIMESTONE
SHALLOW SEAS		CLAY	→ SHALE
SWAMP		PEAT	→ LIGNITE → BITUMINOUS
DRY LAND		SAND	→ SANDSTONE

QUARTZITE
ANTHRACITE
SLATE
LIMESTONE
SLATE
ANTHRACITE
QUARTZITE

PRESSURE FROM FOLDING

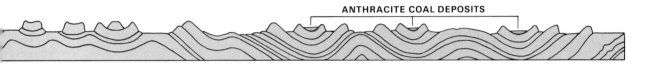

ALLEGHENY MOUNTAINS   RIDGE AND VALLEY PROVINCE

ANTHRACITE COAL DEPOSITS

1907 to 1911 the brothers were brought together at a ceremony called the Gary dinners, where they ate good red meat, drank good red wine and agreed on things—the things The Corporation saw as contributing to the common good. As host —and the industry's undisputed leader—Judge Gary presided at these affairs; over coffee and cigars he delivered gentle homilies on the industry's duty to its country, its workers and its God. Then he got down to the point:

"We as men, as gentlemen, as friends, as neighbors," he said at one dinner, "having been in close communication and contact during the last few years, have reached a point where we entertain for one another respect and affectionate regard. We have reached a position so high in our lines of activity that we are bound to protect one another . . ."

After the applause died down, the friends, neighbors and brothers showed they had gotten the message. "I think . . ." said the representative from Jones & Laughlin, "to talk of reducing the prices ought not to be considered for a moment. . . ." And by and large it was not; nor would there be many serious challenges to the accepted price lines within the industry in the near future. In 1913, for example, the Secretary of the Navy opened some sealed bids for 8,000 tons of armor plate for the battleship *Pennsylvania*. Three companies were in the bidding. "It occasioned no surprise," said a realistic Senator, "to find that the bids did not vary a dollar a ton between the three companies, and that the bids were in fact twenty-five dollars a ton more than the price received by these companies on the last previous contract."

There was little reason why anyone in Washington should have been surprised. For even though a number of the big trusts, notably those in oil and rails, had been under heavy (and often successful) fire by reformers during the period from 1890 to 1914, very few damaging shots had gotten through the protective armor of the Big Steel combines. In fact, from the days of McKinley on through the reform era and into the 1920s, the steel industry was at some pains to keep the key positions in Washington well stocked with men of a friendly persuasion. "On the Thursday before election day," wrote one frustrated reformer, "I saw 5,000 men discharged from one steel plant in western Pennsylvania, with the admonition, given them by the foreman at the gate, that unless Senator [Boies] Penrose were returned [to office], the plant would stay closed indefinitely." Naturally, Senator Penrose was re-elected; and naturally, he did nothing to injure his benefactors.

The Presidents' Cabinets in Washington were also liberally sprinkled with allies of The Corporation. A Pittsburgh lawyer with the name of Philander C. Knox, a close friend of coal-steel tycoon Henry Clay Frick and of Pittsburgh's formidable financier, Andrew W. Mellon, held the important

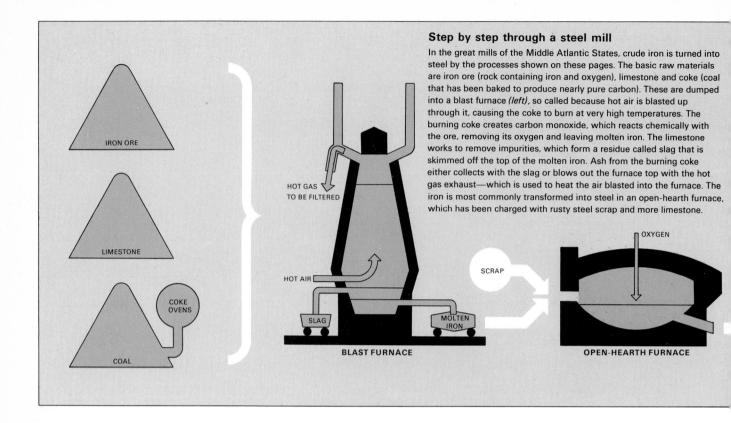

Step by step through a steel mill

In the great mills of the Middle Atlantic States, crude iron is turned into steel by the processes shown on these pages. The basic raw materials are iron ore (rock containing iron and oxygen), limestone and coke (coal that has been baked to produce nearly pure carbon). These are dumped into a blast furnace *(left)*, so called because hot air is blasted up through it, causing the coke to burn at very high temperatures. The burning coke creates carbon monoxide, which reacts chemically with the ore, removing its oxygen and leaving molten iron. The limestone works to remove impurities, which form a residue called slag that is skimmed off the top of the molten iron. Ash from the burning coke either collects with the slag or blows out the furnace top with the hot gas exhaust—which is used to heat the air blasted into the furnace. The iron is most commonly transformed into steel in an open-hearth furnace, which has been charged with rusty steel scrap and more limestone.

office of U.S. Attorney General the year the U.S. Steel trust was formed. At various times Elihu Root, an attorney for the old Carnegie Steel Company, had been McKinley's Secretary of War and held the same position under Teddy Roosevelt before becoming Secretary of State; Robert Bacon, a Morgan partner and director of The Corporation, was Root's Assistant Secretary of State; Truman Newberry, head of a U.S. Steel subsidiary, was Assistant Secretary of the Navy from 1905 to 1908. And Andrew Mellon himself became Secretary of the Treasury under Harding, Coolidge and Hoover. Mellon's appointment was particularly fortuitous for the corporate interests of the Pittsburgh area. For it placed the city's most powerful manipulator of money where he could keep a benign eye on the health not only of the steel business, in which the Mellon family had large holdings, but also of two booming young Pittsburgh enterprises, both Mellon-controlled: the wholly monopolistic, handsomely tariff-protected Aluminum Company of America, and the Gulf Oil Corporation, second-biggest petroleum combine in the world.

One of the more significant aspects of the relationship between Washington and the Pennsylvania-centered industrial machine was the lack of consistent antitrust action from the residents of the White House or the men on the Supreme Court. There is some evidence that this attitude may have been influenced, in part, by Judge Gary's great skill in creating the right impressions in the right places. The judge, occasionally invited to the White House for informal chats, was steadfast in his protestations of the innocent purpose of The Corporation. "It is not intended to obtain control of any line of business," he maintained in one public statement, ". . . or in any way antagonize any principle or policy of the law." Gary was blatant in his flattery of the celebrated trust-buster, Roosevelt. "My dear Mr. President," he wrote, ". . . I think the attitude of the present administration . . . is exactly what this country needs. . . . It is embodied in the sentiment expressed by you: A square deal for all. I do not hesitate to say that your influence as President of this great republic has been of benefit to me personally and I feel equally certain that it is beginning to have a good effect upon others. . . ."

At this time Roosevelt was swinging his antitrust big stick with characteristic vigor, attempting to break up some of the combines of what he called "the malefactors of great wealth." But even Roosevelt's big stick never knocked The Corporation

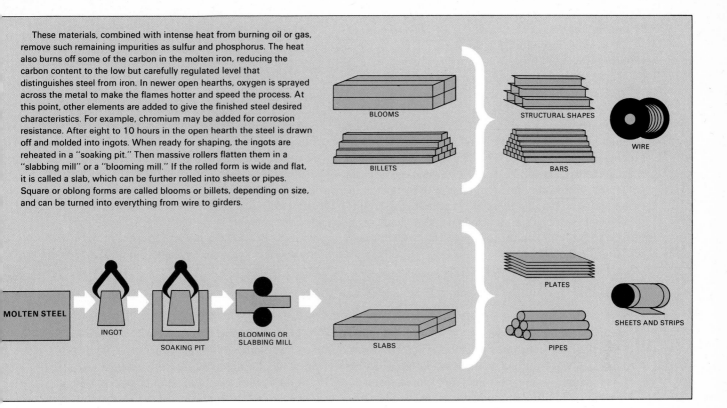

These materials, combined with intense heat from burning oil or gas, remove such remaining impurities as sulfur and phosphorus. The heat also burns off some of the carbon in the molten iron, reducing the carbon content to the low but carefully regulated level that distinguishes steel from iron. In newer open hearths, oxygen is sprayed across the metal to make the flames hotter and speed the process. At this point, other elements are added to give the finished steel desired characteristics. For example, chromium may be added for corrosion resistance. After eight to 10 hours in the open hearth the steel is drawn off and molded into ingots. When ready for shaping, the ingots are reheated in a "soaking pit." Then massive rollers flatten them in a "slabbing mill" or a "blooming mill." If the rolled form is wide and flat, it is called a slab, which can be further rolled into sheets or pipes. Square or oblong forms are called blooms or billets, depending on size, and can be turned into everything from wire to girders.

BLOOMS
BILLETS
STRUCTURAL SHAPES
BARS
WIRE

MOLTEN STEEL
INGOT
SOAKING PIT
BLOOMING OR SLABBING MILL
SLABS
PLATES
PIPES
SHEETS AND STRIPS

down. Nor did the Supreme Court. In 1920, during a serious look at U.S. Steel's activities, the Court stated as follows: "The Corporation . . . did not at any time abuse the power or ascendency it possessed. It resorted to none of the brutalities or tyrannies that the cases illustrate of other combinations. It did not secure freight rebates . . . whatever it did was not at the expense of labor; it did not increase its profits by lowering the quality of its products, nor create an artificial scarcity of them; it did not oppress or coerce its competitors. . . ." So wrote Justices McKenna, Van Devanter, White and Holmes, even as The Corporation was profiting from the Pittsburgh-plus pricing system, and a few months after 20 men and women had been killed in the suppression of an industry-wide steel strike whose two major aims had been union recognition and abolition of the industry's traditional 12-to-14-hour working day.

Thus, in 1920, by a combination of palship, arm twisting and outright possession, the steel companies of Pennsylvania, together with their companion industries, did indeed seem to own everything in sight—including, from time to time, various parts of the United States government. Through this pervasive control, businessmen like Gary and Schwab could do more or less what

they pleased; and what the tycoons pleased to do was keep things very much as they were, much as they had been ever since 1865, when the country had emerged from the Civil War and charged off into a dynamic era of unprecedented expansion.

During this post-Civil War period, with half a continent to be subdued and a host of great cities to build, America had developed a ravenous appetite for iron and steel, of which Pennsylvania then produced the largest portion of the nation's supply. And so long as the need seemed virtually unlimited for rails, bridges, tall buildings, factories, ships, locomotives and other heavy machines, the nation was not inclined to be fussy about the overbearing size of the industries that grew to fill that need—or the methods and morals of the men who ran the businesses. On the contrary. The steel, coal and rail barons were admired in much of the society as symbols of a certain kind of virtue, "the finest flower of competitive society," as a Yale professor once put it glowingly.

There was, in addition, a current notion that the poor were poor because they were lazy, and that any honest, earnest young man was bound to be rewarded. Accordingly, Horatio Alger Jr., one of the most popular writers of the period, cranked out more than 100 versions of his "rags to riches" saga for a believing public. A thoroughgoing financial scoundrel like Jay Gould of New York was piously applauded for his modest self-appraisal: "I began life in a lowly way," said Gould, "and by industry, temperance, and attention to my own business have been successful, perhaps beyond the measure of my deserts."

If some people protested—as the early unionists and other pioneer reformers attempted to do—that Jay Gould was several light-years beyond his just deserts, these reformers found themselves frustrated or beaten down by the bullish mood of society in general, and by the permissive, even impotent stance of a government that had been created in other times to oversee a very different sort of country.

The prevailing attitude in Washington, in Harrisburg and in the lesser seats of civil power during the latter half of the 19th Century was that the best government put the least restraints on people's affairs. It was a philosophy inherited from the days of Thomas Jefferson, when the United States was—and seemed destined always to be—a nation of self-supporting, independent farmers. This laissez-faire attitude hung on while the population of Pennsylvania and other neighboring states began to crowd into urban centers and the balance of the work force shifted from the farm to industry. Meanwhile, the various levels of government developed neither a strong inclination nor sufficient legal instruments to control the brutish forces of an industrialized society. In fact, they were often at some pains to encourage those forces.

Between 1868 and 1872 alone, the suitably bribed General Assembly of Pennsylvania put through more than 40 bills chartering corporations empowered to do virtually anything imaginable in coal mining, transportation, and iron- and steel-making. To be certain that nothing interfered with the smooth workings of these corporations, the Assembly had also passed a coal and iron police bill, by which the companies' hired goons—strikebreakers and the like—became a legal enforcement arm of the state. To one shocked European observer, the Assembly at that time was "a Witches' Sabbath of jobbing, bribing, thieving, and prostitution of legislative power to promote interests."

Aside from this immensely favorable political climate, Pennsylvania was so blessed by geographical position and natural resources that it was plainly destined to become a center of U.S. industrial power. The state itself was dead astride the main transportation routes between the Western U.S. and the major markets and seaports of the East. Northeastern Pennsylvania contained some of the world's most important anthracite coal deposits. Northwestern Pennsylvania held the oil fields that, two years before the Civil War, had already set off the country's first petroleum boom, giving birth initially to the Standard Oil trust, and ultimately to the Gulf, Sun and Atlantic oil companies. But Pittsburgh was the real gem. In and around the city lay at least 200 billion tons (according to one estimate) of bituminous coal, low in sulfur content and hence perfect for conversion into coke—one of the three basic ingredients for making steel. Near the city were generous deposits of iron ore. When these deposits proved inadequate, the steel men reached out to the rich ore of the northern ranges like Minnesota's Mesabi, bringing it in via a fleet of big, new ore boats, which by 1920 were capable of automatically dumping their 12,000-ton loads in a few hours into strings of specially designed ore-carrying rail cars. The other ingredient for steel, limestone to draw off the impurities in the molten metal, lay all over Pennsylvania for the taking.

Into this fertile garden of industry had come the kinds of men who knew how to plant and harvest the seeds of production, men with the strength to build industries big enough to match the nation's need, men with the vision to foresee the importance of iron and steel, coal, oil and rails—growth food for a great industrial nation. These were men, too, for whom personal power felt as natural as the breath of life and to whom immense wealth was an overweening desire. Ultimately, the three industrialists who grew richer and more powerful than any others in the region—and had the greatest effect upon it—were named Mellon, Frick and Carnegie. All were cut to the Horatio Alger mold.

Thomas Mellon came to the Pittsburgh area at the age of five, the son of poor Scotch-Irish farming people. As a young man he worshiped the image of Benjamin Franklin, ". . . poorer than myself, who by industry, thrift and frugality had become learned and wise, and elevated to wealth and fame." By the same kind of industry and thrift, and by buying property and lending money to all the right people at all the right times, Thomas Mellon soon became the sharpest financier and real-estate dealer around Pittsburgh. Before he retired he had set down the foundations of a banking and coal combine that his sons, Andrew and Richard B., would build into as potent a family-held financial empire as any in the nation.

Henry Clay Frick was a fine lad, too, a frail but hard-working Pennsylvania Dutch boy who showed an early bent for business. At 19 he was bookkeeper in the family whiskey-making firm. But even at that early age young Frick could see a much bigger opportunity close at hand—the coal business. In 1871 he borrowed against family holdings to buy his first mining properties. At 21, again short of money but long on ambition, he went to the offices of T. Mellon & Sons to borrow $10,000 to build more coke ovens. The elder Mellon, liking what he saw, gave him the money. Some time later Mellon remarked to his son Andrew that Frick was "able, energetic, industrious, resourceful, self-confident . . . he will go far." That he would, hand in hand with young Andrew.

Within a year he was back for another $10,000, and later for more. With this kind of financing, Frick rode out the Panic of 1873, picking over the bodies of his dead and dying rivals until he had cornered 60 per cent of the coal land in the Pittsburgh region and 80 per cent of the region's coke production. He then shoved the price of coke up from 90 cents a ton (its Depression low) to five dollars, taking a three-dollar profit for himself on each ton, while the iron- and steelmakers screamed in anguished rage at the sudden jump in their costs. By the end of 1879 Frick, aged 30, had become a millionaire, an event he celebrated a few months later by going off on a grand tour of Europe with his good friend young Andrew Mellon. In 1880 the two men returned to Pittsburgh and settled into their lifelong roles as prime drillmasters in the forward march of industry.

The grand master of the whole Pennsylvania industrial parade, however, was a hard-eyed, stocky little gentleman known variously as "the King of the Vulcans," "the Iron Master" and many other titles, some perhaps unprintable. His real name was Andrew Carnegie, and he arrived in Pittsburgh in finest Alger style, aged 13, the son of a weaver. The year was 1848. Carnegie's first notable act was recorded in a local newspaper: "[He] had found in the street a draft for five hundred dollars and, like an honest little fellow, promptly made known the fact and deposited the paper in good hands. . . ." Subsequently his admirable qualities came to the attention of Thomas A. Scott, Western Division superintendent of the Pennsylvania Railroad, and soon to be its president. Scott took to young Andrew, hired him in the dual role of telegraph operator and private secretary, and set out to teach him the ways of the business world. There could hardly have been a better tutor. Besides having the organizational and managerial genius to help build the Pennsy and maneuver it into its position of power, Scott showed other talents and attitudes that an apprentice tycoon could benefit by observing. His hold on the state government in Harrisburg was said to be so tight that the legislature would not adjourn until notified by Mr. Scott that he had "no further business" in the way of new rail franchises, rights-of-way and so forth during that particular session. As to dealing with labor, Scott offered a solution to any disturbances: "Give the workingmen and strikers gun-bullet food. . . ."

Having served under such a teacher, Andrew Carnegie became very receptive to certain other basic lessons whose mastery would be worth millions. Among the first of these lessons was the importance of iron, then the principal metal of industry because there was no way to make steel economically at that time. Carnegie learned that the man who controlled iron production was well on his way toward controlling the entire industrial edifice. By age 30, therefore, with a deft series of acquisitions and maneuvers, Carnegie had bought into an iron mill, a locomotive works, an iron-rail company and an iron-bridge concern. The second lesson came seven years later, after he had resigned from the railroad to devote full time to the iron business. Traveling to London, he met a gentleman named Sir Henry Bessemer, who had devised a process for economically refining iron into its much stronger alloy, steel, by blowing a charge of cold air through the raw materials in the furnace. Carnegie, though reluctant to commit himself, went out to see a demonstration of the Bessemer process; and as the air roared through the furnace, sending aloft a brilliant shower of sparks, he stood transfixed.

"The change that came over the man," wrote a Carnegie biographer, "resembled the religious experience known as conversion. . . . A mind that had lived in apparent darkness was illumined by a sudden flash of light." It was about time. The same flash of light had already been glimpsed by a few of Carnegie's American rivals.

Hopping aboard the first ship for the U.S., Carnegie stormed back to Pittsburgh and, according to one story, rounded up his iron partners and shouted, "The day of iron has passed—Steel is King!" So saying, he built a massive Bessemer steelmaking works at Braddock, Pennsylvania, thoughtfully naming it after J. Edgar Thomson, Scott's predecessor as President of the Pennsylvania Railroad—which would be the new mills'

biggest potential customer. Within a few years the Thomson mill was paying 130 per cent each year on its original investment, returning an annual profit of $1,625,000 and helping to put Andrew Carnegie in the forefront of the burgeoning new industry.

"When was there ever such a business?" he exulted, and drove his mill hands to making the business even better. When a proud plant manager informed him, "Lucy Furnace No. 8 broke all records today," Carnegie shot back, "What were the other 10 furnaces doing?" And to another boast, "We broke all records . . . last week," Carnegie replied, "Congratulations! Why not do it every week?"

While his mills were breaking records, Carnegie learned a third lesson: that really profitable steelmaking demanded control of all phases of production. It was this lesson that led, ultimately, to the biggest pay-off of all. The price of coke had suddenly skyrocketed. And looking beneath the surface of this sudden irritation, he saw the pale, impassive face of Henry Clay Frick, who could not be shoved around by even such a major-league pusher as Andrew Carnegie. "We found that we could not get on without a supply of the fuel . . ." Carnegie wrote later. "The Frick Coke Company had not only the best coal and coke property, but . . . in Mr. Frick himself a man with a positive genius for its management."

After a brief mating dance the two tycoons brought their businesses together. Carnegie took a heavy interest in the coke holdings, and Frick, while remaining in charge of his own concern, eventually moved into the Carnegie organization, becoming in 1889 chairman of what was then called Carnegie Brothers. Under Frick's hard lash, the corporation, subsequently expanded and renamed the Carnegie Steel Company, easily dominated the steel business, while the chief stockholder, who was already contemplating retirement, began spending more and more time abroad, secure in the knowledge that Henry Clay Frick could handle any trouble that came up.

In 1892 there was a very bad spate of trouble at Carnegie's Homestead works, where the workers were striking in protest against the 12-hour day, the frequent seven-day weeks, the low pay scale and Frick's cold refusal to recognize any sort of workingman's union. For five months the mill hands stayed out, at one time fighting a bloody guerrilla war with the company's hired Pinkerton guards. Acting on the governor's orders, the Pennsylvania militia, 8,000-strong, marched on the plant, clapped many of the strike leaders in jail and got the furnaces fired up again under scab labor. Finally the union gave up and the strikers came back to work. Carnegie, in Europe, received the good news in messages from Frick: "Strike officially declared off yesterday. Our victory is now complete and most gratifying. . . . We had to teach our employees a lesson, and we have taught them one that they will never forget. . . . It is hard to estimate what blessings will flow from our complete victory. . . ."

"Life worth living again!" replied Carnegie. ". . . Surprising how pretty Italia—congratulate all around."

By 1900, however, steel's blessings were not at all hard to estimate. The Carnegie company, free of interference from either government or labor, had built itself into a mammoth prototype for all future trusts. To its coke and steel holdings it had added steamship and rail lines and an interest in the ore-rich Mesabi iron range, which Carnegie had leased from "my dear fellow millionaire" John D. Rockefeller. Thus the steel company was building a beautifully integrated enterprise aimed at controlling all phases of production and transportation. Carnegie himself described the business philosophy behind this total concentration of productive effort: "Put all your eggs in one basket—and then watch that basket." When Carnegie counted up his well-watched eggs in 1900, he found that the profits for the company that year totaled $40 million, of which his own share was a cool $25 million.

So rich were the rewards in the steel business that J. P. Morgan, who had previously concentrated on banks and rails, decided the time had come to move in. So did a number of other imaginative businessmen, and suddenly the woods were full of trusts competing with Carnegie. Of all the competitors, the best integrated and most threatening was Federal Steel, which Morgan had pasted together with the help of a young lawyer named Elbert Gary. Carnegie was enraged at this threat to his domain. "A struggle is inevitable and it is a question of the survival of the fittest," he wrote a lieutenant. Then he shot off messages to his various mills and other affiliates. "We should go into making their products at once. . . . Lose not a day . . . crisis has arrived, only one policy open: start at once hoop, rod, wire, nail mills; no halfway about last two. Extend coal and coke roads, announce these; also tubes . . . have no fear as to the result; victory certain. . . ."

Under this kind of assault even so tough a pair of corporate warriors as Morgan and Gary became alarmed. "It is not at all certain," said Gary, some time later, "that . . . the Carnegie Company would not have driven entirely out of business every steel company in the United States." In the face of such a disaster, Morgan sent emissaries to Carnegie to make peace. They did—but in so doing the emissaries made something much better. They made the U.S. Steel Corporation. Using as go-between the smooth-talking young Charles Schwab, a Carnegie lieutenant but a committed proponent of peaceful coexistence, Morgan proposed the formation of the biggest of all industrial combines, whose principal pillars would be the assets of the Carnegie organization and Federal Steel. In all, the mammoth new trust would come to operate 149 separate steel plants and to have a total capitalization of more than $1.4 billion. And its initial share of the nation's steel capacity would be some 65 per cent—all under the control of the Morgan interests.

What, asked Schwab respectfully, might be Mr. Carnegie's price for selling out to Morgan—and thus, in effect, leaving everybody in peace? The old Scotsman pondered for a while and came up with a figure: $492 million. So informed, Morgan said instantly, "I accept." In a later meeting, Morgan said, "I want to congratulate you on being the richest man in the world." Carnegie remarked, "I am the happiest man in the world. I have unloaded this burden on your back and I am off to Europe to play." And off he went, never to head another major industrial enterprise.

With the formation of The Corporation, the pattern of dominance for the steel industry was set. Through steel and its allied heavy industries, an overlapping pattern of control and commitment imposed itself upon Pennsylvania and, for a time, on a large part of the nation as well. In the economy of the U.S. this dominance would last another 25 or 30 years, though by 1920 The Corporation's own monopoly of steel would slide from 65 per cent to less than 50 as Gary gradually cut back his share of the market as one hedge against monopoly proceedings and the fast-growing Bethlehem Steel company took an increasingly stronger hold on Eastern markets.

In the state of Pennsylvania, the fact—and the effects—of the power of heavy industry would not wear off in half a century, for the roots had been planted too deeply. In Pittsburgh, by 1900 a city of 321,600, much of the industrial labor force was in steel alone. Meanwhile, men like Andrew Mellon had begun to branch out to take hold of the area's other heavy enterprises. By 1910 Mellon himself had won control of Alcoa and Gulf and had also established a foothold in the vast Westinghouse Air Brake and Electrical Corporation, whose founder had fumbled his finances into the arms of the bankers. And of course, there was a political machine to help keep the wheels of Pittsburgh industry well oiled. Two master ward heelers, Chris Magee and William Flinn, maintained a city-wide Republican organization—with strong state-wide connections—that Magee claimed was "safe as a bank." This was an apt analogy, since at the outset of each political campaign, bosses like Magee visited the offices of T. Mellon & Sons to get "Uncle Andy's" views on possible candidates and their platforms.

In Philadelphia between 1890 and 1925 the situation was quite similar. The city's economy was wrapped up in heavyweight factories like the Baldwin works, in the Pennsylvania Railroad and its subsidiaries, in the upstate anthracite deposits, and in the crude-oil refineries—Gulf, Sun and the like—along the Delaware. As for a cooperating political machine, it was here that the Vare brothers, George, Edwin and William, boasted, "We can send anybody we want to the Senate—anybody." And anybody is pretty much who they sent.

Baltimore, too, felt the power of steel. Here Bethlehem Steel in 1916 began building up the sprawling Sparrows Point mill, for a time the biggest steelworks in the world and still, today, metropolitan Baltimore's No. 1 private employer and taxpayer. Together with the railroads—the B&O, the C&O, and the ubiquitous Pennsy—the steelmakers would have much to say about affairs in Baltimore and the state of Maryland, too.

Despite all its power, however, and all its control of both the economy and the politics of the region and the nation, the great industrial machine of 1920 was clanking its single-minded way toward a period of deep, deep trouble. For the basic weakness, built into the entire complex, was that most of the elaborate machinery, political as well as industrial, was dedicated not to progress but to making time stand still. The monopoly by The Corporation and its friends, the protective tariffs and the piratical sales methods enabled the aging Bessemer and open-hearth works of Pittsburgh to keep showing profits while other parts of the nation—and other countries as well—were developing more efficient techniques. Finally, the giants came to rely too much on their monopolistic weight alone, rather than on good technological progress and on improved market services. By the

1930s The Corporation's own profits had slid drastically, from a steady 12 per cent in the good old days of Schwab and Morgan to a thin, thin 2.8 per cent. And there was more trouble ahead.

The southerly and westerly drift, both of markets and of manufacturing, would cause Pittsburgh to lose its ancient—and fundamental—geographical advantage. In Pittsburgh itself, the major steelmakers would be reluctant to change over to more modern manufacturing methods, thanks in part to steel's old rallying cry "Pioneering don't pay!," in part to the sheer expense of putting in new equipment and in part to further geographical factors: the narrow ravines where the mills were first set down, to take advantage of both river and rail transport, would be physically too confining to allow for new plant installations.

In much the same way the great power and momentum of the railroads gave a continued impression of dominance, while the young trucking industry was taking little nibbles of the freight business—nibbles that would one day add up to a very formidable bite. And Pennsylvania, by failing to leap in vigorously at the very beginning of the truck and auto boom, had lost an irretrievable opportunity not only to dominate in a new kind of transportation, but also to nail down a major share of the fabricating and assembly-line production that now goes on in Detroit.

The mine operators, too, were deluded by the great surge of coal digging that climaxed with World War I, so that they remained at ease while oil gradually became the country's prime source of heat energy. These same operators were abysmally slow in mending their old, exploitive ways in a shortsighted rush to get the coal out of the earth—and a profit out of the coal. Then the day came when a company abandoned a tired mine and moved across the next ridge, and found there not a virgin coal field but just one more worn-out mine, and another and another. The northeastern and southwestern sectors of the state became darkened, half-ruined regions of torn, burrowed earth and flooded deep mines, of mountains of coal waste burning at the edges of towns like Shenandoah and Connellsville and Carbondale.

Finally, the grip of the politicians on the laws of the society gave a false feeling of quiescence, while in truth the economic situation was slowly heating up in the 1920s to the point of explosion. It would not be long before that explosion went off; and when it did, it would wipe out forever the day when the company could own everything in sight.

THE UNION IRON MILLS, ORGANIZED BY CARNEGIE IN 1865

By all odds the canniest of the steel barons was a stocky, quick-minded Scottish immigrant named Andrew Carnegie, shown below *(left)* with two early associates, his cousin George Lauder Jr. *(center)* and Thomas Miller. Carnegie's career was a perfect model for the improbable Horatio Alger success stories. A bobbin boy in a textile mill at 13, he soon became special assistant to the future president of the Pennsylvania Railroad. Making full use of such contacts, Carnegie leapfrogged from one business to another, finally settling on steel. By the age of 32 he was a millionaire; at 50 he was the most potent figure in the all-powerful steel business. At 65 he had become the richest man in the United States and the key figure in the creation of U.S. Steel.

Steel's grandiose entrepreneurs

During the final decades of the 19th Century, fast-moving, farsighted entrepreneurs such as Andrew Carnegie, shown at left with two favored companions, were fashioning the massive parts of what was to become the biggest business ever created: the United States Steel Corporation. Utilizing the mills left by Pittsburgh's flourishing Civil War-era iron industry, they converted the furnaces to steel production and then reached out for control of railroads, coal fields, ore deposits— of any facilities that affected the manufacture and sale of steel. At first the men behind the steel boom tended to operate as lone wolves, cutting prices—and each other's throats—with one hand while they built up their private industrial principalities with the other. Very soon, however, the shrewdest of the entrepreneurs saw that the potential profits from peaceful coexistence were far greater than the wages of industrial warfare. And so these remarkable men, in a series of power plays that Machiavelli might well have admired, brought together the warring principalities into one potent empire called United States Steel, a combine that on the day of its birth in March 1901 controlled 65 per cent of all the nation's steel production.

CARNEGIE'S EDGAR THOMSON STEEL WORKS AT BRADDOCK, PENNSYLVANIA

At age 52, Carnegie in 1887 married Louise Whitfield, who described the first day of their courtship—they went riding in New York's Central Park—as "the great experience of my life."

A Scottish immigrant proud of his heritage, Carnegie built the Castle of Skibo *(below)* on his native heath. Each morning he was there, a bagpiper awakened the guests for a day of golf or grouse shooting on the 32,000-acre grounds.

A time for big men with big ideas

The America of the late 19th Century was fertile ground for a man like Andrew Carnegie. Shrewd, tough and extremely ambitious, Carnegie once said, "Whatever I engage in, I must push inordinately." And true to his word, he seems never to have done anything halfway. In his private life he built an enormous castle in Scotland and scattered more philanthropic cash than had any other industrialist. His real monument, however, was the steel business, which he plunged into at a time when some investors thought neither the economic climate nor the newly developed Bessemer method for mass-producing steel were particularly promising. In 1873 he began to build a massive new Bessemer steelworks *(above)*, which he named after J. Edgar Thomson, President of the Pennsylvania Railroad, a prime customer. By 1880 Carnegie's furnaces were among the nation's leaders, turning out 10,000 tons of steel rails per month.

At the same time he was moving to the forefront in steel, Carnegie did not neglect his private pleasures, making sure, as these pictures show, that there was always time to enjoy the perquisites of an industrial tycoon. He spent long hours immersed in Shakespeare and Robert Burns, whom he quoted at every opportunity. He threw extravagant parties for his friends. And as his wealth increased, he traveled abroad on a series of vacations that became more extended until, by 1890, he had abdicated the daily supervision of his steel complex to brilliant assistants who would one day take his place at the top.

Devoted to his mother until she died in his 51st year, Carnegie delighted in arranging the most lavish outings for her. Here the steel magnate handles both the whip and the reins of an elegant coach-and-four while his black-bonneted mother sits next to him and a clutch of friends crowd onto the roof behind them.

The antithesis of the miserly Scotsman, as this cartoon shows, Carnegie gave away $330 million, endowing educational institutions and charitable foundations and underwriting 2,800 public libraries, such as that at Paducah, Kentucky.

H. C. FRICK COKE COMPANY

An avid golfer in his later years, Frick, like Carnegie, never did things halfway. He belonged to more than a dozen golf clubs and his memorandum book noted "Golf in the Morning" as often as six days a week.

Top teacher in a very tough school

As tough a man as Andrew Carnegie was, he could, and did, learn lessons in brass-knuckle business dealings from a tight-lipped Pennsylvanian named Henry Clay Frick. The early steel barons like Carnegie rose to the top as independent operators. It was not long, however, before Carnegie discovered the hard way that a lone wolf has too many natural enemies. One of these was Frick, who by 1881 controlled some 80 per cent of the coke ovens in the Pittsburgh area, where Carnegie had his main steelworks. Whenever Carnegie went to buy coke for his furnaces, Frick was likely to jack up the price another dollar or two per ton. Unable profitably to make steel without a cheap supply of coke, Carnegie found himself forced to buy into Frick's company.

He soon discovered, however, that the most valuable asset of his new acquisition was Frick himself, who eventually became board chairman of Carnegie's steel empire. The two men never got along personally, and over the years this coolness gradually sank to outright hostility. Nevertheless, professionally, each man perfectly suited the other's early purposes. Under Frick's management Carnegie Steel Company's earnings jumped in 10 years (1889-1899) from two million dollars to $40 million. Further, Frick, who could not abide the idea of anyone squeezing him as he had squeezed Carnegie, had broadened the company's holdings to include ore deposits, ore-carrying steamships, railroads and fabricating mills—all the components of an integrated steelmaking operation.

As chief officer of the company during a long, bloody strike at Carnegie's Homestead plant in 1892, Frick battled the laborers with a small army of strikebreakers. At the height of the strike, an anarchist agitator named Berkman fired two shots into Frick *(below)*. Frick stoically finished the day's work at his desk, ultimately recovered and broke the strike.

Though he displayed little patience with the frills and formalities of corporate business, Frick nevertheless took care to cultivate key financiers such as George Gould, with whom he is shown below taking a carriage ride at a resort.

ANARCHIST BERKMAN

As his holdings in coke and steel multiplied in value, Frick, too, indulged in mansion building, most notably with a glittering Manhattan town house, one of whose rooms, decorated with wall panels by the French painter Boucher, is shown at far left. An art devotee from boyhood, Frick packed an almost matchless collection of great masterpieces into his New York place. Opened to the public in 1935, largely through the efforts of Frick's daughter, Helen, ''The Frick,'' at Fifth Avenue and 70th Street, boasts such great paintings as Rembrandt's *A Young Artist (top left)* and Vermeer's *Mistress and Maid (below)*. Even in 1935 the collection was valued at $50 million; it is worth many times that today.

MINNESOTA'S RICH MESABI ORE FIELDS

The peace-loving potentate of Wall Street

The man who, more than any other, imposed order on the rough-and-tumble steel industry of Carnegie's and Frick's earlier days was not a steelmaker at all, but a New York financier named J. Pierpont Morgan. As the demand for steel kept skyrocketing, the rewards for dominating the market drove the captains of that industry into a frenzy of competition. At first Carnegie and Frick seemed to have taken command of the industry by arranging long-term leases on the rich ore deposits of Minnesota's Mesabi Range (above) and by grabbing up ore-carrying ships and railroads. But new combines kept rearing up to challenge Carnegie—National Steel, American Steel and Wire, National Tube and, in 1898, a formidable young trust called Federal Steel. Carnegie lustily took up the sword against each competitor, met them price cut for price cut, and when simple undercutting would not suffice, threatened to build hoop, rod, wire and nail mills to flood the market and drown any rivals. Such ruinous competition, while it delighted the highly contentious Carnegie, dismayed the Wall Street financiers, who yearned for a more stable market situation. It was particularly loathesome to Morgan, the biggest financier of them all, whose hugely profitable career had been dedicated to creating peaceful empires out of warring industrial principalities. As a major backer of Federal Steel, Morgan became appalled at the chaos of competition, particularly Carnegie's brand. Therefore he began to look for ways to bring together the combatants and to put an end to the disorder.

72

J. P. Morgan (above) looked every inch the financier. Cartoonists loved to caricature his bulbous nose, but businessmen were struck by the eyes, which seemed to look right through a man.

In his mellower moments Morgan was a highly literate man and a collector of considerable taste. His library (above), now a priceless reference collection, contained some 25,000 books, manuscripts and works of art.

"BET-A-MILLION" GATES

JAMES MOORE

JUDGE WILLIAM H. MOORE

Among Carnegie's major rivals in the climactic war of the steel worlds were such colorful characters as the cigar-chomping John W. "Bet-a-Million" Gates, seen walking with an aide at left, and the freewheeling Moore brothers *(right)*. It was all the proper Morgan could do to bring himself to negotiate with the likes of Gates, who had earned his gambling nickname by such betting escapades as wagering, at $1,000 a throw, on which raindrop would reach the bottom of a window first. But Gates had also gambled his way into a controlling interest in the powerful American Steel and Wire trust, while the Moore brothers had raided and speculated their way to the proprietorship of a combine of four steel concerns. Swallowing his distaste for their flamboyant ways, Morgan brought them under his control as he prepared to sue for peace with Carnegie.

A yachtsman of some renown, Morgan spent much of his leisure time cruising aboard a series of luxurious, rakish, custom-built vessels, all named *Corsair*. *Corsair II (right)*, launched in 1890, was 241 feet long and served Morgan for both pleasure and business. He often commuted on the boat between Wall Street and his estate, Cragston, at Highland Falls on the Hudson River. Eventually he sold *Corsair II* to the U.S. Navy for patrol duty in the Spanish-American War, replacing her with the even more extravagant 302-foot *Corsair III*.

Though his business instincts were basically amicable, Morgan's attitude toward the common people of the country was anything but friendly. A born aristocrat who brooked no invasions of his privacy, Morgan is seen at right taking a swipe with his umbrella at a photographer—who managed to avoid Morgan's charge and make off with this picture. To friends who protested that he should be a bit more tolerant, Morgan growled, "I owe the public nothing."

THE HOMESTEAD STEEL WORKS

The magnificent
steel empire takes shape

Though Morgan yearned for peace in the world of steel, and Carnegie was rumored to be ready to sell out, the two might never have come to terms had it not been for the promotional magic of a superb sales-man and steel master named Charles Schwab. In 1900 Schwab was reputed to be making a million dollars a year as president of Carnegie Steel, having taken over direction of the company after Frick and the proprietor fell out permanently over matters rang-ing from the price of coke to corporate policy. Carnegie had absolute confidence in Schwab and claimed that he "knew more about steel than any oth-er man in the world." In addition, Schwab had an easy, genial way with people: it was he who had ca-joled the men back to work after the bloody strike of 1892 at Carnegie's Homestead mills (above). Most important of all, Schwab had a vision of empire—a steel empire in which the most powerful companies would band together into one dominant, efficient cor-poration. Schwab described this vision one night in December 1900 as the speaker at a banquet at which J. P. Morgan was present. After the dinner Morgan cornered Schwab and fired questions at him. From Schwab's glib answers, Morgan constructed the prac-tical shape of Schwab's visionary corporation. The principal components would be the Carnegie holdings and Federal Steel, as well as the companies owned by the Moores, Gates and the others. The only real ques-tion was Carnegie. "If Andy wants to sell," said Morgan to Schwab, "I'll buy. Go and find his price."

THE MAN WHO MADE THE SALE

Charles Schwab as a young man (above) reflected the poise that enabled him to sell his idea for U.S. Steel to J. P. Morgan. The principal emissary in the negotiations, he ascertained that Carnegie's total price would be $492 million. So informed, Morgan said simply, "I accept." Wrote one historian later: "The deal was consummated with less fuss than commonly went into a horse trade of the era."

Schwab and his wife, Emma (above), were married in 1883 and remained a devoted couple for 56 years, until they both died in 1939. The daughter of a steelworks' chemist and sister of a steel technician, Mrs. Schwab knew enough about the business to share her husband's fascination with the subtleties of making better steel. She often worked with him in a basement chemical laboratory, creating various metallurgical compounds, which he would happily spend his evenings analyzing.

Schwab *(far left)* occupied the U.S. Steel presidency for only two years, resigned and began to build a faltering company called Bethlehem Steel into a powerful concern, second in size to U.S. Steel. Handpicking a young steelworker named Eugene Grace *(dark hat)* as the future Bethlehem president, Schwab pumped such new life into his enterprise that the stock of Bethlehem rose by some 500 points in the first 15 years of his reign. In 1930 Schwab and Grace met with James A. Campbell *(light coat)*, president of Youngstown Sheet and Tube, in one of many efforts to merge the two companies. The merger failed, but Bethlehem remains today the nation's second-biggest steel producer.

In the best steel-magnate tradition Schwab built an elaborate New York mansion, which became his principal home during the last 34 years of his life. The Schwab ménage of some 75 rooms, located at 73rd Street and Riverside Drive, was modeled after a French château. One room contained a $250,000 automatic organ that would play themes from operas or familiar tunes such as "My Old Kentucky Home."

U.S. STEEL'S COMPANY TOWN OF GARY, INDIANA

Benevolent ruler
of a great domain

When U.S. Steel was brought into the world in 1901 by the guiding hand of J. P. Morgan, it was the healthiest industrial baby the world had ever seen: the first billion-dollar corporation in history. It owned outright some 65 per cent of America's steel productive capacity. Very soon, through acquisitions, mergers and common directorates, U.S. Steel controlled the operations of some 200 other companies. Within 15 years it had an annual cash flow greater than that of the U.S. Treasury Department and a work force greater than the country's standing army.

As shown by his early resignation, it was not the kind of place where a man like Charles Schwab, with his consuming interest in the actual work of steelmaking (plus a penchant for gambling) could feel at home. But it was a perfect spot for a corporate servant like Judge Elbert Gary, whom Morgan had installed as chairman of U.S. Steel's Executive Committee. Upon Schwab's departure in 1903, Gary also became The Corporation's chief operating officer and immediately set off on a remarkably successful campaign to make his industrial giant seem as benevolent as possible in the eyes both of the public and of the Justice Department's antitrust division. He broke an industry precedent by publishing earnings reports, sermonized on The Corporation's good intentions, denied any monopolistic aims and protested that all his workers were happy antiunion men. And he was successful: in 26 years under Gary the nation's biggest company was never prosecuted successfully as a trust.

Strait-laced and cautious, Gary *(above)* was called by social commentator H. L. Mencken "The Christian Hired Man." Modesty was Gary's stock in trade, and though he permitted a new Indiana steel town *(above left)* to be named in his honor, his loudest public words tended to be in praise of others who might be useful to U.S. Steel.

Gary married his second wife, the former Emma Townsend *(above)*, three years after the first Mrs. Gary died in 1902. The new Mrs. Gary shared ardently in her husband's business interests. In fact she was a booster of The Corporation in her own right, reportedly giving away shares of preferred steel stock as bridge prizes.

Gathered around a banquet table set up in the shape of a huge steel rail, 89 officials of the Carnegie Steel Company sat down in New York on the evening of January 9, 1901, to celebrate the formation of U.S. Steel. The dinner marked the climax in the growth of steel from a tiny handcraft enterprise to the world's biggest business. Carnegie himself, the single man most responsible for the rising power of the industry, had long since become bored with corporate triumphs and did not bother to attend the dinner. However, he sent the celebrants his best wishes and predicted that steel's future would "eclipse its past."

Flames sweep a Pittsburgh rail yard in this sketch of havoc during the railway strike of 1877, one of the bloodiest in the region's history of labor turmoil. For two days, wrote a reporter, the city was roamed by "a howling mob."

4

A Place
in the Sun

The view from the bottom of a coal mine is not quite so good as it is from the board room of a great corporation. In fact, from the bottom of a coal mine the view has never been very good at all. One day, some years ago, a stranger to the coal fields went down into a deep mine, just for a lark, to see what it was like inside the earth. Squeezing onto a crude, cagelike elevator, he found himself dropped like a rock through the sudden darkness of an access shaft, 300 feet straight down past slate walls dripping black water, until the cage came to a sudden stop only inches from the bottom. There, the visitor took an unsteady step out onto the floor of the main tunnel, peered for a moment into the bowels of the mine and sank to his knees screaming, "The dark! The dark! Take me out!"

The miners led him out; and so, except for the darkness, the man saw nothing. Had he stayed,

however, until his eyes and his mind became used to the pervasive gloom of the shafts and tunnels, he would have known—as the miners already knew— that in 1932, from coal camps all across the U.S., the outlook for the miners was in every way as bad as it could possibly have been, and for Pennsylvania, where as many as a quarter of a million men had depended on coal for their living, the situation was rapidly becoming hopeless.

To begin with, mining was, as it always had been, a hard and dangerous business. The hours were brutally long, employment no steadier than the unpredictable market, the pay generally not much higher than 50 cents an hour—and no pay at all for the hours spent riding elevators and empty dump cars through miles of shafts and tunnels to the depths of the mine.

When a coal miner and his buddy—for the men

usually operated in pairs—arrived in the working area, they would duck walk or crawl into a workroom off the main tunnel, at the end of which lay the naked face of the coal seam. There they would stay all day, sometimes in ankle-deep water, sometimes lying on their sides in a dry spot to hack away at the coal, in a silence broken only by staccato bursts from the cutting machines or by the chunk of their picks and the scurrying feet of rats and mice that lived along the tunnels, feeding off grain spilled from feed bags of the horses and mules still pulling carts in the older mines. Sometimes there would be the muted thump of a dynamite blast, as the men in a neighboring tunnel shot down a heavy load of coal from another part of the seam. At other times there would be an even deeper noise, nearer, louder, repeating itself, like thunder on a summer evening.

"The top is talking," the miners would say, meaning that the slate strata above their heads were beginning to break down and that sometime —in a minute, or in three days, or right now—the whole tunnel was going to cave in. When he first heard the sound, a new man was likely to run or just break down in terror. An old hand would stay put, digging away at the weakening structure of the face, for the looser the rock strata, the easier the coal was to take out. Finally, the roof timbers of the tunnel would start to splinter—the final warning— and the veteran miner, timing his move for the last possible moment, would roll, crawl or scramble back to safety.

Too often he did not make it. From 1910 to 1933, of every 1,000 men who went down to take their living from the mines, at least 3.3 would die in the deep tunnels each year. In all, during that period, more than 50,000 miners were killed, and more than a million injured, most of them from cave-ins. But there were other ways to die down there. A dynamite charge that had loosened coal in the working face might also produce a deadly dividend of carbon-monoxide gas. The miner would breathe the odorless gas and go to sleep. Or still more terrible, a random stroke of the pick would let out an invisible cloud of explosive methane gas—"firedamp," the miners called it. One spark from a blasting fuse or from the electric overhead wiring, and the gas would explode, incinerating the miner where he stood, then rolling and hissing in shock waves along the tunnels, the secondary waves of the explosion compressed into a spear of flame traveling at 1,000 feet a second.

One rescued miner told what an explosion had been like for him. When he first heard the blast he groped through the smoke and foul air, out into the main tunnel. There he came upon a pile of wrecked coal cars and dead men, whose legs and arms jutted out of the mess at grotesque angles. "Look like I can't do nothing," recalled the saved miner, a Slovak-American. "Try to pray. Can't do that neither, so I think, 'This is all. I'm finished!' and I lie down on the ground." Lying there, he smelled good air, close to the ground. Sniffing like a dog, he tried for a time to follow the air, hoping for a passage to safety. Hours later he gave up and sat down on a dead mule, sure that soon he would be just as dead. At that moment, by purest chance, the rescue party stumbled upon him. But in the same mine 195 men died, and some of these were never found.

That is the way it had been to work in the mines —often lethal, always dangerous and always very hard even in the better times, when business was booming. But in 1932 the miners' lot was as bad as it had been in any man's memory. The whole country was in a bad way that year, at the nadir of the deepest economic depression in its history. Of the 154,000 men who had been working America's anthracite mines—all of which were in Pennsylvania—during the profitable years of World War I, only 50,000, according to one authority, were still digging hard coal by 1931. In the bituminous fields 4,000 mines had gradually been shut down and production was hardly more than half what it had been in 1918. A fair number of the few remaining jobs were in nonunion mines, where, even in the better-paying coal camps of western Pennsylvania, a man spent 10 or more hours a day underground for 40 cents an hour or less.

As the market kept falling, some of the coal companies simply boarded over the mine shafts, tore down or burned the surrounding shanties and disappeared from the hillside mining camps. In many ways the companies had no choice, since the trouble with coal ran far deeper than the obvious consequences of the overall economic slump. Right after the boom year of 1918, when America still depended on coal to supply three quarters of the nation's heat energy, the industry had started a long, fast, downward slide from which it has not truly recovered to this day. Oil and gas began to replace coal as sources of industrial energy and heat, automobiles were pulling passengers off the coal-burning railroads, and better techniques for making coke and smelting iron were reducing the steel mills' demand for coal. In the mines themselves, cutting machines and the first of the automatic loaders and conveyor belts were replacing the men. Thus the industry, which had always been fundamentally exploitive and had also been geared to overproduction in boom years, was sinking through the floor of a permanently depressed market. And the miners' jobs were vanishing, many of them forever.

"Coal is a sick industry," John Brophy, a union leader from Pennsylvania's coal fields, had said. "There are too many mines, too many miners." And in 1932 neither John Brophy nor even John L. Lewis, the tough, resourceful President of the United Mine Workers' union, seemed to have an immediate answer. During the winter of that year, neither did the federal government nor the Statehouse of Pennsylvania.

Where the winding engines and clashing coal breakers had stood in boom times, now there were only rusted rail sidings, tumble-down buildings, and weed trees growing in the silent mine yards. Even in the face of such conditions, some of the miners refused to leave the dead villages, believing that the mines would open again. Besides, where could they go? Perhaps half of all Pennsylvania miners were immigrants or first-generation Americans, mainly from Italy and Eastern Europe, and many had come over just to dig coal. It was all they knew how to do, all they had ever done in the U.S. In fact, it was just about all there was to do in the remote world of the patches—the miners' word for the weatherboard settlements clustered around the machinery at the mouths of the shafts.

So the men stayed on; and in the coking patches around Connellsville, Pennsylvania, they moved their families into the only available shelters, the filthy, abandoned coke ovens, where the women and children somehow existed through the winter months, many of them walking barefoot out to the privy or to the well. Meanwhile, the men pried open the boarded-over mine shafts and crawled, alone, down into the cold, silent pits to scratch out a few lumps of bootleg coal to keep their families warm—and a few lumps more that a man might sell in town if he had the strength to carry a sack of them in on his back. In all the deprivation and agony, perhaps the bitterest fact of the miners' life was that, outside of the patch towns themselves, not enough people seemed to know, or to care, about these half a million men and their families—in all perhaps a million and a half Americans spread across the coal fields of the United States.

"Oh, they are Polacks; they are used to that," said one coal-region businessman, using the common, derisive term for Polish immigrants, a group of whom were standing barefoot on frozen ground nearby. This callous lack of concern had been endemic in the coal industry for decades. In 1928 Richard B. Mellon, major stockholder in the Pennsylvania bituminous fields, when asked whether he had ever done anything to alleviate the miners' suffering or destitution, had replied, "I do not go out feeding them or anything. I would not be out there, way out in the mines."

Nor were any of his fellows from the board rooms of the great corporations "way out in the mines," where they might have understood, first-hand, the plight of the coal industry as represented by the patch towns of 1932. This lack of close observation was accompanied by an astonishing inability to appreciate, or deal effectively with, the overpowering fact that coal would never again recover its relative standing in the economy.

Just as astonishing was the failure of business leaders to face or fully understand the plight of the steel industry: in 1933 fifty-six per cent of American steelworkers were laid off, the mills operating at a bare 14 per cent of capacity. U.S. Steel admitted that it had barely a single full-time laborer in its whole domain. Jobs were, in fact, so scarce and so desperately needed that some of the workers began to bribe the hiring bosses to get a week's work. One foreman at Jones & Laughlin was later found to have picked up $10,000 in kickbacks from the men—at a time when the annual take-home pay for many a mill hand in a town like Duquesne, Pennsylvania, was $378.

The cause of steel's distress was strikingly similar to that of coal, with roots reaching far below the economic wreckage of the Depression. Like the coal barons, the big men in steel had overbuilt their productive capacity so as to be able to skim off every possible dollar in years when the market boomed, as it had in World War I. When demand leveled off, or a depression rolled in, or new kinds of metals supplanted steel, the overgrown mills had to slow down or stop altogether. In the slumps of 1908 and 1921-1922, steel had been able to coast through on its control of both market and prices. But in the years leading up to the Depression, the overbuilding, coupled with a fundamental shift in markets, had become so bad that even a production-worshiper like Bethlehem's Charles Schwab was forced to take a reappraising look at the industry's habits. What he saw amounted to a revelation—though a somewhat belated one. Rising at a meeting of his fellow steel men, Schwab deplored the "hunger for tonnage and desire to operate at capacity which is now and always has been one of the fundamental mistakes in our industry." Later he went on to recommend a "moratorium on all new building of plants." He added, "We must pause in our foolish race for building capacity."

The pause had come too late to be of much help in the early 1930s. Besides, the steel business had other ailments whose residual effects would remain with the industry through the decade of the 1960s. One was a ponderous lethargy toward innovation, particularly in the technology of steelmaking.

"A huge organization is too clumsy to take up the development of an original idea," reported the authoritative *Engineering News*, only 10 years after the founding of U.S. Steel. "Our trusts do not want the bother of developing anything new." Twenty years later the trusts had learned very little and were losing business to smaller and more flexible competitors.

There was another problem, too, most immediate for the Pittsburgh area: the railroads had virtually stopped ordering steel. In the years between 1915 and 1932, railroad routes in America reached their greatest extent; from then on mileage shrank and there was a long, relatively steady drop in total steel orders for new rails, track replacements and new rolling equipment. The automobile makers' demand for steel would, in time, take up the slack left by the rail falloff—but not enough in the moneyless days of 1932, and never completely in Pittsburgh. For the auto makers' needs could be met more easily (and more cheaply) by the newer mills of the Midwest. One auto magnate, Henry Ford, had even shown the incredible bad manners to build his own steel plants in Michigan, rather than buy from the established mills, as the well-behaved older customers, such as the rail people, had always been at pains to do.

Hence, the tradition-bound steel industry, especially in Pennsylvania, was sinking to the floor of the depressed market. And the millworkers' jobs, like those of the miners, were vanishing, partly because of shrinking or displaced markets, partly because of growing competition from other metals, and partly because the technological innovations steel did manage to embrace resulted in putting more and more men out of work. In Pennsylvania, between 1923 and 1929, some 27,000 steel- and ironworkers were permanently laid off.

Those jobs that were left around the mills and furnaces were as difficult, and in some cases as dangerous, as the ones in the mines. "When you work by a furnace," said one veteran mill hand, "the front of you is burning and, in winter, the back is freezing. Those mills make old men out of young men." A steelworker was considered well on

his way to being "burned out" when he was 40. Many companies, in fact, had a rule against hiring any man over 45.

Sometimes a man was through long before 40. The extreme contrasts of heat and cold in American steel mills bred more than 2,000 cases of pneumonia each year, and in summer months the furnaces caused severe—sometimes even fatal—heat prostration. The "hot-mill cramps," as the laborers called the malady, once killed six men in a week at the great Sparrows Point mill outside Baltimore, while at Charleroi, Pennsylvania, 127 workers were knocked out of one shift.

In addition to these hazards, the workers for many years had been driven by the mill bosses beyond the limits of common sense, to get the greatest possible tonnage out of them in the hours they were at the mill. Early in the century an immigrant laborer, weary of dodging the engines that brought ore to the furnaces and carried off raw steel, described their heedless progress this way: "No choo choo! No ling ling! No God damn you get out of the way! Just run over!" Another man, long past any sardonic mirth, remembered with terrible clarity the day he was operating a crane that carried ladles of molten steel across the mill and suddenly saw a ladle slip off its hook, spilling a stream of white-hot metal. The craneman stopped his machine and clambered to the floor. There, he saw a man lying face down, being roasted by the metal spilling out of the pot. "At that time," said the craneman, "I did not know [who it was]. It was not till I turned him over that I recognized him. Then I saw it was my brother. . . ."

By 1930, conditions in some of the mills had improved. Nevertheless, some 200 men were still being killed in the mills annually, another 1,200 permanently disabled and 21,000 injured to lesser degrees.

For the mill hands, however, as for the miners, the bitterest fact of their existence, worse even than the danger of the work or the spreading unemployment, was the oppression and the degradation of their lives under the great companies. "Hundreds are laid off forever," wrote one observer, "for months on end more hundreds have no work at all, and thousands work one, two, or three days a week. Human demoralization follows. . . . The police blotter records the rise of petty crime, abandoned families, suicide."

More than a third of the laborers were of immigrant stock, and many others in the region—particularly those with deeper American roots—persisted in seeing these immigrant laborers as hardly human. "These hunkies. They don't seem like men to me," said one Anglo-Saxon native, picking up the derisive nickname for all Slavic immigrants. Said another native, "The hunkies? They're more like cattle."

When the mill- and mineworkers, immigrant or otherwise, tried to break out of the pattern of poverty, they found they had no means to do so. In fact, their employers had deprived them, so far as was possible, of even the right to protest against their situation. In many of the company towns there was no free assembly, no right of free speech. There was, in fact, not much right of anything—except the company's right. "You would have thought the Constitution of the United States was suspended in western Pennsylvania," said one visitor. The labor unions had been harried and starved to the point of virtual impotence, lest they call strikes that would result in higher production costs for the companies. The United Mine Workers' union was bankrupt, its membership shrunk from 400,000 in 1920 to an estimated 150,000—and probably less than that; the Amalgamated Association of Iron, Steel and Tin Workers was down below 6,000 members.

The companies tried to see that the unions stayed that way. Many of the mill towns and coal camps were sealed off against labor organizers—or even casual visitors—by the companies' police forces. "All automobiles or wagons attempting to enter these strongholds were searched, their occupants cross-examined some distance from town by the police patrols mounted on horses trained for riot duty," observed one writer. "These animals had the unpleasant habit of rearing up at the touch of a spur, pawing the air with their front legs. . . ."

In some towns roving police patrols broke up any street-corner gathering of more than two or three men. If a crowd did happen to form, and trouble started, men were likely to be shot—and sometimes women and children, too. A Mrs. Englert, noted another report, "told the story of the iron and coal police shooting into a group of school children in which two of her children were coming home from school. . . ." A union official trying to enter a coal camp was told, "There's a machine gun waiting for you." Another union man simply disappeared, to turn up later locked in an insane asylum through the connivance of state officials. Several of the coal camps were even ringed with barbed wire; at night, searchlights, machine guns mounted beneath them, swept their yellow-white beams over the streets and the shacks of the sealed enclosure.

Mary Harris "Mother" Jones, a little old lady in a black bonnet, with curly white hair and flashing gray eyes, devoted more than 50 years of her long life to fighting relentlessly on the side of labor in its long, epic struggle with management. She was campaigning for child-labor laws in Pittsburgh during the savage Pittsburgh riots of the 1877 railroad strike *(pages 78-79)* and witnessed the Haymarket tragedy in Chicago in 1894, when a peaceful labor protest evolved into a bloody riot. During the violent West Virginia coal strikes of 1900 and 1902, she organized the wives of striking workers, who, armed with mops and brooms, marched to the mine in a show of solidarity with the strikers. She rallied support for the steel strike of 1919 and, in 1923, when she was 93 years old, traveled to West Virginia to join the striking coal miners there. On her 100th birthday, in 1930, congratulations and good wishes poured in from all over the country, from labor and management leaders alike. She died six months later.

"About all you can do," confided one miner, "is to go by night to your room, lock the door, and pray, in a whisper. . . ." Earlier a steel-town politician had said, "Jesus Christ himself could not speak in Duquesne for the A. F. of L." Nor at that time was it safe to talk much in Pittsburgh, where the county sheriff was the brother of an American Sheet and Tinplate supervisor.

Such oppression, and the rock-bottom wage levels it was designed to maintain, had been the rule in American steel and coal towns for 50 years. In trying to protest through their unions, the industrial workers were reaching for something more fundamental than simply higher wages, shorter hours, safer working conditions and the right to collective bargaining. They were fighting for civil rights, for human rights, for the rights that had been guaranteed them long ago in the U.S. Constitution—rights that were now suspended, apparently, with the consent and often the support of various branches of the very government that had sprung from the Constitution.

Long ago William Penn had said, "Governments, like clocks, go from the motion men give them, and as governments are made and moved by men, so by them are they ruined, too . . . if men be bad, let the government be never so good, they will endeavor to warp and spoil it to their turn.'' In the decades leading up to 1932, the Constitution, if not suspended altogether, had at least been warped to the turn of heavy industry.

Pushing hard from the bottom, the workers had tried from time to time for half a century to bend it back. But before they could succeed, a new balance of political power would have to be created, new laws passed and fresh instruments of government created so that the flexible, ambiguous articles of the Constitution could properly regulate the forces of an industrialized society. The battle for this redress of power and the basic freedom accompanying it had been by no means confined to the miners and mill hands of Pennsylvania. It had broken out in violent starts all across the country—and it amounted to nothing less than the beginnings of a major social revolution.

Nowhere, however, had the struggle been more bitter; and, in time, nowhere was the outcome to be more decisive to the cause of labor than in the Middle Atlantic States. The most spectacular flareup in the region had occurred as far back as 1877, when the Pennsylvania and B&O Railroads had ordered a 10 per cent cut in the men's weekly paycheck, and double duty for freight crews on some of the difficult mountain runs. The first riots broke out in the Baltimore yards and spread quickly north and west across Pennsylvania, leaving a litter of wreckage and death in their wake. Eventually the storm center settled over Pittsburgh. At the request of the Governor, 650 militiamen moved upon the strikebound city, opened fire and killed some 20 men. Enraged mill hands, hearing the sound of the guns, poured out of the steelworks, pillaged the Great Western Gun Works and then attacked the troops. For two days mobs surged through the city's streets, looting stores, and roared through the Pennsylvania's rail yards, where they wrecked 1,449 rail cars and 104 locomotives and burned down numerous buildings, including a roundhouse that the soldiers had occupied.

Finally President Rutherford B. Hayes called in federal troops—as President Washington had done during western Pennsylvania's Whiskey Rebellion 83 years before—and order was restored. The final score: 26 dead, five million dollars in property damage for the city and the railroad, and a legacy of hate and suspicion for the whole community.

"The Pittsburgh rioting," wrote one historian, "had been more violent and destructive than any [labor disturbance] the country had ever seen." For the first time in industrial warfare federal troops had been used to quell a strike. And for the

Some early labor leaders

John Mitchell, who in 1902 led the United Mine Workers in the victorious strike for an eight-hour day, began working in the mines in 1882, when he was 12. He joined the UMW when it was first formed, quickly rose through the union ranks and became its fifth president in 1898. His definitive book on labor problems, *The Wage Earner* (1913), focused the nation's attention on the plight of the workers.

first time it was obvious that the strike had been about much more than a worker's wage cut. In a study of the disturbance a Professor N. J. Ware called it a "revolt of the community against the Pennsylvania Railroad."

The early power of the rail workers was drained by the Pittsburgh revolt. However, the labor movement was carried forward by the steelworkers and, most effectively, by the coal miners. During the 65 years following the Pittsburgh riots, the coal miners went out on major strikes no less than 15 times, the steelworkers six times. In the guerrilla fighting of those years, most of labor's gains were won by the miners, whose hard apprenticeship in the art of digging coal turned out to be perfect training for the art of industrial warfare.

Down in the mines every man had to work and think not just for himself, but for his buddy, for the men working in the neighboring tunnels and for the men on the top, too. It had to be that way: one careless spark, a neglected winch brake or a badly timed dynamite charge, and hundreds of men might die. Whenever disaster struck, there was a miners' tradition that every surviving hand stayed on to dig through the debris, to search the choked tunnels until every last living or dead man was accounted for. Thus a remarkable feeling of solidarity

William Z. Foster, a militant organizer for the American Federation of Labor, helped spark the strike of 1919 against the steel industry. A radical labor leader, Foster saw the workers' problems in Marxist terms and became an early member of the U.S. Communist Party. He ran three times as the party's candidate for U.S. President.

Philip Murray was a soft-spoken but effective negotiator. During the 1930s, while an officer of the UMW, he and John L. Lewis accomplished a task that had defeated many before them —organizing labor in the steel industry. He was later president of both the United Steelworkers and the Congress of Industrial Organizations.

had developed in the mines, as the men made common cause in their bitter struggle against the earth.

When labor trouble flared, the solidarity of the deep mine was transferred to solidarity on the picket line. The miners, the winchmen and all the other laborers in the industry banded together almost by instinct. They shared the stolid resolution of men who lived every day with danger and were not likely to back off from a trooper's club. Finally, the miners were blessed with a series of shrewd, vigorous leaders who knew how to channel the workers' outrage and to time strikes so that the cohesive force of the miners could be put to best effect. In 1900 and again in 1902, dark, fiery young John Mitchell—"Johnny da Mitch" to his worshipful followers—pulled more than 100,000 men out of the anthracite mines under the banner of the United Mine Workers' union and won an eight-to-nine-hour working day plus a 10 per cent wage boost. In 1914, thanks to the foundation laid by Mitchell, the UMW counted 378,000 members, and even the hostile mineowners of Pennsylvania were willing to recognize it as the official bargaining agent for the men. By 1923, now under the leadership of a dictatorial ex-miner named John L. Lewis, the northern coal diggers demanded and got—at least temporarily—an average minimum daily wage of some

$7.50. As a result of these intermittent victories, the coal miners earned the nickname of "the shock troops of labor," and they earned, too, the grudging respect, if not the love, of the coal operators.

The steelworkers, on the other hand, had won very little but blood and tears. The Homestead strike of 1892, broken by Henry Clay Frick—and by 8,000 militiamen—had been a disaster for labor. It set a pattern of futility and defeat both for the mill hands and for their union, the somewhat disoriented Amalgamated Association of Iron, Steel and Tin Workers. Unlike the UMW, which welcomed every workingman in the coal industry—and was thus a true industrial union—the Amalgamated was organized along old-fashioned craft lines, recruiting only skilled labor and speaking only for the aims of skilled men. This made no sense whatever in the world of the steel industry, where by 1900 changes in production methods had eliminated many handcrafting operations so that more than half the workers were unskilled.

Whenever there was a strike, the company could drive a wedge between the men, giving concessions to the organized minority of skilled laborers and convincing them not to make common cause with the unskilled masses. The line between skilled and unskilled usually broke down, unfortunately, along ethnic lines, the high-paying skilled jobs going, for the most part, to entrenched English, Welsh and Irish workers and the low-paying scut work to the armies of newly arrived Italians and Slavs. Hence, it was also easy for management to brand any strike a "hunky uprising," stirred up by foreigners who had no allegiance to the good old American ways. In time, the more imaginative industrialists managed to conjure up the image of Karl Marx reaching across the Atlantic to embrace the "socialist vermin . . . Reds, and radicals" who were waging war on U.S. industry.

Because of the union's fragmented nature—and particularly because of its unawareness of the growing role of unskilled labor—in 1901 U.S. Steel was able to force the union to sign a form of "yellow-dog" agreement, by which the union promised not to take in any new members. In 1909 a notice was posted at the 12 unionized mills of U.S. Steel announcing that "all plants after June 30, 1909, will be operated as 'open' plants"—meaning that The Corporation would have no further dealings with unions. The independent steel companies quickly fell in line. In the course of these imposed agreements, the industrialists assured the community at large—and each other—that their destruction of the unions would, in the long run, be the best thing for everybody. Under the benevolent rule of The Corporation, said Gary later, there was "no necessity for labor unions." This same philosophy had been espoused much earlier by George Baer, President of the Reading Railroad, who said, "The rights and interests of the laboring man will be protected and cared for—not by labor agitators but by the Christian men to whom God in his infinite wisdom has given the control of the property interests of the country, and upon the successful management of which so much depends."

In case this celestial insight might not provide sufficient guidance for the mill foremen in their dealings with labor, one steel magnate—thought to be Charles Schwab of Bethlehem—had more specific instructions: "If a workman sticks up his head, hit it!"

In September of 1919 the Amalgamated stuck up its head in protest once more, and the industrial barons hit it very hard. With union ranks temporarily swelled by a postwar organizing campaign, the Amalgamated led a walkout primarily aimed at abolishing the still-prevalent 12-hour working day and the murderous "long turn," the 24-hour stint that each man worked every two weeks when the mills rotated the shifts. Most importantly, the Amalgamated asked for recognition as bargaining

agent. The unskilled men walked out, too, and soon there was a stoppage in steel mills all over the country. Within nine days 350,000 men were out. The coal miners would soon go out on a strike of their own.

Potentially, the steel strike, coinciding as it did with the mine walkout, was the most powerful single protest ever mounted by U.S. labor. But it was doomed from the first. The Amalgamated, for all its new members, was still not an industry-wide union, but a jumble of craft locals with "about as much cohesion as a load of furniture," as one union official gloomily phrased it. Further, one of the union's organizers, William Z. Foster, had been friendly with various radical groups and was on his way to becoming an outright Communist. The companies naturally lost no opportunity to splatter Foster with red paint and to once again brand the uprising as a Slovak strike, the work of foreign agitators. People spoke darkly of Moscow gold and urged that it was "the patriotic duty of all good citizens to use their every effort to stem the tide of unrest if possible." Meanwhile, the coal and iron police, and the Cossacks—the workers' name for mounted troopers—moved against the laborers.

As the strike opened, 25,000 strikebreakers had been put under arms in southern Allegheny County alone, and civil rights were suspended in Pittsburgh and in the mill towns and mining camps. Mounted police ranged the streets, clubbing down strikers, suspected strikers or just anyone who happened to get in the way. In more than one case the riders charged their horses right through the front doors of laborers' houses and then went to work on the terrified people inside. In West Natrona, near Pittsburgh, a woman named Fannie Sellins pulled some children away from the danger of a picket line and then ran to plead with an officer who was clubbing a prostrate striker. Another officer struck her down, and when she tried to rise, a trooper shouted, "Kill that Goddamn whore." Three shots hit the woman. Then, according to the affidavit of a witness, ". . . one of the deputies, standing over the motionless body, held his gun down and . . . fired into her once more. [Another deputy] picked up her hat, placed it on his head, danced a step, and said to the crowd: 'I'm Fannie Sellins, now.'"

By November the strike had been beaten down and by the end of December the streets of Pittsburgh were plastered with posters saying "Go Back to Work!—*Idite Natrag Na Posao!—Chodte Nazad do Roboty*," in a total of seven languages, so that no hunky could possibly fail to understand. "It is useless to fight the big corporations," said a mill

John L. Lewis: "Mr. Labor"

To several generations of Americans the name John L. Lewis is virtually synonymous with organized labor, for the career of this tough individualist was linked for a tumultuous half century with the workingman's struggle. Born in Iowa in 1880 to an immigrant Welsh mining family, Lewis climbed to national eminence through his successful efforts at unionizing the coal and steel industries. By 1921 Lewis, recently elected President of the United Mine Workers *(top photograph, second from left),* was being consulted by men such as Herbert Hoover *(second from right),* then Secretary of Commerce, on labor matters. Lewis built the UMW into one of the nation's strongest unions, and in 1935 he helped create the Committee for Industrial Organization, which succeeded in organizing workers on an industry-wide basis in such fields as autos and steel. Five years later he stepped down from the presidency of the Congress of Industrial Organizations (as the CIO had come to be called) over the issue of President Franklin D. Roosevelt's third term. His emotional resignation speech *(center photograph)* reduced his daughter, Kathryn, to tears. Through World War II and the postwar years Lewis concentrated on his Mine Workers activities, such as visiting a mine disaster in West Frankfort, Illinois, in 1951 *(bottom left)* and on his role as a labor adviser to government. When he resigned his UMW presidency in 1960 he was made President Emeritus of that union. The 1963 photograph below shows him at age 83.

hand in McKeesport, Pennsylvania. "They have the constabulary, the courts, the state government, and the city government on their side." There was no question that this was so, and the great corporations, secure in the knowledge, went back to business as usual. In 1923, as the result of a prior plea by President Harding, U.S. Steel and the independent companies did finally give up the "long turn" and the 12-hour day. But otherwise, right through the market crash and on into 1932, the big millowners' labor policies remained as callously unimaginative and as unchanging as their attitudes toward technological innovation and enlightened marketing practices. In the meantime, the UMW, whose finances and resolve had been badly debilitated by the Depression, had been forced to back off from many of its earlier gains. So that by late winter of 1932 the union movement had receded almost to the point of extinction.

It was at this time, however, with labor's fortunes so low, that the tide began to turn. The first impetus for change came not from within the labor movement as such, but from the general public, which went to the polls to register its disgust with the Depression. In the first series of major elections since the market crash, the voters of Pennsylvania installed a known liberal, Gifford Pinchot, as governor. One of Pinchot's earliest acts was to revoke the commissions of all the private company police and to refuse to issue any new ones.

In Washington, Congress, harking to the distant drum of the Depression-bound public's changing attitude toward labor, passed the milestone Norris-LaGuardia Act, which outlawed yellow-dog union contracts and curtailed the ability of the courts to issue antistrike injunctions. The act also implied the right of workers to "association, self-organization, and designation of representatives of their own choosing to negotiate the terms and conditions of their employment." Then, in the fall of 1932, Franklin D. Roosevelt carried the national election, pulling along with him a large Democratic majority in Congress pledged to carry out the Presidential program of a New Deal all across the board. Now, in the nation's capital, as in the Statehouse at Harrisburg, there was an administration that would not answer so readily to the demands and persuasions of heavy industry. A fresh balance of political power had at last been created that would enable the U.S. labor movement to achieve its freedom.

Labor lost no time in doing so. John L. Lewis conferred with Roosevelt's advisers on the shape of a program of country-wide economic revival called the National Industrial Recovery Act, and in these conferences Lewis made certain that labor got its due. "I was the only representative of organized labor present," he said. "I insisted on the inclusion of what later came to be known as Section Seven A." This section, picking up from the recent Norris-LaGuardia Act, categorically guaranteed the right of workingmen to organize and to bargain collectively through "representatives of their own choosing."

Through this single section of the law, which Lewis proudly called Labor's Magna Carta, the federal government took a giant step across the no man's land of industrial warfare and began to line up some of its power behind labor. "I fought for [Section 7A]," said the tough, self-assured Lewis, "and got it." With this legislation in hand, the President of the UMW launched a massive new recruiting drive to revive his union. Hundreds of organizers, protected now by federal law, fanned out through the coal fields, shouting, "The President wants you to join the union. Your government says 'Join the United Mine Workers!'"

And the miners joined. "Within 90 days the industry was organized," recalled labor leader John Brophy. Within a few months 300,000 miners had signed up and paid their dues, so that the union not only was revived as a bargaining force but became sufficiently solvent to last through any major strike that might come. With the shock troops of labor once again lined up in solid array and Washington clearly in their camp, a majority of the bituminous coal operators caved in without a real struggle, signing the historic First Appalachian Joint Wage Agreement, which granted a seven-hour day, time and a half for overtime, a solid minimum day's wage, recognition of the union and arbitration of disputes. Later, a second agreement went so far as to concede a closed shop, the companies guaranteeing to hire only union members. With the enactment of such legal protection for union activities as the Wagner Act and the Fair Labor Standards Act, organized labor was at last beginning to stand at equal weights with the heads of industry.

It had all happened so fast that the miners themselves could hardly believe it. And some of the die-hard coal operators, particularly in the captive mines belonging to the steel companies, could not either, refusing at first to go along. At a vicious strike in the captive mines of the Frick Coke Company—where, despite a company-dominated union, working conditions had, in fact, been substantially improved—hardhanded union organizers clashed with company men and 16 people were wounded. Various of the other coal and steel concerns, girding for a long struggle, placed orders of $15,000 and more with an arms broker called Federal Laboratories for guns and tear gas. Mayor Jim Crawford of Duquesne, Pennsylvania, said, "We're not going to stand for any Goddamn hoodlums coming into town. We're going to meet them at the bridge and break their Goddamned heads!" Leaflets appeared in Duquesne, describing the union organizers as a "bunch of Communists, a bunch of hoodlums, hunkies, and a few Negroes." And the *Duquesne Times* knew just what to do with such vermin. "There are plenty of vacant trees," said the *Times*, "and hemp can easily be procured."

It sounded just like old times—but it was too late. Governor Pinchot jumped into the dispute on the miners' side, proclaiming first, "The fight which you [miners] and I must fight together is against the grasping money lords," and he followed this by pledging that the National Guard of Pennsylvania would henceforth be the impartial friend of all citizens. Finally, from Washington, President Roosevelt himself moved in to help settle the Frick strike and subsequently acted as the principal go-between in settling the miners' demands. At length, unions won recognition at 19 of 28 captive mines. It would take several more years before all the captive mines came over, but by 1942 every single commercial coal mine in the U.S. was operating as a closed union shop under the banner of the United Mine Workers.

Meanwhile, using the new power of his UMW as a lever, John Lewis had set in motion a broad campaign whose aim was nothing less than the organization of every U.S. laborer, skilled or unskilled, into a single, national industrial union. "I had learned the bitter lesson," reflected Lewis, "that so long as the great mass of workers was unorganized, so long would it be impossible for organized labor to achieve its legitimate goals." In going after his particular goal of a broad-based national union, Lewis made the steel industry his primary target. In so doing he turned over the coin minted some time ago by the captains of industry and their financial advisers.

As Gary, Morgan, Mellon and the others had once done, Lewis was reaching out for control over the whole industrial edifice. And Lewis came to realize, as had others before him, that the man who would control industry must first control steel. Furthermore, Lewis had also absorbed the useful lesson that in creating any kind of monopoly, it would be very helpful to establish some hold on the market outlets. By the mid-1930s the automobile industry was becoming the No. 1 market for steel. Therefore, as part of his strategy for conquering steel, Lewis planned to move in on the auto makers. First, however, he had to deal with the conservative craft unionists in the old American Federation of Labor, who were dead set against the principle of an across-the-board union for all the men in the big mass-production industries.

At the 1935 convention of the A. F. of L., Lewis challenged the membership to move ahead with a campaign of industrial organization. The craft unionists refused—loudly, vocally, and at one point so bitterly that Lewis bounded from his seat and smashed his fist into the face of a heckler. That single punch put an end to any chances that an industrial union would form inside the A. F. of L. Lewis immediately pulled together six unions with his own UMW to create the framework of a new combine called the Committee for Industrial Organization—the CIO. Turning over $500,000 in funds to the new union, Lewis put his old friend Philip Murray in charge of a concerted drive to organize the steelworkers. At the same time, with superb generalship, Lewis reached out to Detroit to help the United Automobile Workers unionize steel's top customer.

Once again the captains of big industry girded for war, and once again the war was short and vicious, resulting in a victory for Lewis. By February 1937 there were more than 100,000 new steelworkers in the Steel Workers Organizing Committee (which was later to become the United Steelworkers of America). But the real test was in Detroit, where Lewis came in to negotiate an immense sit-down strike that paralyzed General Motors. From the mill towns of Pennsylvania came the word: "The workers regard the General Motors sit-down as a test of the CIO." And from steelworkers still outside the new union: "Wait till you win the auto strike. Then we'll join."

Within 40 days General Motors had capitulated. Chrysler followed—after a sit-down strike of its own—and back in the mill towns Steel Worker membership was moving toward 200,000. Lewis now zeroed in on the biggest adversary of all, U.S. Steel. But to the nation's astonishment, The Corporation, heretofore the blood enemy of labor and the industry-wide leader in maintaining every aspect of the status quo, ran up the white flag without firing a shot. The surrender of Big Steel came about after a chance meeting at the Mayflower Hotel in Washington, D.C., between Lewis and Myron Taylor, the man who now held the position once occupied by the late Judge Gary at the head of U.S. Steel. Entering the hotel dining room, Taylor happened to see Lewis eating at a nearby table; and to the astonishment of the other diners, many of whom recognized both men, Taylor shook hands warmly and invited the contentious labor leader to sit with him for a time after the meal. Against all the probabilities, the two men quickly became friends.

For the next two months they were in close touch on the matter of The Corporation's attitude toward recognition of the Steel Workers Organizing Committee as a bargaining agent, and Taylor proved a far more tractable man than old Judge Gary. First, the new head of The Corporation had ideas about community and industrial responsibility that were far more progressive. Second, the steel industry, after five years of almost unbroken distress, was beginning to revive, principally on the surge of European armaments orders. "The cost of a strike to the Corporation, to the public and to the men would have been incalculable," Taylor explained later. And finally, Taylor was aware that times were truly changing and the old rules under which Judge Gary had run the game would no longer do.

The White House was clearly on labor's side. A Senate Civil Liberties Committee was whetting its knife for any signs of the old company repressions. Another liberal governor was sitting in Harrisburg. The Slavic workers, once cast out from the community as foreigners, had begun to blend in with the rest of the American labor force and could no longer be represented to the public as a creeping Red menace sent over from Marxist cells in Europe. John Lewis himself was by any measure "a foeman worthy of U.S. Steel," as one reporter described him. And finally The Corporation's control of the economy and the people had been swept away both by the Depression and by the rapidly changing political winds: "It appears that we [at U.S. Steel]," admitted Taylor gloomily in 1932, "are at the mercy of [fluctuations in the economy] just like any other corporation."

By a complete reversal of the traditional power structure, The Corporation now appeared to be at the mercy, also, of a labor leader named John L. Lewis. For the talks between Lewis and Taylor had reached a climax, and on March 1, 1937, word got to the ravine towns that there was to be a settlement, that the union might even win. At first the steelworkers thought it could not be so. In the steel fortress of Aliquippa, an incredulous union man put in a call to Phil Murray in Pittsburgh. "One of the steelworkers just came in," shouted the caller, "and said he heard over the radio that U.S. Steel was meeting with the CIO. I told him he was crazy and kicked him out of the office."

"Well, don't kick him out," replied Murray. "It's true." And it was. Lewis had accepted Taylor's proposed formula for recognizing the Steel Workers and the CIO. The formula was quite similar to the Appalachian agreement—acceptance of the union as bargaining agent for the workers, a 40-hour week, an eight-hour day, and time and a half for overtime.

If this sounds a bit tame today, it was a triumph in 1937. At the signing of a contract under the new agreement, one of the union men, in an attempt at small talk, asked a company official, "Who is that in the oil portrait behind you?"

The company man replied, "He wasn't there yesterday."

"Is that so?" said the union representative. "Whose picture was there yesterday?"

"Old H. C. Frick," was the response. "They took him out. Didn't think he could stand it."

On that sardonic note, and with a few strokes of the pen, the war was over. There was still some bloody mopping up to do. The major independent steel companies—Bethlehem, Republic, Youngstown and National—took four years to fall in line behind The Corporation's new labor policy. But the struggle for recognition, for the rights of the workers, for a place in the sun, was substantially over. In 1941 there would be 600,000 men in the United Steelworkers and 600,000 men in the United Mine Workers; by 1945 fifteen million men and women would be signed into labor unions as a whole, the most powerful single voting bloc in the nation. And back in the sooty ravine towns of Pennsylvania, where industry had once had its most paralyzing hold, and where the deadliest labor battles had since been fought, the view from the mills and the mines seemed finally to be clearing. In the course of the union victory over The Corporation, 17 Pennsylvania towns, including Clairton and Duquesne, tossed out the incumbent industrial politicians and installed union-backed mayors, burgesses and other representatives. The Secretary-Treasurer of the UMW, Thomas Kennedy, doubled as the lieutenant governor of the state. Between 1939 and 1943 a former slate picker and anthracite mine mule driver, Arthur H. James, served as governor of Pennsylvania. And in Aliquippa, where the company had once owned everything in sight, a steelworker noted proudly that now you could "walk down the main street in Aliquippa, talk to anyone you want about anything you like, and feel that you are a citizen."

At eight years of age to the breaker I first went
To learn the occupation of a slave;
I certainly was delighted, and on picking slate was bent—
My ambition it was noble, strong, and brave.

"THE OLD MINER'S REFRAIN"

In the cold, sooty screening room of a coal-crushing plant called a breaker, small boys separate worthless slate from the coal.

Bitter memories of mines and mills

During the years from 1870 to World War I, Pennsylvania spawned a great combine of mines and mills that supplied the steel and coal for America's industrial pre-eminence. At the same time these booming industries ground down the workers, especially recent immigrants, who gave the industrial complex its strength. Eight-year-old boys shivered through exhausting days for 25 cents in wages. Grown men got little more, and the women struggled to raise families in festering slums. The memory of those terrible years is still preserved in stark pictures, many taken by crusading photographer Lewis Hine in the early 1900s *(see following pages),* and in the workers' own bitter and ironic ballads.

The Homestead steel mill dominates its Pennsylvania town, where workers lived in rows of company houses or hillside shanties.

We are asking one another
  as we pass the time of day,
Why workingmen resort to arms
  to get their proper pay,
And why our labor unions
  they must not be recognized,
Whilst the actions of a syndicate
  must not be criticized.

Now the troubles down at Homestead
  were brought about this way.
When a grasping corporation
  had the audacity to say:
"You must all renounce your union
  and foreswear your liberty
And we will give you a chance
  to live and die in slavery."

"THE HOMESTEAD STRIKE"

The pervasive power of the companies

In the halcyon days of the coal and steel industries, the lives of the laborers were dominated by the powerful companies that owned the mines and mills. In a town like Homestead, Pennsylvania, the steel mill was the main source of livelihood for most of the people. But that livelihood usually amounted to bare subsistence, or less. In return for working 12 hours a day, often seven days a week—including a brutal, round-the-clock "long turn" when the shifts changed every two weeks—a mill hand might make as little as $350 a year. Too often, particularly in the smaller mill and mining towns, he never saw a cent of that, at least not in cash. In many company-controlled towns, currency took the form of certificates called company scrip, redeemable in overpriced goods sold at the company store—usually the only store in town. The scrip might also be used to pay rent on the laborer's company-owned house, one of a row of bleak weatherboard shacks. Unions were usually outlawed, and any attempts to organize were suppressed, violently. When the workers at Homestead tried to strike in 1892, Henry Clay Frick, the steel company's top executive on the scene, called in a detachment of hired gunmen. In a battle between these guards and the strikers, 16 people were killed and scores injured.

Workers' children play among the ragtag tenements in Pittsburgh's Soho District, named after London's once-infamous slum.

Me troubles are o'er, Missis Murphy,
For the Ditchman next door told me straight,
That the breaker starts full time on Monday,
That's what he told me at any rate.
Sure the boss he told Mickey this morning,
When he's 'bout to enter the mines,
That the coal was quite scarce
 [down] 'bout New York,
And the breaker would start on full time.

And it's oh-ho-ho, my, if the news be true,
Me store bill's the first thing I'll pay,
A new parlor shuit and a lounge I will buy,
And an organ for Bridgie, hurray!
Me calico shirt I'll throw into the dirt
And in silk ones won't I cut a shine?
Chear up, Missis Murphy, we all will ate turkey,
When the breaker starts up on full time.

"WHEN THE BREAKER STARTS UP FULL TIME"

A bleak existence in the industrial towns

Though the companies boasted that they could—and did—take proper care of their laborers, the truth was that in most of the mill and mining towns of Pennsylvania living conditions, especially for the foreign-born, were crowded, sordid and disease-ridden. Sickness festered in the fouled stream and sewage ditches. In one Homestead ward occupied largely by recent immigrants, one baby of every three born to mill hands' wives died before it reached the age of two. And Pittsburgh from 1898 to 1907 had the highest typhoid rate of any U.S. city: 130 deaths per 100,000 people per year. On top of that, there never seemed to be enough nourishing food. In the smaller mining "patches," the workers had no rights or privacy. At any hour private police might burst in to search their company houses, where, one survey noted, "a tenant had fewer rights than the occupant of a flophouse."

A worker, with wife and baby, surveys his one-room home, heated by a crude stove and equipped with a tub for all washing and bathing.

94

Children play in the back yards of Kingston, Pennsylvania, amid a filthy jumble of privies, open sewage ditches and rubbish.

Miners and wives line up for handouts during a famine that swept Pennsylvania's coal fields while a 1902 strike shut the mines.

Vell, me belong for union,
I'm good citizen,
Seven, mebbe 'leven year,
I'm vorkin' in beeg, beeg 'Merica;
I'm vorkin' fer de Black Heat,
Down in de Lytle Shaft,
In de Nottingham, Conyngham
And every place like dat.
I'm got lotsa money,
Nine hoondret mebbe ten,
And shtrike kin come, like son-of-a-gun
I'm Johnny Mitchell man.

Vell, I'm-a dunt afraid for nottink,
Dat's me never shcare,
Come on shtrike tomorra night
Dat's de business, I dunt care.
Right-a here I'm tell you,
Me not shcabby fella.
I'm a good union citizen,
I'm Johnny Mitchell man.

"ME JOHNNY MITCHELL MAN"

GERMAN STEELWORKER WELSH MINER SLAVIC STEELWORKER

SLOVAK STEELWORKER ITALIAN STEELWORKER IRISH IRONWORKER

The immigrant's struggle
for a decent life

People sufficiently tough—or desperate—to live under these often appalling conditions never seemed to be in short supply. Indeed, there was a constant surplus of laborers as wave after wave of European immigrants flooded into the country after 1880. In 1907 alone some 187,000 immigrants, like those shown at left and below, headed for the Pittsburgh area. An estimated 95 per cent of Pittsburgh's newcomers had no knowledge of industrial machinery, and very few understood either the English language or their rights as potential citizens.

Worst off at first were the immigrant coal miners, who were herded into the seamiest parts of the company towns. Their willingness to work for low wages depressed the general pay scale, and they were easy game for mining-town politicians, who bought their votes with a scuttle full of coal or a basket of food. It was not long, however, before these miners rallied behind a fiery union organizer named John Mitchell, who took them out on strike in 1902 until the mine operators conceded an eight- or nine-hour day and a 10 per cent wage increase. But the steelworkers never got a leader like Mitchell, and their misery went generally unheeded until the New Deal years after 1932.

Pittsburgh's Russian Progressive Labor Club meets in about 1907. Such clubs gave immigrants solidarity in preunion days.

The crushed body of a miner, his head resting on his lifeless hand, lies underneath the debris of a 1917 cave-in at Kingston, Pennsylvania.

O to $200.

O to $300.

O to $225.

O to $100.

The low cost of life and limb

Death and disfiguration were gruesomely common events in the mines and mills of the turn of the century. Often there was no compensation at all for a mangled arm or a lost eye. Even those companies that did compensate employees for injuries paid them what now seem shockingly small sums.

In 1908 researchers for the "Pittsburgh Survey," a pioneering social science investigation, decorated a photograph of Constantin Meunier's famous sculpture, *The Puddler (left),* with the amounts that a Pennsylvania steelmaker might get for the loss of an eye ($200 or less), an arm ($300), a leg ($225) or two fingers ($100).

The same research team composed the chilling "Death Calendar" shown at right, documenting the dates of industrial deaths that occurred in Allegheny County during 12 months in the years 1906 and 1907. The total: 526. Among the most frequent—and feared—killers in the steel mills were the overhead cranes whose great ladles full of white-hot metal had a deadly habit of slipping off the carrying hooks. In the mines the worst danger was from cave-ins. But the men who worked the mines were fatalistic about the peril under which they lived: after one terrible explosion that killed 72 men, a spokesman for the miners said simply: "The law of averages just caught up with them."

The threat of death in the mills and mine shafts

When a coal miner sang, in such songs as the one at right, that his working life was more dangerous than that of a soldier or sailor, he was merely telling the truth. Between 1880 and 1936 about 43,000 miners were killed in Pennsylvania alone, almost as many as the U.S. Army lost in battle in World War I. Many of them were crushed by cave-ins like the one shown at left. And the common laborer in a steel mill was not much safer. An investigator of 1908 commented, "When I mentioned to a priest a plant that had a bad reputation, he said, 'Oh, that is the slaughter-house; they kill them there every day. . . .' " They killed them every day in other plants, too: each year in the U.S. some 1,400 mill hands were killed or maimed.

Safety measures were something that people talked about, usually in the wake of a major disaster like the Twin Shaft cave-in at Pittson, Pennsylvania, where 58 men were drowned. But rarely were adequate measures taken before the fact. For safety cost money, in terms of both equipment and the extra time a man needed to be cautious. And therefore, in that harsh era a workman's life tended to be precarious.

You can talk about the railroaders,
the danger they go through,
Warriors and sailor boys,
I know it's very true.
They have good air to work in,
for the roof they have the sky:
There's no one braves the danger
like the poor miner boy.

They have bad air to work in,
shattered pillars and bad top,
They don't know the moment
when a fall on them might drop,
A little lamp to show them light—
that is their brightest hope,
See the danger they go through
coming up a shaft or slope.

"THE MINER'S LIFE"

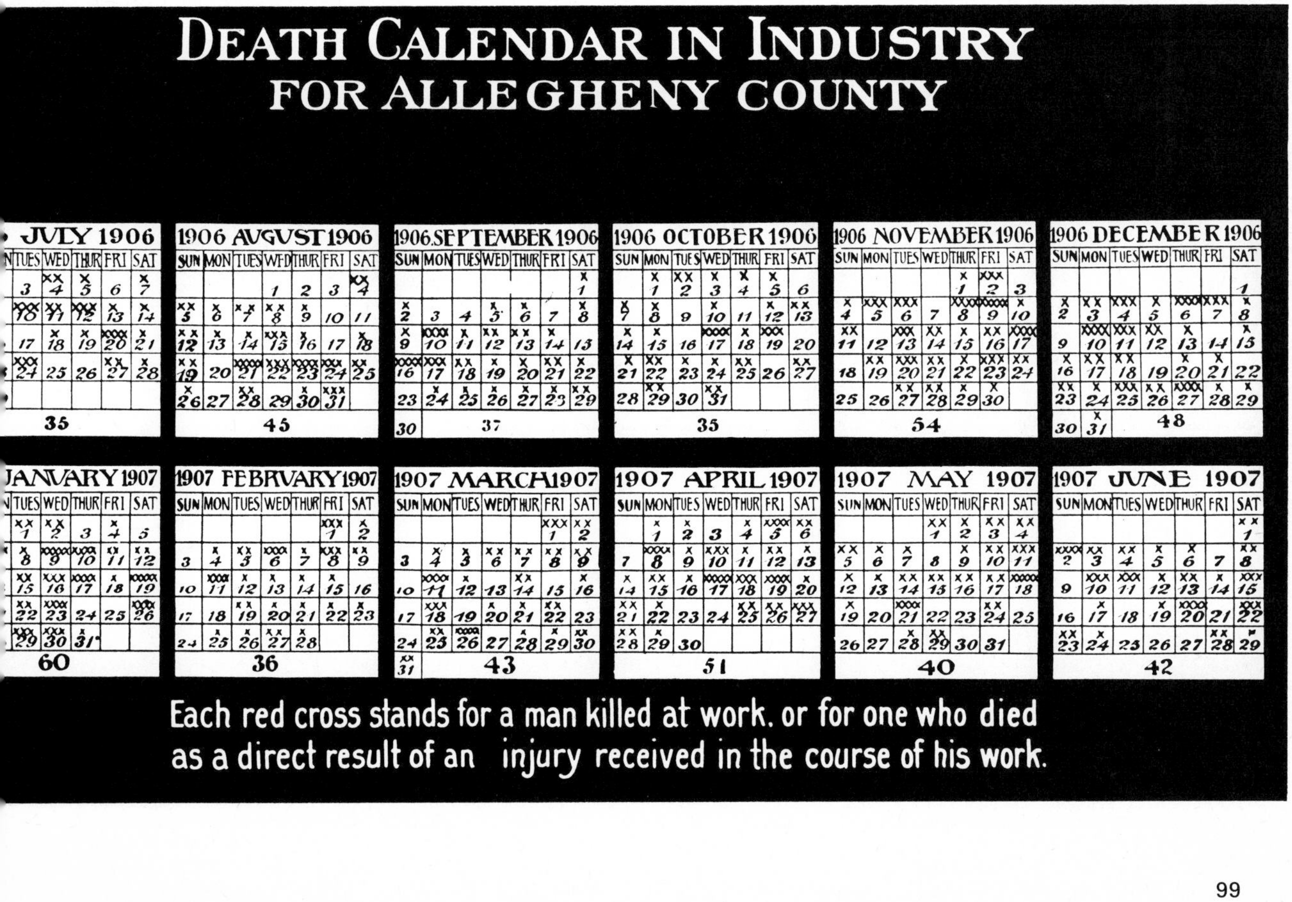

DEATH CALENDAR IN INDUSTRY FOR ALLEGHENY COUNTY

Each red cross stands for a man killed at work. or for one who died as a direct result of an injury received in the course of his work.

When daylight comes I go to work,
When dark I go to bed,
The money that my labor earns,
Keeps us in meat and bread.
Poor father he was killed one day,
Yet mother for him pines,
And that is why you see me here,
A white slave of the mine.

"A WHITE SLAVE OF THE MINE"

Miner boys: the most tragic victims of all

Because the people of the coal camps were so desperately poor, and because Pennsylvania had no child-labor laws for the coal fields until 1909, boys were often put into the mines when they were barely eight years old—so small, remembers one miner, that "I was carried into the mines on my father's back." The youngest worked as breaker boys, picking slate out of the coal after it was crushed. At 10 or 11 they might become "trappers," spending 10 hours in the darkness of the mine while tending the entry doors to the deep shafts. Then they would graduate to mule drivers, or, like the tired lad at right, to bona fide miners, with all the privileges—low pay, lung disease, and the prospect of death from a cave-in or an explosion.

Deep in an anthracite mine a trapper boy keeps watch at an entry door as the flash camera illuminates his lonely vigil.

Dressed in the sooty clothes, heavy gloves and head lamp of the full-fledged miner, a proud but weary Pennsylvania boy finishes a day's work.

Downtown Pittsburgh fades into a smothering haze of dense smog in this 1947 photograph, taken when the city's attack on air pollution was just beginning. Within 10 years the smoke was down 89 per cent, and the business district was being rebuilt.

5

New Heart for the City

At the end of World War II the basic structure of the Middle Atlantic region was dangerously overripe in some sectors and just ·plain rotten in others. The larger cities were grimy and, in several cases, corrupt, filled with the concentrated flotsam of a century-long industrial revolution. The productive muscles of these urban centers had been given a brief shot of adrenaline by the demands of war. But now that the war orders were gone, the cities had become textbook illustrations of the social and economic decay that can overtake a society whose main passion has been production and whose leaders have failed to see the changing shape of the industrial future.

The population of each of the three principal metropolitan areas—Philadelphia, Baltimore and Pittsburgh—had long since passed a million. Philadelphia was, in fact, twice that size, and across the region some 40 per cent of all the people now lived in urban centers of more than 25,000. Yet these cities had grown with no coherent notion, and surely no plan, of becoming decent places to live or of comfortably carrying out any enlightened kind of white-collar business.

Baltimore was a prime example. Born as a seaport and later nurtured as a railhead with a heavy stake in the coal and steel industries, it had become as ugly and as nearly inoperable as any major U.S. city. Its harborside was—and still is—a hideous mélange of skeletal steel cranes, rust-streaked, old concrete docks and ancient warehouses. Its downtown buildings, both office and residential, were low, dark, black-roofed and, in Baltimore's muggy summers, almost unendurably hot. In the central city the grid pattern of narrow streets, laid down for horse traffic and interlaced with railroad tracks, was a frustration for through drivers and a dangerous obstacle course even for a sharp-eyed native. Along Aliceana, President, Pratt and many of the other streets near the harbor, a driver could round a corner and be cut off by a string of Baltimore and Ohio freight cars rumbling over a midstreet track, or he could find himself suddenly eyeball to eyeball with a massive, smoke-spewing Pennsylvania locomotive nosing its ponderous way from an unloading platform out toward the yards. Nor was there much chance of an immediate change in the general look of the harbor area, since the railroads dominated the real estate and reportedly refused to sell land unless the customer would guarantee a good measure of rail business.

Though in times past, Baltimore, less intensively industrialized than some of the other Middle Atlantic cities, had managed to avoid the worst aspects of slum crowding, recently the housing situation had been pushed toward the critical point by the concentration of thousands of undereducated, dirt-poor people, both white and Negro, from the farms of the South. "We got a lot of those poor whites," said a Baltimorean, many years later, "mothers and fathers who could neither read nor write." Another citizen, this one thoroughly unenlightened, complained further that there were "a lot of colored who didn't even know they *ought* to be able to read and write." The latter comment reflected one of Baltimore's basic social dilemmas: half Confederate in its sympathies during the Civil War, the city had never broken away from its ancient prejudices. Negroes still ate at segregated restaurants, were not permitted to try on garments at department stores and were generally handed scut work anywhere they applied for a job.

Politically, the city—in fact all of Maryland—was suffering from another kind of hang-over from the old days, when the economy was geared to agrarian commerce and when men of rural persuasion had carved out a state constitution that was still in force. Because of this constitution, the electoral districts were so lopsidedly apportioned that eventually, with the bulk of the voters having migrated to urban centers, one state legislator from Somerset County, on the Eastern Shore of Chesapeake Bay, would represent 6,000 people while a delegate from Baltimore would stand for 82,000.

State-wide, a conservative, staunchly rural 24 per cent of the electorate could mount a majority in the state legislature at Annapolis.

In the face of this unfavorable political climate, Baltimore, possessing only limited political autonomy, had to go to Annapolis to get permission for everything from money-raising bond issues to off-street parking regulations. "When we went to the brothers in Annapolis to get authority for a constructive change affecting only or chiefly the city," reflected Theodore R. McKeldin, twice mayor of Baltimore and a two-term Maryland governor, "again and again there has been a price to pay, in votes for something that shouldn't have gone through. We have had to pay plenty."

Meanwhile, the old families of Baltimore, who had guided the city's commercial and industrial growth, had moved their residences out of town, to the rich, horsy suburbs of Ruxton and Worthington Valley. On weekends and early evenings these easygoing, comfortable people went golfing or riding, or drove to the nearby Chesapeake to shoot waterfowl, to sail or to fish for rock bass. Weekdays they went downtown to their businesses, blissfully unconcerned with the city's problems and blandly certain that if everyone would just relax—as so many Baltimoreans always had—things would work out fine. Life was, in all, so easy, the pleasurable escapes from care so near at hand, that hardly anyone stopped to look at what was happening to the core of the metropolitan area. If any burning issue arose, the city, half Northern and half Southern in its ancient ideas, half urban and half suburban in its later mood, tended to take a safe middle position—or no position at all. "This is a great town for middle of the roaders," said one citizen. "I'm a great middle roader. That's why I love it here."

A hundred miles north along the four-track line of the Pennsylvania Railroad, Philadelphia was suffering some of the same pains, plus a few special ones of its own. The reformer Lincoln Steffens had once characterized Philadelphia as "corrupt and contented," a description that still fit in the years just after World War II. Like Baltimore, the city of Philadelphia had a ruling class that came into town as little as possible, preferring to sit in almost paralyzing contentment on the estates and tennis-club lawns of suburban communities. At the same time, these heirs of the business barons and old mercantile grandees kept a tight financial hold on the city's industrial and slum properties, skimming profits from the declining central business districts but abdicating firsthand responsibility for running the city to the political hacks who infested City Hall. "It makes little difference to us what happens in the city," said one suburbanite, whose detached attitude was all the more shocking since he was at the same time president of a major Philadelphia industrial concern.

In 1946 the resident hack in the mayor's chair at Philadelphia's City Hall was a pudgy little handshaker named Bernard "Barney" Samuel, who had come up through the notorious local political machine, a Republican organization nearing the 70th year of an almost unbroken run of municipal power. This machine had been so thoroughly in control of the city's politics that it had even paid the rent for Democratic headquarters and given out bundles of cash to rival-party members who might be growing restless in their thralldom.

Like any good machine-made mayor, Barney Samuel had too much patience with the venalities of his brothers within the organization. As an administrator he was little more than what one observer called "the city housekeeper," and its No. 1 ribbon cutter and speechmaker. He is reported to have made more than 4,000 speeches while in office and, according to one observer, "probably talked more and said less than any other mayor in the city's history." In older times, when Samuel was a rising young ward heeler, he had learned the classic formula for keeping slum voters happy: a load of coal and a basket of food at Christmastime, with maybe a job around the ward for someone's uncle. New Deal welfare programs had cut deeply into the favor trading. And the voters had begun to want a lot more from City Hall than a load of coal. But the Mayor and his fellow politicians had not managed to shake off their old notions of scattered largess or to provide any real plans to meet the urgent needs of the city and its people.

In this general nonfeasance, City Hall had long enjoyed the support or at least the tolerance of most of Philadelphia's old-money families, which approved of the inexpensive way the party looked after the town and were gratified by the friendly eye that city officials seemed willing to keep on absentee-owned slum and industrial properties.

The fact that in 1946 a few of the vested heirs were becoming restive to the point of outrage at the city's decay had not yet ruffled the calm exterior of Barney Samuel. Very shortly, however, it would. But until Philadelphia's upper-class businessmen got ready to move in concert for reform, the city's landscape, its living conditions and its economy kept sinking downward. Intensifying the effects of the decline, Philadelphia, like Baltimore, was being struck by a heavy immigration of disadvantaged Southern Negroes, who put a critical strain on the city's housing, school and social-service facilities, while contributing little to the city's tax resources. And finally, as with Baltimore, Philadelphia's occasional impulses toward renewal had been further hampered by a rural-dominated state legislature, as hostile as ever to the needs of that classic enemy of all honest farming men, the Wicked City. Thus "the cold and sower temper of the back counties" that Gouverneur Morris had feared at the time of the Grand Convention in 1787 was still making life difficult for a Philadelphian with fresh notions.

Pittsburgh, too, had had its troubles with the sour temper of the rural interests and with the anachronisms of a state constitution that the town's most powerful citizen, Richard King Mellon, was to call "one of the nation's worst." But Mellon and Pittsburgh had more immediate worries than the shortcomings of state government.

"The war had left Pittsburgh a dying city—the dirtiest slag pile in the United States," said David Leo Lawrence, boss of the state Democratic machine and a kingmaker in national Democratic Party politics. In 1946 Pittsburgh was overlaid by such a heavy cloud of gray industrial smog that the streetlights sometimes had to be left on all day and businessmen planning to dine out had to carry a second shirt downtown for the evening. One woman remembers as a little girl "stumbling to school each morning through darkness, with the city smelling like a tunnel." In downtown Pittsburgh 40 per cent of the office buildings were either blighted or empty, no new construction had been started for nearly 20 years, streets were potholed, and assessed tax values had been dropping at the rate of some $18 million a year. Downtown at the Point, where the green waters of the Allegheny joined the brown of the Monongahela, there was an industrial slum as decrepit as Baltimore's old port area. Only 10 years previously the rivers had risen in a disastrous flood during which, according to the *Pittsburgh Sun-Telegraph*, "Deaths mounted every hour. Houses were swept loose from their foundations. Power went off. . . . Phone lines went down. Fires broke out all over the district. . . ." At the end, 135,000 were homeless.

Surveying this dank, smoggy wreck of a city in the mid 1940s, the architect Frank Lloyd Wright was asked what he thought might be done to renew Pittsburgh. Wright replied coldly, "It would be cheaper to abandon it. . . ."

Yet there were some people—important people —whose commitments and personal affection for

Pittsburgh, despite its grimy failings, were far too strong to permit any thoughts of leaving. "We have a lot of property here," said Richard Mellon, the richest, most influential citizen in the town. "We can't very well move out banks." Mellon held a good deal more in Pittsburgh than banks, for it was an axiom of the Mellon investment policy that any company controlled by or heavily indebted to the family interests ought to be headquartered in Pittsburgh. Thus Gulf Oil, Koppers, Consolidation Coal, Alcoa and Westinghouse had some major facilities that were more or less rooted to the spot. So did a lot of big companies outside of Mellon's control, such as Jones & Laughlin, Allegheny Ludlum, Pittsburgh Steel and various divisions of the U.S. Steel Corporation, none of which wanted to move from the old home grounds if there was any sensible way to stay where they were. Nor was there really any sane possibility of following architect Wright's offhand proposal to abandon all these multimillion-dollar plants. Some better solution had to be found for the city, and quickly. "Pittsburgh was in a state of real desperation then," one resident remembers, "and it was a question of survival." But the real question was, What could, specifically, be done?

Richard Mellon and David Lawrence, each in his separate, potent way, had already been in pursuit of some answers. As far back as 1941 the City Council had passed a smoke-control ordinance. But with Pearl Harbor the new law had been shelved until the end of the war as a possible hindrance to production. That same year, Mellon had taken on the presidency of a civic organization called the Pittsburgh Regional Planning Association, whose staff director, Wallace Richards, had convinced him of the need to recruit the community's top men from both business and politics in a long-range campaign to rebuild the floundering city. Out of Richards' suggestion, and a subsequent series of meetings among Pittsburgh's ruling powers, came the Allegheny Conference on Community Development, a unique coalition of citizens with no official public authority but with the power to get things done. Besides the force of the Mellon interests, the Conference embraced such shakers and movers as Benjamin Fairless of U.S. Steel; H. J. Heinz II of the 57 Varieties company; Edgar Kaufmann, head of the city's leading department store; and Dr. Robert Doherty, President of the Carnegie Institute of Technology.

While the Allegheny Conference began to carve out its plans, David Lawrence put his considerable weight behind a new state urban-development law

that would grant Pennsylvania cities broad powers of eminent domain to acquire properties needed for renewal projects.

Now the kings and the knights were being moved into position for the renewal campaign. Lawrence himself, who had never before gone after a major elective office, decided to come out of the back room and run for mayor, where he could help lead any fight that might take place in pushing through the program. When he first confided this intent to his friend Fiorello LaGuardia, the tough New York mayor replied, "You're a damn fool." Lawrence growled that he had no interest in hearing that, ran for mayor on a renewal platform and won.

The platform was broad and bold, with some planks that would fall heavily upon the toes of the slum lords and old-line industrialists:

• Drastic enforcement of the 1941 smoke-control ordinance, whose suspension was legally scheduled to end with the war.

• A complete cleanout of the Point, where a state park and superhighway would replace the old industrial jungle.

• A continuing program of office and industrial renewal, picking up at the edge of the new park.

By no coincidence whatever the renewal platform of Lawrence the Democrat was identical to the fast-developing plans of the Republican businessmen of the Allegheny Conference. For in Pittsburgh the moving power within the city had become so balanced between politicians and big business that neither could work effectively without some help from the other. Realizing this early in the game, Mellon had quietly walked over to Lawrence's City Hall office and said, "If you ever need my help, I'm no farther away than that telephone."

Lawrence took up the offer and the two men joined forces. In so doing they pulled together the town's main powers into final battle array. At the same time, they added another dimension to Pittsburgh's pioneering formula for carrying out renewal: a union of both major political parties, of business and of labor under the umbrella of a single civic organization, in this case the Allegheny Conference. "We had political leadership in one vest pocket of the program," said a Conference staffer, "and the biggest taxpayers in the community in the other." No American city had ever before put together so effective a coalition or set down such bold goals. Significantly, the organization and its plans had been created outside the existing framework of established state and local government, which had proved inadequate to the needs of a city in crisis. Now that the combine had been created, however, other big towns, like Philadelphia and Baltimore, would be watching closely to see whether this Pittsburgh formula might be the answer to their own problems.

Though Pittsburgh launched its program on a wide front, the Allegheny Conference generally regarded the smoke-control issue as its critical early test. "That was our first crisis," recalled Ed Magee, a key Conference staffer. "It was a fork in the road, and we could have stopped dead."

There was indeed an effort in some quarters to make the renewal stop dead on smoke control, just as there would be opposition later at other points. But in almost every case the opponents would have been well advised to step aside before they got hurt. Because the technique the Pittsburgh revivalists fixed upon to reach their objectives was a series of good, old-fashioned Pittsburgh power plays, whose execution was reminiscent of the headlong style of the old robber barons.

For example, in best get-it-done fashion, it was Mayor David Lawrence—rather than the President of the United States—who first proclaimed that World War II was actually over. Lawrence made his drumhead pronouncement in order to start Pittsburgh's smoke-control campaign, which was not yet moving ahead even though the shooting part of the war had ended. "As no peace treaty had been signed," Lawrence recalled later, "technically the war was not over yet. Now I—together with members of the City Council—declared that the war was over and we fixed a date [October 1, 1946] for the ordinance to go into effect."

Mellon, meanwhile, passed the word through his industrial holdings that he was much in favor of smoke control. "Mr. Mellon's prestige with them was great," reported Lawrence, in a classic understatement. "He is a sort of bell cow in Pittsburgh." "Once you get the word out that R. K. is for [something]," said a Conference staff member, "the troops just fall in line."

At one point the Pennsylvania Railroad stepped out of line by lobbying against a bill that would force the road to use smoke-arresting equipment. "I understand," wrote Lawrence, "that after this Mr. Mellon called the president of the Pennsylvania Railroad, who happened to be in Florida, and told him in no uncertain terms that the Pennsylvania Railroad must change its position," reminding him that other railroads besides the Pennsylvania would be quite content to ship the products of the many Mellon enterprises. Shortly after this exercise of pressure, a batch of brand-new smokeless diesel locomotives with the Pennsy's distinctive

PRR markings appeared in the Pittsburgh area.

The overall drive for smoke control went so fast, in fact, that within a few years Pittsburgh's suffocating gray-black shroud had been almost entirely torn away. Squads of men were soon scrubbing and steam-blasting decades of grime from the façades of midtown buildings. One white shirt was plenty for a late night in the city. The air no longer smelled like the effluvium of a mine tunnel. And for the first time, really, in the 20th Century, Pittsburgh had pushed its head up into the sun.

While the smog bank was being blown away, the rest of the renewal program moved forward—often to the accompaniment of some more heavy arm twisting. When a new highway and a grassy park had first been proposed as the main instruments for cleaning up the Point, the conservative politicians in Harrisburg had pulled back sharply from the initial $61 million price tag (the eventual cost would be more than three times that figure). Whereupon a Mellon deputy, who also happened to be Finance Chairman of the Republican County Committee, reminded Harrisburg that money flowed in two directions, and an investment in the Point might well bring a cash return for the party from Pittsburgh's grateful businessmen. Support for the Point project soon followed.

A short time later the men within and behind the Allegheny Conference began putting together a package of laws that, if it could be pushed through the legislature, would free Pittsburgh from the need to continually resort to all this arm twisting and favor trading. Critical provisions in the package were for the creation of several new public bodies with the authority to carry forward renewal programs without having to request permission in Harrisburg before making each new move. It was the kind of legislation that only the powerful men of the Allegheny Conference could have forced through.

"We could muster a hell of a lot of strength on both sides of the aisle," said Ed Magee, and that is precisely what was done. At a dinner before the package went to the legislature, Mayor Lawrence addressed the Assemblymen and state Senators from the Pittsburgh area, aiming his most pointed remarks at the local Republican representatives. "If you want to help me politically," he said, sweeping a cold eye over the GOP contingent, "oppose the bills. The Governor will sign them anyway." The bills were duly passed. Later the Governor signed them as predicted.

With that act, the initial battle in the war to save Pittsburgh was virtually over. And although the war for total renewal was a long way from won, the city now had the ways—and was free to raise the means—to complete the first phase of the campaign. The 36 acres at the Point and an additional 23 bordering acres were swept clean of their industrial sludge, and the Equitable Life Assurance Society put up $43 million for construction of three modern, landscaped office buildings in the area. About the same time, the Mellon family carried renewal another step forward by donating $4.4 million toward the creation of a center-city park. On one end of this new park, U.S. Steel built a brand-new 41-story headquarters skyscraper, and at the other end Alcoa put up a 30-story headquarters of its own.

Farther uptown, plans were hatching to clean out 95 acres of slums in a squalid patch called the Lower Hill, replacing them with 600 units of high-rise apartments and a $20 million, 14,000-seat auditorium whose gleaming dome, 415 feet in diameter, could be rolled back for summer evening concerts. In all, the Allegheny Conference had started Pittsburgh on a spending spree that eventually would involve $850 million in private money alone. By the mid-1960s total expenditures would climb toward three billion dollars. The heart of the city would be remade, and the mood of the city would change from despair to deep pride. "I knew we had it made . . ." said a Conference member, "when a cabdriver picked me up at a hotel, thought I was from out of town, and insisted on taking me off the route to show me Gateway Center. When he said, 'I want to show you what we're doing,' I knew the renaissance was a success, because he had identified it as his own."

Outside of Pittsburgh, too, the spirit of the renaissance was taking hold, most notably in Philadelphia, where another broad renewal program was underway. There, a citizens' organization called the Greater Philadelphia Movement (GPM) had been put together. Like the Allegheny Conference, it was made up of the top executives in locally owned companies, the sort of men, said one charter member, who "didn't have to check back with Papa" after they made a decision. These men decided to follow the formula laid down in Pittsburgh —"to concentrate on the heart of the problem in the core of the city, because . . . if you can't do it here—forget it."

"With the suburban pull," said one leader of the Philadelphia version of the movement, "you've got to do something to hold the center of the city together, because the center of the city provides your tax base." Without a sound base of tax revenues,

Two of the men most responsible for Pittsburgh's renaissance, David Lawrence *(left)* and Richard K. Mellon, look across Mellon Square Park, a downtown plaza they created. Mellon donated $4.4 million to develop the space; then Mayor Lawrence used his political power to line up city-wide support for the project.

which can come most readily from a healthy central business district, a city cannot provide either proper services or an adequate physical environment for its people. Under the guidance of the men who were to form the backbone of the GPM, a rebuilding plan more elaborate even than Pittsburgh's, and more carefully integrated, was laid down. Then, as a first step toward convincing the city's people that planning would work, a 30-by-14-foot scale model showing how a rebuilt center city could look was put on display in Gimbels department store, along with other elaborate exhibits. In two months 400,000 people trooped past the model—the design of urban architects Oskar Stonorov and the lean, messianic Edmund Bacon—staring at a dazzling panorama of green parks, airy apartment houses, and lovingly restored buildings of the colonial and Federal periods. In the model the central business district was a complex of tall, glassy towers, rather than the familiar jumble of aged buildings split by the grim barrier of stone and steel (often called "the Chinese Wall") that carried the Pennsylvania Railroad's line to its Broad Street terminal. Overall, the public was shown that the rusted image of the city could be recast as a 20th Century realization of William Penn's dream of a "greene countrie towne." It was hard, at first, for the postwar citizens of Penn's town to believe that anything like this could happen. "For years Philadelphia had thought of itself as hopeless," said Bacon. "The idea that the city could be exciting was an enormous shock." But, added one of the other main planners, the "exhibit made people see the city as solvable."

Before a real city could be built according to this or any other model, however, Philadelphia had to establish locally one more critical element of the renaissance formula: an alliance between businessmen and politicians. In the process a thorough fumigation of municipal government would have to be carried out, since the incumbent crew of Barney Samuel and company, conspiring beneath City Hall's brooding, corroded statue of Father Penn, were hardly to be sought as allies for any sort of urban reform movement. What Philadelphia needed was some political crusaders, and as if by summons, they appeared in the form of Joseph Sill Clark and Richardson Dilworth, as unlikely a pair of political white knights as the city had ever seen.

Each was, by birth, a proper socialite, with a long Pennsylvania heritage. Each had set out on the path to proper prep schools and thence to Harvard (Clark) and Yale (Dilworth). Later they had both gone into the law, as so many good Philadelphians always had. Despite this careful grooming, however, Clark and Dilworth acquired some odd quirks. They became Democrats and developed a passionate interest in their city.

In 1947 Dilworth ran for mayor on a reform ticket with Clark as his campaign manager. Riding through the city on a sound truck, jumping down onto street corners, the shouting, gesticulating Dilworth shook City Hall to its foundations as he bellowed chapter and verse on municipal corruption. He passed out leaflets entitled "Who Got the Graft?" and "Questions the Mayor Won't Answer"; and then he himself answered those questions, naming the grafters and racketeers.

On election day Barney Samuel still managed to beat Dilworth, but that was the organization's last hurrah. Dilworth's shotgun charges on corruption had taken such deadly effect that the machine, even in victory, began to fall apart. A committee looking into ways to raise municipal salaries found something else: somebody had been dipping into the till. The farther down the committee dug, the more grubby hands they found. Suddenly an embezzler in the Amusement Tax Office committed suicide, leaving behind a written roster of his fellow conspirators. A rash of suspensions and a grand jury investigation followed.

"People began jumping out windows," as one lawyer close to the scandals described the lethal chaos around City Hall. In a grim climax the chief of the Vice Squad also killed himself.

By now even the most sluggish, contented Philadelphian was awake to the fact that there was something very wrong with his city besides a drab, declining downtown. And for the first time in almost 70 years the voters began to believe the time had arrived for a drastic change. In the off-year elections of 1949 Dilworth and Clark were elected city treasurer and controller, respectively. From these two key offices they kept up their fire upon the vestiges of the Republican machine. But even more important, the critical alliance was consummated between the reform politicians and the businessmen of the Greater Philadelphia Movement, whose renewal goals could not be achieved without strong, enlightened political support.

The benefits of the alliance were decidedly mutual, since Clark and Dilworth, emerging as the town's two hottest politicians, were hatching bigger plans of their own for municipal reform and very much needed the bipartisan backing that could come only from union with the GPM. While they were acquiring that backing, the reformers had lobbied the state legislature into granting the city the right to draw up a brand-new charter for home-rule government, enabling them to establish a strong mayor's office, an improved civil service to replace the old spoils system and a powerful planning commission to carry forward the new capital-investment programs. Then, after a rousing 1951 campaign, Clark and Dilworth were swept into office as mayor and district attorney, respectively. The victory was strikingly bipartisan: even the stodgy *Philadelphia Inquirer*, which had always been a pillar of support for Republicans no matter how unattractive, gave a lusty editorial cheer for the success of the two liberal reformers.

The men in the Greater Philadelphia Movement cheered even more loudly, not only because their adopted candidates were in office but also because several months earlier the new charter had been adopted by a rousing 120,000 majority of the voters. Ed Bacon was perhaps most ecstatic of all, eventually describing the charter, a bit grandly, as "one of the greatest instruments of municipal government in the free world."

Ed Bacon was likely to think so, since, as executive director of the newly strengthened City Planning Commission, he could now get on much more effectively with the business of rebuilding the heart of the city. And that, with the support

Philadelphia's resuscitation

Before and after views of two major urban-renewal projects in Philadelphia suggest the extent of the city's redevelopment program. In what has been called the most comprehensive rebuilding scheme in the U.S., planners have laid out designs that will guide the city's growth through the 1980s. The photograph at right looks north past Independence Hall toward the new Mall. This Mall, designed to attract pedestrians, replaced the four blocks of decaying buildings shown below.

Penn Center *(left)* is Philadelphia's most ambitious downtown renewal project. This $120 million complex of offices, hotels, apartments and walkways replaced the mile-long muddle of elevated railroad tracks known as the "Chinese Wall" *(above)*. The tracks now run underground. Many urban planners believe that the first thing that must be done to resuscitate a city is to transform it from a cold canyon of buildings into a spacious, open complex where the individual does not feel lost. Philadelphia's Independence Mall and Penn Center are successful examples of such transformation.

of the coalition, is pretty much what he did. With-in a year the Pennsylvania Railroad's "Chinese Wall" of elevated tracks began to come down to be replaced by a complex of landscaped office and residence buildings called Penn Center. Close to the Delaware, a foul, sprawling wholesale produce depot was moved out, and the restoration of the historic part of the city was pushed forward.

One by one the massive pieces of the overall renewal plan were put in place, with such careful coordination and execution that by the early 1960s the once grubby center of Philadelphia was emerging as a modern model of William Penn's "greene countrie towne." And proud citizens—perhaps a bit defensive about Pittsburgh's pioneering role in the renaissance movement—were saying, as one did, "You can go to almost any other city and find more spectacular individual projects. . . . But in Philadelphia we have the only place where we've tried to tie these things together."

Down in Baltimore the citizens, jolted into action by the spreading spirit of renaissance, were feeling just as chauvinistic about their own local renewal program. Although the Baltimore movement did not hit its full stride until 1960, it gained momentum so fast that by 1962 almost $465 million had been spent on projects covering 775 acres. The showpiece was Charles Center, a center-city business-residence complex on the order of Penn Center in Philadelphia, but carried out—so say Baltimoreans—with a good deal more speed and verve. "I've been in urban renewal for almost fifteen years," said one planner, "and I've never seen a project like Charles Center move so fast."

"We've started to build a new city right in the middle of the city," added Jerold C. Hoffberger, a boosterish local businessman and charter member of the energizing Greater Baltimore Committee. "The leaders of this community realize there's something to be done. . . ."

Just as important to the old border city has been its peaceful progress in race relations. When the Supreme Court passed down its school integration judgment in 1954, there was a real danger that Baltimore, with a Negro population growing toward 40 per cent, would explode in riots as bad as those that have since shaken Watts, Newark and other cities. But when the first test occurred in the schools, traditionally temperate Baltimore showed marked unanimity and wisdom in rising above the vestiges of its prejudices.

"We decided to . . . integrate the schools," says Walter Sondheim Jr., former school-board member, "and that's what we did. We had a law

here, requiring us to have separate schools, but that was nullified. And the thing is, Baltimore has a fairly young tradition of no violence. A lot of people who didn't necessarily agree with integration were repelled by violence."

During the early weeks of school in the fall of 1954, the Police Commissioner, Beverly Ober, went on television to announce that there would be no interference with the peaceful operation of the schools. "Some pickets went out," said Sondheim, "and Ober said [to them], 'Okay, the bell's rung, school has started.' And that was it."

"I think the thing is," added Sondheim, "that people in Baltimore felt 'This is the law, and constitutional rights are not a matter of choice.' And today I don't think people want to turn the clock back." Nor is it likely they will. After the initial success in the schools, Baltimore went on to integrate virtually all its public facilities and then set up an enforcing agency called the Community Relations Commission to see that they remained so. A prime mover behind much of the city's continued social progress has been its wise but very tough former Mayor, Theodore R. McKeldin. "I'm what my enemies call a nigger-lover," chuckled McKeldin. Then he added proudly, "We're the only major city with *this* kind of population that hasn't had a major riot." And indeed Baltimore has remained quiescent during the past decade of integration.

In an effort to keep abreast of other aspects of its social problems, Baltimore has become a national leader in both neighborhood renewal and in low-cost public housing. "These things," says Sondheim, "are just as important as the more dramatic moves like Charles Center." To date, some 20 renewal projects, using both local and federal funds, have gotten underway in areas covering more than 900 acres, and public housing has gone up for more than 41,000 people. Baltimore still has miles to go in this and other fields before it sleeps—if, indeed, the city should ever again choose to drowse off. But after its recent achievements, and the upsurge of local pride that has gone with them, there are strong indications that the old border city is determined to carve out a leading place in the national culture.

"I have faith in Baltimore," said McKeldin, just before he stepped down as Baltimore's mayor at the close of 1967. "In a place like this, where people do essentially know each other . . . people do care. By and large, this city is very much on the move, on the way up. You wait, great things will come out of here in years ahead."

Its beauty unmarred by power poles or electric wires, an Amish farm adorns the Pennsylvania Dutch countryside. A feature of these farms is the enormous "bank barn" *(far left)*, which contains fodder, livestock and farm equipment.

Old ways of the Pennsylvania Dutch

Among the richest and most beautiful farmlands in America are those in southeastern Pennsylvania, home of the Pennsylvania Dutch. Industrious, devout, faithful to old-fashioned ways, these remarkable people have given the area a unique regional flavor.

The original Pennsylvania Dutch were mainly Rhineland Germans—the term "Dutch" comes from *Deitsch* or *Deutsch,* meaning "German"— who came to America to escape religious persecution. Many of their descendants have taken to urban life, but others, especially members of the Mennonite and Amish sects, have stayed on the land. Skillful farmers, the Pennsylvania Dutch of all religious persuasions have made their area extremely fruitful and, with their ancient crafts and customs, have preserved a peaceful, bucolic air from the past.

Photographs by Richard Noble

Like a figure out of the past, an Amish farmer, his face shielded from the sun by a homemade straw hat of traditional design, sits placidly on the seat of his mule-drawn plow. The more strict among the Amish, in common with members of some other Pennsylvania Dutch sects, will not use tractors or other modern gear. "Tractors and electricity are not in the Bible," they say, and therefore they find no need for them. On some of the richest farms in Pennsylvania the only piece of modern machinery is a gasoline engine that powers the milking equipment.

Using a handmade tool of simple design—a piece of bent steel with a leather grip—a Pennsylvania Dutch farmer husks an ear of corn. These people plant corn in April or May and harvest during October and November, but it is not one of their principal cash crops. Any corn that does not turn up at farmhouse dinner tables as corn relish or corn pie is likely to be fed to the livestock. The main cash crops are broad-leaf tobacco and wheat; by intensive cultivation of their rich, if relatively small, fields, the hard-working farmers make these high-value crops pay off handsomely.

No matter where I take my guests, it seems they like my kitchen best," goes the Pennsylvania Dutch saying. After viewing the feast laid out below by Mrs. Mark Feinour, no one would wonder why. As in the Feinour household, the kitchen is usually the largest room in a Pennsylvania Dutch home—the center of its activity. Enormous, multicourse meals are served there three times a day. Everything from soup to dessert is placed on the table at once since these people particularly enjoy a bit of pie along with a piece of sausage. There is always an abundance of everything—for any dish to be "all," or empty, is a cause for shame and lamentation.

Canned fruits and vegetables are put up each summer by Pennsylvania Dutch housewives and their daughters. The shelves below contain a number of favorites. From left to right and top to bottom, they are beans, black cherries, chowchow, apricots, string beans, pickles, red beets, lima beans, pickle rings, pears, sliced pickles and peaches. Besides cupboards loaded with canned goods, a house prepared for winter has crocks of "puddins"—a delicious mixture of beef and pork scraps—and jugs of homemade wine stored in the cellar. Hanging from the rafters in the attics are usually smoked sausages and bags of dried apples.

Since many of the Pennsylvania Dutch—notably the Amish and the Old Order Mennonites—still use wagons and buggies instead of automobiles and trucks, craftsmen such as blacksmiths and harness makers can still be found in almost every community. Adam Beam *(below)* has been a blacksmith in Talmage, Pennsylvania, for more than 65 years and he still reshoes 40 to 70 horses each week. He also does welding and can make or repair almost any metal implement. Harvey Menkel *(right)* stands amid the clutter of an old-fashioned harness-making shop in Topton, Pennsylvania, owned by Ivan Leid. Not a member of one of the stricter Pennsylvania Dutch sects, Menkel agreed to be photographed because Leid, an Old Order Mennonite, had refused, heeding the Mennonite stricture against pictures.

Auctions, or "vendues," as the Pennsylvania Dutch call them (the term derives, oddly enough, from an old French word for a sale), are popular events, for these people take special pride in obtaining a useful item at a bargain price. At the auction shown above, the possessions of an elderly woman are being auctioned off by her children at her request. Since she intended to live with one of her children, she held the auction rather than risk a family squabble over the division of such possessions as tables and chairs.

Gifted artisans, a group of Pennsylvania Dutch women (*left*) proudly pose behind a prizewinning quilt. Quilts like this one are usually made during the winter months when farm work makes fewer demands on the women. They are decorated with motifs taken from nature, history or religion—the most popular design is the tulip, often applied in triple clusters thought to symbolize the Trinity. Some are made to be sold and can be seen on display in the community markets of towns like Lancaster and Lebanon.

The Mennonites and the Amish, the pious "plain people" of the Pennsylvania Dutch country, form the backbone of this old-fashioned rural area. It is their dedication to tradition, to the old way of life, that does most to preserve the flavor of the Pennsylvania Dutch style of living.

The Mennonites—the term comes from Menno Simons, the name of an early leader among Anabaptist dissenters—were the first Germans to settle in the area. The Amish (named for the sect's founder, Jacob Amman) were an offshoot of the Mennonites and remain even stricter in their practices. The Amish not only eschew machines but also stick to the simple clothing their forebears wore. Both groups practice a fundamental, Bible-centered religion.

One of the most obvious differences between the Mennonites and the Amish is the beard worn by every Amish married man; Mennonites are often clean-shaven. Older Amish men like the one above resemble Old Testament patriarchs. Yet despite his beard, he has a clean-shaven upper lip: to the peaceful Amish, the mustache is the sign of the military man, and therefore is forbidden.

Each Sunday morning Amish and Mennonite alike flock to their simple churches—a Mennonite meetinghouse is shown at left—for the weekly service. The lay preacher delivers a sermon in Pennsylvania Dutch—a unique blend of English and German. While there is no instrumental music, hymns are sung lustily by the entire congregation.

Leaning against a split-rail fence, Amish and Mennonite children smile cheerfully during recess in front of their one-room schoolhouse. This school is one of the more than 40 run by the "plain people" in Pennsylvania, many of whom insist on educating their children their own way—an attitude that has led to conflict with state authorities.

Believing that their children are destined to be farmers and housewives, the stricter Amish and Mennonites think that high-school education, let alone college, is needless. Their schools, therefore, include only the first eight grades, and the pupils commonly leave at about age 14. Pennsylvania law, however, requires children to stay in school until 16. The matter came to a crisis in 1956 when a group of Amish fathers were fined and jailed for taking their children out of school too soon. Immediately the cry of religious persecution was heard. Political pressures rose and the Governor arranged a compromise; it stipulated that the children could leave their schools when they had completed the eighth grade, but they had to continue their study of academic subjects for three hours each week until reaching age 16.

The stricter Amish and Mennonite fathers believe, quite naturally, that any higher education will tend to make the children dissatisfied with their traditional ways of life and inevitably doom the unique culture that they have preserved so diligently for so long. Compromise has smoothed over the dispute but has not resolved the problems that caused it. State authorities point out that not all the children of even these devoted farming folk stay on the land; those who leave, in particular, must be prepared to cope with the problems they will face in modern U.S. society.

So far, although Pennsylvania Dutch youths continue to melt into the common U.S. pattern, enough have stayed on the farms to carry on the life of their fathers. In doing so, they have kept the beautiful rolling hills of this part of Pennsylvania an almost unchanging island of peace and plenty amid the tumult of mobile modern America.

6

Tiny Delaware's Giant Enterprise

The hills of northern Delaware descend in rolling terraces for a dozen miles from the arc of the Pennsylvania border through a succession of prosperous little suburbs to the city of Wilmington at the edge of tidewater on the Delaware River. On many of these hills, crowned by their clusters of tall oak, the grass is close-cropped by orderly bands of cows and sheep or by even more orderly bands of grounds keepers who roam within the bordering stone walls of estates, and of estates lately turned country clubs or charitable foundations, scattered along the meandering tar roads. This is a corner of the world abounding in money: old money, new money, money carefully held; but above all, money dedicated to an ethic that might appropriately be defined as Better Living. The living here is, in fact, so much better than in most other places that, for example, one local ménage just across the Pennsylvania border employs a force of 87 gardeners to maintain its formal gardens and most particularly to pamper the plant life inside a greenhouse whose floor area covers some three and a half acres. These

gardens have been open to the public since the estate—Longwood—became a foundation in 1946. In other times, however, the master of the place would prowl the greenhouse alone, peering at his exotic blooms while a hired concert artist made soothing sounds upon the world's largest privately owned pipe organ.

Closer to Wilmington, bordering Delaware's premier suburban area of Greenville, stands a mansion with more than 100 rooms, all of them decorated with period pieces from American history; each chair, floor board, curtain and spoon in the various rooms is an authentic antique matched to the décor of the individual room. Some years back, a guest who tried with a friend to explore this enormous mansion reported: "It was all so big, so monstrously big, and there were so many rooms, corridors and staircases that we got completely lost. Fortunately we found a telephone and called for help. We were asked what number we were calling from and told not to budge from the spot until someone got there. . . . After some time a footman arrived. But he got lost, too, and called from another station to find out the route back."

Nearby is an estate whose late owner lies buried beneath a 223-foot-high carillon tower built according to his own specifications. Next to him are

Members of the du Pont clan, gathered at a family estate in Delaware in 1950, celebrate the 150th anniversary of the arrival in America of the first du Pont, Pierre Samuel du Pont de Nemours. His son, Eleuthère Irénée, founded the Du Pont Company.

the mortal remains of his mongrel dog. Near the mansion rises a full-sized Temple of Love modeled after one that stands in the world-famous gardens at Versailles. The two bronze gates leading into the grounds are emblazoned with the motto *Aimer et connaître*—"To love and to know." But those gates are the only break in an encircling wall 10 feet high and topped by embedded shards of broken glass, put there by the owner to indicate that he desired the love and knowledge of very few people.

Approaching the city limits, the mansioned properties give way to quietly prosperous subdivisions, such as Westover Hills and Woodbrook— clusters of conventional brick or stone houses set on single-acre plots and rigidly zoned against any kind of commercial building. In these tight little communities, uniformed day help walk the small children along the byways. Here and there among the houses a wire fence marks the front of a well-supported high school or a private academy where, on fall afternoons, clusters of girls in matching wool exercise suits scurry about playing that most representative of rich Eastern girls' school sports, field hockey. At the fringe of the business center of Wilmington the grass plots are reduced to quarter acres, but the houses are no less neat or orderly, the newer neighborhoods having the cheery, tree-lined aspect of a motion-picture set, complete with newsboy on bike followed by a small, yapping dog.

"People live well here," confirmed one local executive, in a typically understated Wilmington way. And then, in fuller explanation he added, "Du Pont pays well, and people live well."

E. I. du Pont de Nemours & Company, Inc., has paid well indeed, and in consequence a fair portion of the state of Delaware has lived very well, too, ever since the company made a farsighted decision half a century ago to diversify out of the explosives business—in which it had been almost wholly absorbed for more than a century—and to venture into the young and then relatively unexplored world of synthetic chemistry. Because of the diversification program, and the broad campaign of pioneering laboratory research that went with it, Du Pont today is the world's biggest chemical company, with annual sales of some three billion dollars. Its operations and its influence extend outward from the company's headquarters in Wilmington to embrace 150 plants in 29 states and 15 foreign countries. Unlike many of the corporate giants in the other Middle Atlantic States, however, Du Pont has used its size, its power and its prosperity with remarkable wisdom and foresight.

Instead of turning its home territory into a repressive corporate fief, prone to all the bitterness and dislocations of labor upheavals, Du Pont has handled its employees and their community with an enlightened care that the exploitive industries in neighbor states would have done well to observe. The payroll in the headquarters area alone is so high that per capita income in the state of Delaware is second in the United States. And the positive contributions of the company extend into almost every phase of community life, penetrating more subtly—though no less deeply—than even the crucial influence of personal income.

Besides creating an enlightened model of corporate behavior, Du Pont has also pioneered in establishing a progressive concept of industrial growth. Productivity has been based primarily on brain power rather than on muscle power, and the orientation has been toward the discovery of new products rather than toward the massive production and heavy-handed selling of the same old line. Acting on the corporate motto of *Better Things for Better Living . . . Through Chemistry*, Du Pont's nationwide army of 6,000 degree-holding scientists have brewed up 1,200 basic Better Things, half of which did not exist before World War II.

Yet these Du Pont products are now so commonplace that they are part of the bettered lives of almost everyone in the U.S. For instance, when an American couple wake up in the morning, it is not unlikely that they will rise from a mattress of Du Pont polyurethane foam and throw off a blanket of Du Pont Orlon colored with Du Pont dyes. The wife may then wriggle into a girdle of Lycra spandex (by Du Pont), smooth a pair of Cantrece stockings over her legs and put on a slip of nylon— the most widely used synthetic cloth ever produced. Her husband, meanwhile, may don a suit of Dacron and wool, button up a spotless white shirt bleached with Oxone and perhaps lace on new shoes of Corfam, the leather substitute with which Du Pont hopes to pick off an eventual 25 per cent of the six-billion-dollar U.S. footwear market.

At breakfast the couple is still hip-deep in Du Pont products, many named with the help of a computer that maintains a list of 153,000 catchy— and copyrightable—nonsense words as a source of labels for new products. To start the morning meal the wife opens the refrigerator—cooled by Freon gas—takes out a half pound of bacon wrapped in Mylar and tosses a few strips into a frying pan coated with nonstick Teflon. As the husband leaves for work, he picks up his raincoat waterproofed with Zelan and steps into a car whose body is very likely painted with Lucite (Du Pont invented the original spray-on lacquer from which standard auto body paints have been derived). Rolling down the driveway on tires reinforced by nylon cord, he may cast a prideful glance back at the house, with its coating of waterproof Tedlar, and at the lawn from which crab grass has been purged by a dose of Oust. And if either person should feel influenza coming on, he could pop into his mouth a pill of Symmetrel, a newly marketed virus retardant that Du Pont researchers have evolved from a chlorinated compound originally made in the company's now de-emphasized explosives department.

In the course of this day the couple may never see a Du Pont trademark or be otherwise aware of the effect on their lives of the products developed by the company's scientists. Only about 5 per cent of Du Pont's output goes direct to customers over a retail counter. The rest is sold to manufacturers who market the finished products under their own names. Thus the pervasive presence of the world's largest chemical firm is barely noticed by most Americans. In the state of Delaware, however, and especially in the Wilmington area, the name Du Pont and the company bearing that label are the dominant facts of daily life—and as one appraising citizen (himself not an employee) put it—"The community's number-one asset."

The corporate headquarters of E. I. du Pont de Nemours is in a massive pair of concrete buildings that cast their maternal shadow over Wilmington from the top of its highest midtown hill. The main structure is called, not too surprisingly, the Du Pont Building. It is umbilically connected by an overstreet passageway to the Nemours Building on the adjoining block. Six thousand people work here, from 8 in the morning until 5 p.m. And when they leave for their homes in the suburbs, the central part of the city, which has only five modern apartment houses, is suddenly very empty. "This town is dead," says one employee, of Wilmington's night life. "You could fire a French seventy-five down the middle of the street at nine o'clock Saturday night and not hit a goddamned thing."

Wilmington dies after dark, and on weekends too, because the business of the Du Pont Company and two of its former subsidiaries, the Hercules and Atlas Chemical companies, spun off long ago in an antitrust divestiture, is about the only activity of any real importance in the central city. On any night when there is a gentle breeze from the northwest, Wilmington is so still, the passage of cars and buses so infrequent, that the faint smell of manure from the farms and horsy estates beyond the city line is discernible at the main entrance of the Du Pont Building. Among these farms at the edge of town and beyond are Du Pont's main research laboratories, the operating base for the company's central corps of 1,300 scientists and technicians, who are backed up by 2,700 assistants and other support personnel. Elsewhere around the city Du Pont has half a dozen producing plants, for a total work force of 26,000 in the Wilmington area, far more than any other employer in the state. The total payroll for this work force is $260 million. And the individual paychecks, for the most part, are, in the words of a typical Du Pont employee, "very, very generous." It is this generosity that makes the suburbs of the northern district of Delaware the very quintessence, as we have seen, of Better Living.

The scrubbed, movie-set suburbs on Wilmington's city line are home grounds for Du Pont's minor supervisors and young scientists, who draw down base salaries reported to be $15,000 plus, a figure substantially increased by bonuses. Lately even a fresh-minted Ph.D. right from a university has been able to start out in suburban comfort, since Du Pont now offers upward of $13,000 to top-level science graduates. As he moves up the ladder into middle management and to a middle salary of more than $25,000, the Du Pont employee tends to move out to the greener pastures of Westover Hills and environs. Finally, if all goes well, he will reach the ultimate suburb of Greenville and its environs. There he will settle among the top managers and scientists, whose incomes only begin with their $50,000-plus salaries and can be tripled by Du Pont's munificent bonus system, which has made millionaires of the men who have turned up the company's most successful products.

There, too, if all goes particularly well, he will come in contact with the du Pont family itself, which still holds substantial ownership and maintains effective control over the company originally founded in 1802 by Eleuthère Irénée du Pont as a tiny black-powder mill. In 1968 five of the eight members of the firm's Finance Committee, which passes on all investments over one million dollars, were du Ponts or du Pont in-laws. The Finance Committee's chairman was Crawford Greenewalt, an in-law. The Chairman of the Board was Lammot du Pont Copeland, son of a du Pont lady and one of the largest stockholders in the staggeringly wealthy Christiana Securities Corporation, a family-run holding company that owns 29 per cent of the voting stock in E. I. du Pont de Nemours.

Like most other members of the inner family circle, Chairman Copeland has always been dead serious about his position in the company and talks earnestly about Du Pont's role in bringing Better Living to the American community at large and to Delaware in particular: "It's fascinating," he said recently, "to speculate on the impact the things you make have on society. . . . Where our things give people a better product at a better price, we are making a real contribution to the world." And like virtually all du Ponts who have advanced to key positions, he is a hard, effective worker. The less effective du Ponts are shunted into harmless so-called "drag" jobs, where, as one close observer put it, they are "left to age quietly, like a Chinese egg, in a cool, dark place." Or they may be prevailed upon to stay out of the firm altogether. One du Pont recalls, "At a family cocktail party years ago [I] said [to a company director], 'Honestly . . . what do you think my prospects are with the company?' He put his hand on my shoulder and he said to me, 'Why don't you take up boating?' "

As befits a leader of a great company, Copeland's private life is the epitome of elegance. He spends his holidays salmon fishing in Scotland or duck shooting on the Chesapeake. His weekends are taken up overseeing the Angus cattle on his 3,000-acre Maryland farm, which he pleads with a reporter to describe not as an estate but as "an old Victorian house where my wife and I camp out." His principal domicile, however, is a 20-room Greenville mansion whose 300 acres are manicured by 14 gardeners and protected against bugs and blight by Du Pont agricultural chemicals. The big neighboring properties are almost all under title to the du Pont family. For Greenville is also known as du Pont Château Country. It is here that the tribe began to spread out years ago on a string of estates, many of which adjoin one another to form a magnificent preserve for shooting, riding or just being away from the world among other du Ponts.

The Temple of Love and the wall with broken glass are, of course, in the Greenville area, having been put there more than 50 years ago by Alfred I. du Pont, a passionate, erratic man who, with his cousins Pierre S. and Coleman, saved control of the company when an outside syndicate very nearly bought it away from the family in 1902. Another big estate, the one with the three-and-a-half-acre greenhouse and the pipe organ, was built only a few miles away by Pierre S., who was president of the company during World War I and is credited with having helped to change the firm from a tightly held, one-product enterprise to a widely diversified corporation with a fundamental commitment to research. Henry Francis du Pont, the grandson

Eleuthère Irénée du Pont, seen on the right in the painting above with Lavoisier, the celebrated French chemist, was the founder of E. I. du Pont de Nemours & Company, the Delaware-based firm that is the present-day giant of the chemical industry. Coming to the U.S. in 1800, the young du Pont shortly set up a small gunpowder plant near Wilmington, Delaware. The company expanded quickly both before and after the Civil War—its size in 1881 can be seen in the sketch at right—but it did not become the colossus it is today until it diversified into many areas of chemistry after World War I.

of old Henry du Pont, who ran the business in the latter half of the 19th Century, lives in a massive "cottage" next to the 100-room Greenville mansion where the guest once became lost in the labyrinth of antique rooms. And though the original owners of these properties are dead, and the main portions of the estates given over to foundations that maintain them, the rest of the Château Country is very much alive with du Ponts who are vigorously active both in the company and outside it.

Next to Copeland's house are sprawling establishments with names like Chevannes, Louviers and Bois des Fossés, titles reflecting the family's pride in its French Huguenot ancestry. The interiors of these houses, whose owners are at least as sports-minded as Copeland, are spotted with African big-game trophies, photographs of du Pont boats like the 1964 America's Cup contender *American Eagle*, and trophies won by du Pont race horses, most notably Mrs. Richard du Pont's Kelso, the first thoroughbred to be named Horse of the Year over three consecutive seasons. In fact Kelso, a huge, lovable beast whose favorite food is chocolate ice-cream sundaes, is so much a part of the family that his doting owner says, "If he were small enough we'd keep him in the house."

Unlike most institutions whose prosperity is so

thoroughly established, neither the Du Pont Company nor the du Pont family has become bogged down in the complacency or smug disinterest that so often accompanies success. Rather, they have both tended to maintain a continuing awareness of their role in helping to create a kind of new-wave industrial community.

Within the company, management's relationship with blue-collar employees has been a model of soft-handed consideration, especially when contrasted with the mailed-fist tactics of some of the industrialists in the other Middle Atlantic States. For decades Du Pont has kept its wages and benefits for blue-collar workers even with or well ahead of most reasonable union demands. As a result, only some 4.1 per cent of Du Pont's blue-collar men, across the country, have felt the need to join national unions. Furthermore, the number of man-hours lost through strikes over the years has been far below that of the big companies in coal and steel, and, says one forthright executive, "The amount of money we've saved by not having work stoppages has been enormous."

Perhaps the most important benefits for Du Pont's hourly wage earners have come from the company's nationwide diversification of production, which has reduced the cyclical unemployment still suffered by some undiversified industries. Even Du Pont's textile-fiber plants, the most sensitive of its facilities to market demand, normally operate at an estimated 77 per cent of capacity. Moreover, the continual flow of new products coming out of the laboratories helps to provide new job opportunities for workers who may be in an obsolescent corner of the fast-moving chemical industry. For example, some 25 years ago Du Pont was among the country's biggest manufacturers of rayon, an artificial fiber that provided thousands of men and women with employment inside the company. Today, rayon production has been completely phased out; but instead of simply closing plants and laying off people permanently, Du Pont has created 25,000 fresh jobs in its nylon, Dacron, Orlon, Lycra and other fiber facilities. These built-in policies of product renewal and good employee relations have helped to keep the economic base of the community growing and to produce the degree of harmony between management and labor that was so disastrously lacking in the coal-steel towns.

Another upgrading and renewing influence on the Wilmington community has been the presence of large numbers of company scientists and degree-bearing executives. Du Pont has more than 1,800 people with Ph.D.s in the Wilmington area alone, divided between the laboratories and management headquarters. "The community expands intellectually through these people," says an employee. "For one thing, they demand better schools. Years ago the public schools here were very bad. One survey rated them down fortieth or forty-fifth among all the states in academic standards and teacher pay. Now we're around the top."

"I moved here three years ago," says another, "and I had the option of sending my kids to either public or private school. I investigated very intensively, and the only reason for sending them to the private school would have been for the business of smaller classes; the education is no better. And so my kids are in public school." Some 70 per cent of high schoolers in Wilmington's select suburbs go on to further education.

The most conspicuous contributors to the community, of course, and the most consistent, have been the members of the du Pont family. There are 12 major family foundations, and an uncounted number of minor ones, that channel a continuous flow of support toward the welfare, the education and the health of the people of Delaware. Of the 32 trustees of the University of Delaware, nine are family members or top company officers, and one of these is the university's leading benefactor—to the tune of $30 million. In his lifetime Pierre S. du Pont alone spent four million dollars to improve education and replace run-down school buildings. At one time he served as a vigorous and effective state tax commissioner. And today state revenues provide up to 77 per cent of the budget for public elementary-secondary schools (whereas Pennsylvania state aid in 1967 was still below 45 per cent). Alfred du Pont, in a characteristic burst of impatience at Delaware's slow progress toward old-age pensions, pushed a pension bill into the legislature and then grandly financed the entire plan out of his own checking account for two years until the bill was finally passed. Coleman du Pont conceived the plan for Delaware's first modern highway, paid in full for the first 20 miles and then backed the remaining construction with 44,000 of his own dollars per mile, thus creating a critical link of modern transportation between Wilmington and the patchwork of truck farms and chicken hatcheries that still dominates the state's southern reaches.

Today this sort of grand gesture by a single family member has all but disappeared, partly for tax reasons and partly because both the family and the company have developed a hair-trigger sensitivity about possible overdominance of the community. The more caustic local wits, noting the family's

influence on both Wilmington newspapers (and an absence of unfavorable editorial comment about Du Pont), have nicknamed the *Morning News* the *Daily Better Living*. A number of years ago a radio disk jockey who persisted in heckling the du Pont interests was referred to locally as Radio Free Wilmington. Aside from these gibes and a few minor incidents, however, the du Ponts have succeeded fairly well in becoming a benevolent presence rather than an overpowering force.

"They lean over backward not to dominate," says one Wilmingtonian.

"They don't want to be accused of pushing people around," says a newspaperman anonymously.

"They want to play down the du Pont factor," says a leading Wilmington urban planner. "And after all, they're not a negative factor. They're a plus. They're here, and that's good and we ought to capitalize on it."

Wilmington has managed to capitalize very handsomely upon the du Pont presence, right up to the point of recruiting company officials as a guiding force behind the city's current program of urban rebuilding. For despite all the benefits exuding from the world's biggest chemical firm, Wilmington has suffered from the urban decay that has overtaken virtually all other Eastern cities. However, the situation in this small (the city proper has only 85,000 people) and very prosperous town is far less severe than elsewhere. "Wilmington has never had a real crisis like Pittsburgh or Philadelphia or Baltimore, although we may be getting to one," says a state legislator. "So far the success of the Du Pont Company, and the du Pont family, has helped keep the state out of the sludge."

In the company's early history there were very few indications that Du Pont would ever have either the inclination or the ability to keep anyone out of the sludge. "Up until about 1920," says a Du Pont executive, "we were a company that concentrated on a fundamental tool for the economy— blasting powder, for mining iron ore, building railroads, taking out coal." In this respect, and in its means of operating, Du Pont then was remarkably similar to the heavy industries, some of them Du Pont customers, that held sway in the neighboring states. Like the other big companies, its emphasis was on a single product and its corporate impulses were monopolistic. By the first decade of the 20th Century, Du Pont had wiped out or absorbed more than 60 former competitors. Earlier, through a Du Pont-dominated pool called the Gunpowder Trade Association, the Wilmington firm and several friendly competitors had divided the United States into seven sales districts within which were distributed some 90 per cent of the nation's blasting powder and 95 per cent of its powder for rifle ammunition.

"We make our own powder, and we make our own price at which it shall be sold," Henry du Pont had written in 1889 as he energetically helped to knit together the monopoly. "We do our own dictating . . . If we choose, we can as quickly as wires can carry the orders change the price at each and every point in the world where Du Pont powder is for sale. . . . " Du Pont was also moving into cartels with foreign firms. Eventually the company would make agreements with Germany's I. G. Farben company, Britain's Imperial Chemical Industries and Japan's chemical combine Mitsui whereby the globe would be cut into spheres of influence, complete with fixed prices and gentlemen's agreements against trespassing on the other fellow's business. Within these territorial lines the rules against underselling became just as rigid as those that Judge Gary of U.S. Steel once imposed on the U.S. steel industry.

In these monopolistic times Du Pont had taken other pages from what might be called the Middle Atlantic book of industrial ethics. For along with economic dominance in its narrow field of business, the du Pont family exercised a degree of political dominance over the state from which that business was controlled. In 1916 one U.S. Senator from Delaware was the son of Henry du Pont. The other was a du Pont in-law, Willard Saulsbury, who, though a relative, was politically opposed to Henry du Pont. Some years later the voters of Delaware were visited with the marvelous spectacle of Saulsbury backing the campaign of another du Pont in-law against a natural-born du Pont on a paradoxical kind of freedom ticket. "Shall Delaware belong to the du Ponts?" they asked the electorate. "Are we a free people or shall we permit ourselves to be crushed under the weight of du Pont wealth?" Whereupon the voters declared for freedom, electing the Saulsbury-backed in-law.

"Now it also happened," explains a present-day Du Pont executive, "that the industrial tool we were manufacturing at that time was instrumental for fighting wars." Historically, the company had always been ready to take advantage of this particular happenstance. As early as the War of 1812, when Eleuthère Irénée du Pont received orders from President James Madison's Administration for 400 tons of black powder, the Du Pont Company had been the leading U.S. manufacturer of military explosives. In the Mexican War of 1848 the company fulfilled government contracts for a million pounds of gunpowder, at the same time turning down a circuitous order for 200,000 more pounds from the Mexican government—and all the while piously deploring the whole wicked business of war. "However shameful [the U.S.] invasion of Mexican territory," wrote one family member at the time, "we cannot make powder to be used against our own country." But there was no apparent objection to making powder for use against selected parts of the country, as the Confederacy discovered to its sorrow during the Civil War, since Du Pont supplied more than three and a half million pounds of powder for the Union armies. It was not until World War I, however, that the company realized its full potential as a munitions maker: from 1914 to 1918 forty per cent of the explosives for all Allied artillery came from Du Pont. The rewards from the munitions business were enormous. During World War I, Du Pont's average annual profit was $59 million, compared to a modest five million dollars in prewar years. In this same four-year period the company expanded from 5,000 employees to more than 85,000.

Despite this booming prosperity, Pierre S. du Pont and others realized that when the war's end shut off the munitions business, there might suddenly be no work for thousands of people. And for the company, there would be the prospect of falling back—as steel, coal and rails were already doing—into the traditional industrial rut of doing the same old thing the same old way. Therefore the du Ponts made the fundamental decision to change the company's ways, to sharply reduce their commitment to the explosives business and to embark on the new course of creating better things for better living through chemistry.

"We knew a lot about chemistry—nitric acid and nitrocellulose—from the explosives business," explained a Du Pont man, in retrospect.

"We took a position that we would look into and make anything where we could make a contribution and a profit," said another. "A comparable thing the steel industry might have done was to begin thinking of itself broadly as a structural materials company. This, conceivably, could have led it into being a leader in plastics. And if the Interstate Commerce Commission had allowed the Pennsylvania Railroad to develop not just as a railroad but as a transportation company, *think* what they could have done in the automobile business, or in airplanes." But steel and rails kept on concentrating on their old single-minded ways of doing

A cornucopia of chemicals

This chart shows three families of chemical products made by Delaware's mammoth Du Pont Company. Each family illustrates the genealogy of technologically interrelated, and much used, compounds. The blue-colored family tree, for instance, traces the evolution of products as diverse as Corfam and Lucite from the company's original product, gunpowder. Similarly, advances in chemical technology made by Du Pont experts while producing rayon and cellophane enabled the company to exploit the discovery of nylon. Nylon in turn helped give birth to other products such as Dacron and Orlon (green family tree). Product names are given in capital letters when they are Du Pont trademarks; the dates indicate either when that compound was discovered by the company or when Du Pont acquired manufacturing rights to it.

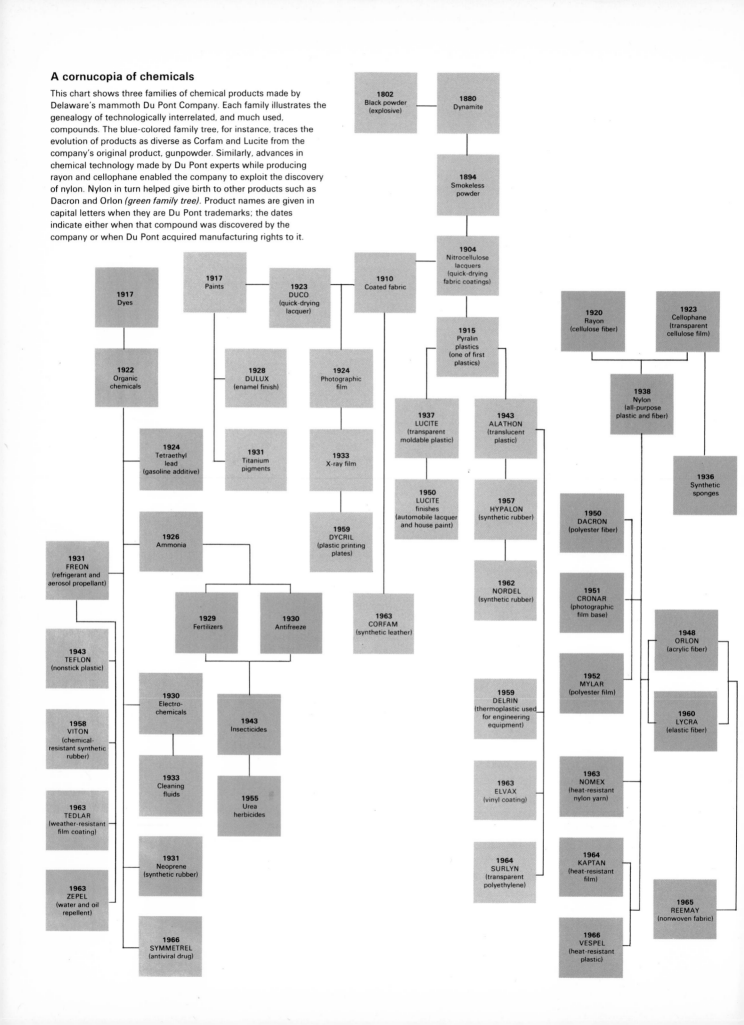

things, and sliding—along with their dependent communities—into the sludge.

These were other days, however, and in the context of the times the decision to diversify was by no means easy to make, even for Du Pont. Not only was there the natural tendency to stay in a familiar and basically simple business, but also there were some indications that better things—for the company, at least—might not be found through chemistry. In an earlier, tentative effort to discover what kinds of new product might be derived from its knowledge of chemistry, Du Pont had set up two small experimental laboratories and had established a Development Department to search out promising new fields of business. But all that had come out of these new facilities, so far, was a driblet of paint and varnish business, the manufacture of an artificial leather that Du Pont has since abandoned and a start into commercial dyes that for a time would prove woefully unprofitable. Nevertheless, Pierre S. du Pont, along with his brothers Irénée and Lammot and a brilliant organizer named Walter Carpenter, turned the company around and set off in the fresh direction. The payoff was almost immediate and, as it has turned out, continuous. In the first instance, however, the payoff was partly accidental.

During the summer of 1920, a group of Du Pont's chemists, dabbling in some experiments with motion-picture film emulsion, were mixing up a new nitrocellulose composition in a barrel. In the midst of the experiment there was an electrical power failure in the lab and the barrel was left outside where it sat in the hot sun for three days. When they went to retrieve the barrel, they found that the sun had reduced the cellulose jelly to a soupy liquid. This liquid became the base on which Du Pont subsequently developed its immense volume of commercial lacquers for automobile body paint.

Aside from rare, cheerful accidents such as this, Du Pont's innovations have been the result of shrewd marketing insight or meticulous laboratory work, or both. The same year as the paint discovery, the company picked up a license to produce a French-invented silk substitute called rayon. The ability of Du Pont and others to produce and market the product was so successful that one observer called this early major venture into artificial fibers "the greatest textile revolution since the invention of the cotton gin." Three years later Du Pont took hold of a transparent packaging film called cellophane, gave it a moistureproof coating in 1927, and was soon selling one of the world's most widely used wrappers for food, cigarettes and other consumer items. Shortly thereafter the company maneuvered itself into a proprietary position in the sale of the gasoline additive, tetraethyl lead, and discovered neoprene, the first commercially successful U.S. synthetic rubber. Then, in the early 1930s, a team of Du Pont researchers headed by Dr. Wallace Carothers turned up the company's most important discovery of all.

Seeking radically new synthetic fibers, they had begun to explore the structure of polymers—molecules made up in the form of very long chains, as are the molecules of natural fibers like silk and cotton. During the research-and-development program, one of the chemists, handling a molten solution of one particularly promising polymer, noticed that when he stuck a rod into the solution and pulled it out, a thin, fibrous strand would adhere to the rod. To create more such strands, he put some molten polymer into a hypodermic needle and then squeezed it. With further development, the strand seemed to have just the properties of strength and uniformity that an excellent textile fiber should have. Out of these experiments came a tough gossamer thread that, under the name of nylon, again revolutionized the fabric industry.

Today Du Pont's main line of research is conducted within a wire-fenced 100-acre Experimental Station set on a bluff above Brandywine Creek, overlooking the original family powder mill. A neat, symmetrical complex of brick buildings and clipped lawns, the station looks for all the world like a small college—and boasts as many Ph.D.s as many good-sized universities. On this corporate campus, endowed with an annual research budget of more than $40 million, Du Pont's crack researchers spend their days delving into anything from finding better materials for making milk containers to synthesizing new drugs that might improve a man's memory capability. There is even some speculation on finding ways to slow down in aging people the physiological deterioration of some parts of the brain. "I'm sure," says one scientist, "that this sort of thing can be an influence in pharmacology. But remember, we're not talking about weeks and months with such things. We're talking about years and years."

In its research Du Pont always talks in terms of years and years. A chemist at the Experimental Station may stay on a single exploration for as long as three years, then drop it and come back many months later with a refreshed approach. In the end he may strike another rich chemical lode, such as Mylar, the new packaging film, which took 16 years to perfect. He may find a better version of the drug Symmetrel, whose formula was the result of screening 20,000 compounds. He may unlock the secret to another Corfam, a product that required 30 years of searching and $30 million before it reached the market. Or he may find just one more substance whose scientific properties are fascinating but whose market value is zero. In any one year Du Pont scientists may come up with some 950 such worthless compounds, as against perhaps 50 that see the light of commercial profitability.

For the most part, the company is undismayed by the high incidence of failures, since a number of their scientists are specifically urged to forget about short-range profits and concentrate on exploring the far reaches of their special fields. "We don't have the foggiest notion of what [this project] means for a product," said a researcher cheerfully of one far-out experiment, "but we're looking into it." "You don't even know whether you're being original," explains a supervisor at the station, "unless you know where the frontiers are."

Other Du Pont scientists, with their feet pressed firmly upon the ground, feel they are on the way to bringing in such practical, immensely profitable products as an auto lubricant that never needs to be changed, clothing that lasts a lifetime, preservatives that keep food fresh for years without freezing and paint that does not chip or wear.

In recent years, while not attempting to discourage basic research, Du Pont's top management has been pressing for a faster, higher yield from its huge investment in research and development, both at the Experimental Station and in the field laboratories of its worldwide network of plants. For in the cold realities of the marketplace, Du Pont has found that after decades of being comfortably ahead of any major American competitors in chemistry, suddenly it is being surrounded by bright, vigorous rivals whose research techniques are every bit as good as Du Pont's. "We are not used to having research labs compete against us," said one discommoded Wilmingtonian in 1963, when the competition was beginning to make a serious dent in Du Pont's sales growth.

"It is no longer easy for a chemical firm to get out in front with a fundamental discovery," said another, thinking perhaps of the fact that Du Pont remained in front with its nylon discovery for almost 15 years before anyone else was able to cut into the market with a competing synthetic. Today Du Pont estimates its lead time on a product like Corfam is no more than one to three years. Most of this pressure for products and profits has come from predictable sources, such as Celanese, Union Carbide, Allied Chemical and other chemical companies that have learned how to develop their own better things, and also how to quickly imitate or improve on someone else's brand-new compound without infringing patents. However, there has been an increasing challenge from a growing string of the most unlikely rivals.

In neighboring Pennsylvania, for example, the Sun Oil Corporation, traditionally a conservative crude-oil company, has recently doubled its financial commitment to research and development with an eye to extracting new chemical compounds from petroleum. Already a group of Sun's chemists are working on new agricultural pesticides and fungicides. Other scientists have evolved a naphthalene compound that Sun feels may be an important textile fiber. "We believe the material probably will make . . . garments [that] could be washed at boiling water temperatures without removing a natural press," says a Sun spokesman. Another Sun project involves a potential antiviral compound—the very kind of thing that Du Pont developed in its first invasion of the rich pharmaceutical market.

In Pittsburgh Gulf Oil is investing some $30 million a year in research and has acquired the habit of putting up a chemical plant wherever possible when it installs a new refinery. Besides the chemical pesticides, fertilizers and tires it already has on the market, Gulf has moved into plastics and is researching a process for extracting a protein food supplement from crude oil.

Finally, it appears, the urge to do Better Things has begun to overtake even those once unbending institutions, the coal and steel industries, which are taking tentative steps down the path marked out by Du Pont in breaking away from the old habit of concentration on the same old product. U.S. Steel in 1966 announced the formation of a new division called U.S. Chemicals, from which a line of fertilizers has begun to emerge. And in 1967 the coal industry began a research program whose aim is to create liquid fuels from coal. Neither coal nor steel has yet made any startling progress in its new direction (although each had acquired some prior chemical experience, primarily in processing the by-products of coke ovens). However, they are at least launched on embryo diversification programs that could lead, in time, to benefits both for the industries and for the communities in which they are based. The time may come when the still-dismal ravine towns of Pennsylvania, like the hill district of northern Delaware, will reap a rich harvest of Better Living through the ways of Chemistry.

Marinas jammed with pleasure craft line the banks of the Sassafras River, one of Chesapeake Bay's many tributaries. Increasingly, powerboats, like those in the foreground, are overwhelming the bay's graceful sailing craft.

The special magic of a great bay

Few places in America are as peaceful, handsome and historic as the Middle Atlantic States' great inland sea, the Chesapeake Bay. Breaching the Virginia coast and splitting Maryland in two, the bay has so many estuaries, creeks and inlets that its shoreline, if straightened out, would reach across the continent and back.

The great bay is part of the mind and soul of every Marylander. Thousands of Baltimoreans have "a little place on the Eastern Shore," and for them, almost as much as for the Chesapeake's year-round residents, the bay, with its sailing, fishing and duck shooting, is a way of life. But the bay is also part of every American's heritage. It was one of the first areas to be explored, has been the scene of crucial battles, has served as a highway for clipper ships and remains a vital avenue for seagoing commerce.

John Smith's first exploration

Every American school child is taught the story of Captain John Smith *(left)* and Pocahontas. But in the bay area Smith is better known for his charting of the Chesapeake. After spending the winter of 1607-1608 helping establish England's first permanent settlement in the New World—at Jamestown, near the mouth of Chesapeake Bay—Smith turned his attention to the great body of water that stretched away to the north. The old lithograph at the right shows him with his small crew after they had set out from Jamestown in "an open barge" early in the summer of 1608. Theirs was not the first penetration of the bay by white men. During the preceding century, both John Cabot and Giovanni Verrazano, among others, explored the area, and in 1588 Captain Vincente Gonzales, a Spaniard, is known to have sailed to the very head of the bay, but none left a useful record of his exploits. Smith's exploration, however, resulted in a vivid written account of his adventures as well as a map, astonishing in its detail, that was published in Oxford, England, in 1612. This map became a basis for further English exploration and led, in 1634, to Lord Baltimore's being granted the right to colonize the territory that is now Maryland.

An early landmark named for Smith

The Smith Island fisherman coming ashore at dusk with a crab pot on his shoulder walks the path of his father and his father before him. Change comes slowly to this out-of-the-way Chesapeake island, which boasts the distinction of being the first landmark in Maryland mentioned by Captain John Smith in his chronicle of exploration and to which, taking first things first, he gave his name. Most of Smith Island's 800 inhabitants trace their ancestry back to the English (especially Cornish) and Dutch families that settled there in the 1640s. Though they do not scorn such innovations as electricity or engines for their boats, they hew to old-fashioned ways in an old-fashioned trade. They remain a society of fishermen—or to use their own word, watermen—people who live by their knowledge of the tides, currents, winds and clouds. On the mainland the breed is fading out. Perhaps better than any other inhabitants of the bay area, Smith Islanders in their remoteness know the Chesapeake as their illustrious namesake described it: "Heaven and earth never agreed better to frame a place for mans habitation," wrote Smith in 1608. "Here are mountaines, hils, plaines, valleyes, rivers and brookes all running most pleasantly into a faire Bay compassed but for the mouth with fruitful and delightsome land."

Work boats for a busy waterway

When the first bay colonists arrived, they quickly put their great waterway to use. Modifying the Indian log canoe, adding mast, sail and other improvements, they produced a vessel destined to foster a long line of hard-working heirs. Four of the most famous are pictured with the canoe at the right. Their low, graceful lines, forthright bows, raked masts and overall aura of speed make the family resemblance unmistakable. For two and a half centuries the log canoe served as the work horse of the bay. But soon after the Civil War the demand for a larger, inexpensive vessel for dredging oysters resulted in a new type, the bugeye, essentially an oversized canoe with planking. The seagoing Baltimore clipper of the 19th Century became the heavyweight of the family. A smaller version, the pungy, was used for work inside the bay. Today, the lone survivor of the clan is the skipjack, still used to dredge oysters, since conservation measures forbid the use of powerboats for that purpose.

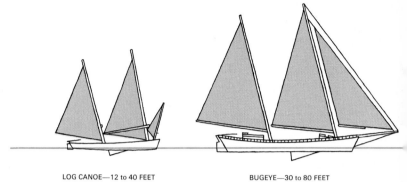

LOG CANOE—12 to 40 FEET   BUGEYE—30 to 80 FEET

The pleasures of sail

Except for the skipjacks of the oyster-dredging fleet, sailing craft are no longer used for practical purposes on Chesapeake Bay. But the three Luders yawls at the right, sweeping downwind past Greenbury Point Light at the mouth of the Severn River, remind us that man is not an entirely practical animal. So long as he accepts the challenge of a race or finds serenity and escape in the clean power of wind on water, the bay will continue to be dotted with sail. It has been estimated that in 1910, when cargo was still being moved around the bay by sail, some 3,000 wind-driven boats graced the Chesapeake. Today there are several times that number, but with the exception of the dwindling skipjacks and one or two museum pieces, all are pleasure craft owned by the bay's eager, even passionate, weekend sailors. The bay is ideally suited for such racing and cruising. There are literally hundreds of rivers, creeks and inlets that make snug harbors for fleets of small boats and an endless variety of cruising destinations for larger craft. The bay offers a long season, from May through October, and, unlike the New England coast, has few dangerous rocks, little fog and a tide that ranges no more than two feet.

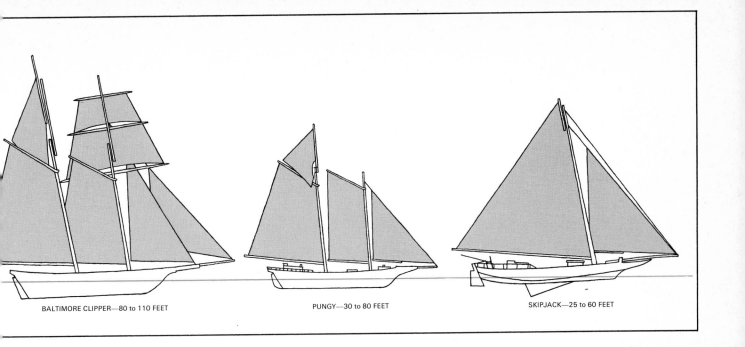

BALTIMORE CLIPPER—80 to 110 FEET

PUNGY—30 to 80 FEET

SKIPJACK—25 to 60 FEET

Baltimore's great fleet

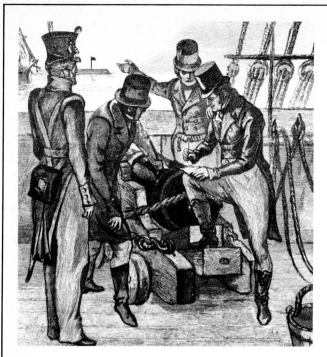

The busy port of Baltimore as it appeared in 1850, with its famous signal tower *(right)*, might have looked quite different had it not, 36 years before, passed its first severe test with flying colors. In September 1814, during the War of 1812, some 50 British warships threatened the city. Only weeks before, this same force had burned much of Washington, D.C. Now, if Baltimore, home of the swift Baltimore clippers that were so successfully harrying the mighty British Navy, suffered the same fate, the fledgling United States, its armies already in rout, would be left helpless. On September 12 the British warships began a bombardment of Fort McHenry, which guarded the mouth of the harbor's Northwest Branch. All through the day and well into the night, rockets were hurled at the fort. An anxious observer of the battle, on board a ship in the harbor, was the young Maryland lawyer Francis Scott Key. By the dawn's first light he was able to see the Stars and Stripes still flying over the fort *(left)*. The attack had failed. Inspired, Key penned on the back of an envelope the words for what later became the U.S. national anthem.

Growth of a mammoth port

In 1729, the year Baltimore was incorporated, Philadelphia was already 48 years old and New York had celebrated its centennial. Baltimore's rival on Chesapeake Bay was 80-year-old Annapolis, but the younger port made up for its late start by its better location. The main north-south road of the day passed through it, as did the only practical road from the Eastern Seaboard to the Ohio Valley. Moreover, Baltimore was 30 miles closer than Annapolis to the mouth of the Susquehanna River, down which Pennsylvania farmers shipped their grain by barge. Once established, Baltimore grew rapidly. By 1790 it was the third-largest city in the new republic, and it retained that position until 1850. Today it ranks seventh in the country. The extent of the modern port, which grew from a nucleus of piers located at the head of the Northwest Branch, can be seen at the right. In the early days, individual merchants owned and operated both ships and piers. But beginning with the founding of the Baltimore and Ohio Railroad, which brought its tracks in at Locust Point during the 1850s, the port became largely railroad-owned and -operated.

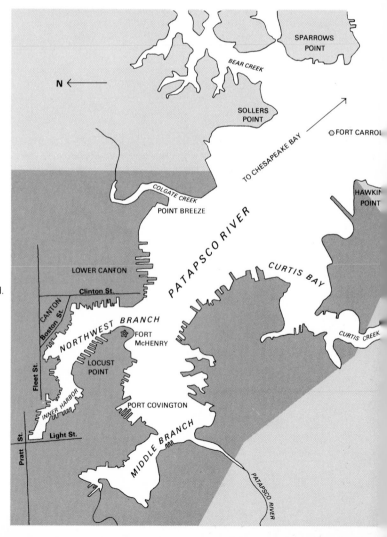

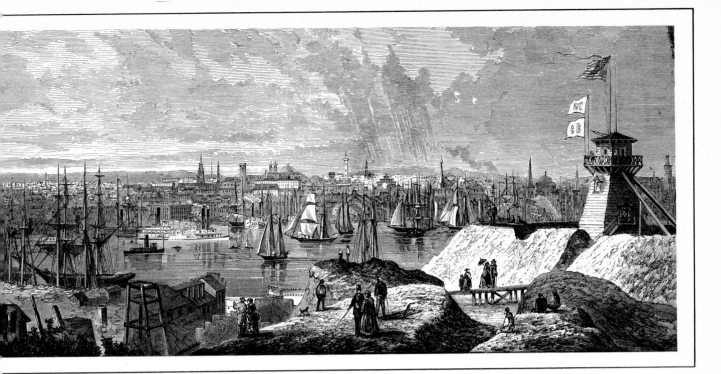

A century and a quarter have wrought enormous changes on the harbor pictured in the old lithograph above. Sailing ships that might take as long as six weeks to cross the Atlantic have been replaced by huge modern freighters that make the trip in a matter of days. The wooden tower on Federal Hill, from which spotters had a view of the outer harbor and could appraise shipowners of the arrival of their vessels by flying signal flags, has long since been supplanted by radio, and the hill is now surrounded by downtown Baltimore. The aerial photograph of the Northwest Branch at the left shows how completely the works of man have encrusted every available inch of the surrounding coastline, while the waterway itself is half choked with long finger piers. Today the port's 45 miles of waterfront handle more than 100 ships each week from all over the world. A list of the goods delivered to the docks includes such varied items as teakwood, iron ore, manganese, coffee, bananas, tea, spices, rubber, firecrackers, goat hair, chinaware and olives. And for export to foreign lands the ships carry away grain from the Midwest, coal mined in the Appalachian Mountains and canned tomatoes from Maryland's abundant truck gardens, to name but a few.

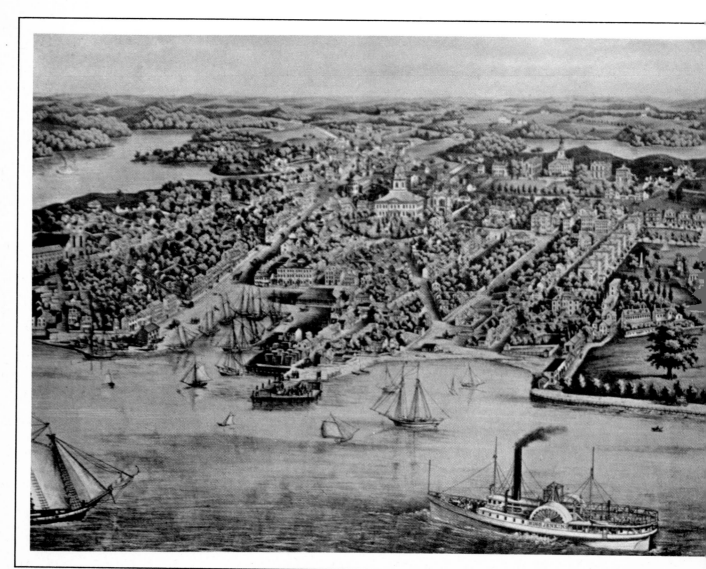

A cradle for midshipmen at Annapolis

In the days before steam, midshipmen were trained at sea. The handling of sailing ships and men was best taught by doing, not by theorizing. Such salty lore became outmoded as naval science grew more complex. In 1845 the Secretary of the Navy directed a board of officers to consider the founding of a naval academy ashore. There was no debate over what body of water the school should grace; clearly it belonged on the Chesapeake. But should it be in Virginia, in Maryland or perhaps on an island? Annapolis was chosen because training ships could be moored there and the Navy could acquire the site of an old Army fort. The first class entered in October 1845, and except for the disruption of the Civil War, the academy grew steadily. In 1881 President Garfield reviewed the graduating class *(left)*. At the right, midshipmen "learn the ropes" aboard the academy training ship *Constitution*.

A preserve of colonial architecture

Unlike Baltimore, Annapolis has not always kept pace with the times. Instead, it ages gracefully on a small peninsula at the mouth of the Severn River on the Chesapeake's western shore. Founded in 1649, it became the capital of Maryland 45 years later, reaching lusty maturity as an 18th Century shipping center for tobacco. It was still an active port a century later, as seen in the 1858 lithograph at left. Then commerce, riding on steam-powered trains and vessels, passed it by, and with only its two distinguished boarders, the Naval Academy and the state government, to sustain it, the city settled back into its colonial lineaments to watch the world go by. Therein lies its charm today. A view up Cornhill Street *(above)* shows a 17th Century brick sidewalk bordering a graceful colonial façade. The State House, begun in 1772, the oldest in continuous use in the U.S., is seen at the top right of the photograph and dominates the center of the lithograph. Also prominent in the lithograph are the early buildings of the Naval Academy, standing in rows on the open ground at the right.

Working the "protein factory"

The professional Chesapeake Bay oystermen wielding their long-handled tongs at right are practicing a craft little changed in 200 years. The waters they work, described by the Baltimore writer H. L. Mencken as an "immense protein factory" out of which his native city "ate divinely," have long been known for their superb oysters and for their excellent crabs as well. The bay water, rich in organic sediment, provides the mollusks with near-perfect conditions. Early settlers reported oysters with shells measuring more than a foot across and bodies "the size of a horse's hoof." Most of the early colonists scorned oysters as food, but by the middle of the 19th Century, Americans had acquired a taste for them that amounted to a passion. Large fleets put out from Baltimore and other bay ports, often with crews shanghaied along Baltimore's tough waterfront, to work the dredges ("drudges" they called them) in the winter months when oysters are at their prime. During the season of 1884-1885, fifteen million bushels were taken out of the Chesapeake. This record has not been equaled since, for although the supply seemed inexhaustible, it was not. Early attempts at conservation were fought bitterly by the oystermen, but eventually nature imposed its own inexorable rule. With oysters harder and harder to find, the industry survives today only by adhering to strict conservation laws. They include the mandatory use of sailboats in those areas where oystermen are permitted to employ dredges to harvest their oysters, the use of the old-fashioned and less efficient tongs in other areas, and the putting off-limits of still other parts of the bay.

The ancient art of the watermen

When early white settlers arrived in the Chesapeake Bay, they found the resident aborigines, members of the Chesepiuc tribe of Indians, already adept at gathering food from its waters. As early as 1585, when the Ralph Lane expedition sailed up the bay, one of its members, an English artist named John White, did a drawing of Indian activities from which the engraving at left was later made. The fire in the log canoe, around which two Indian crewmen are warming themselves, is burning on a bed of wet sand. In the upper part of the picture other Indians are seen standing in the shallow water spearing fish and trapping them in weirs made of interwoven branches. Recognizable in the foreground are a blue crab, a horseshoe crab, a turtle, a sturgeon, a sting ray and an eel.

OYSTER HAND TONGS

As a conservation measure in many parts of the bay, the only tools permitted oystermen are the relatively inefficient hand tongs *(left)*. Essentially, these are a pair of long-handled rakes, hinged like pliers and fitted with shallow baskets above the tines. Oystermen rake together a quarter of a bushel of oysters at a time, then pull them aboard. Marketable oysters must measure at least three inches.

The crab pot *(right)* is another common tool used by tidewater fishermen. Made out of poultry wire, it is baited with fresh fish. The pot, attached to a buoy, is then set in depths of water ranging from 15 to 30 feet. To get at the bait, crabs enter the pot through funnels and then are unable to find their way out again. The minimum legal size for hard-shelled crabs is five inches measured across the back of the shell.

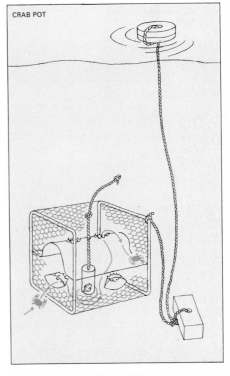

CRAB POT

Hunting the Chesapeake's wildfowl

The Chesapeake not only breeds superb crabs and oysters; it is also a great wintering ground for millions of ducks and geese—and therefore a paradise for hunters. Flying east and south from summer breeding areas in the north-central states and Canada, the birds seek the ample food and relatively temperate climes of the bay. The duck most esteemed by the hunters, both for its succulence and for its challenge as a target, is the canvasback. This large, wary, fast-flying bird once smoked up the November skies over the Susquehanna Flats, but now it is counted only in the thousands. Mindless killing in earlier decades is partially responsible. The real evil, however, is pollution, which is killing the wild celery on which this duck once fed so handsomely. But there are still plenty of birds of this and other varieties for the hunters to pursue, including the great Canada goose, which may run as heavy as 13 pounds. And the hunters do pursue them from duckblind or rowboat, despite the fogs and chill of winter, with unflagging zeal.

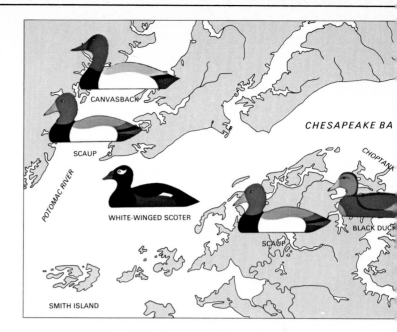

Hidden hunters lying in wait

A bone-chilling mist shrouds two hunters crouching at dawn in a blind on the Choptank River, only their gun barrels visible above the reeds at the far left of the photograph at right. These men, waiting for the decoys they have placed in the water to attract a chance flight of ducks, are indulging in a sport now hemmed in by many rules. They may not, for instance, shoot sitting ducks from a powerboat, nor may they shoot earlier than one half hour before sunrise; they may not kill more than one canvasback a day, or two black ducks; their guns may not be larger than 10 gauge; they may not sell what they shoot; and those are just a few of the numerous things they may not do.

In earlier times, however, when it was both legal and economically feasible for a man to shoot waterfowl commercially, gunning was often undertaken on a quite different scale. On a cold, still November night a professional hunter might mount a colossal shotgun, weighing about 100 pounds and having a two-inch bore, in the stern of a punt. Then, locating a flock of ducks resting on the water, he would surreptitiously paddle close and ready his gun. Suddenly he would ripple the water, and the ducks, reacting instinctively, would sink, leaving only their heads protruding. Firing his immense gun, the hunter might kill 50 birds, each one shot neatly through the head.

Such methods, of course, would in time have annihilated the Chesapeake's winter bird population. Happily, such wholesale slaughter has long been banned, and with the stringent conservation laws strictly enforced, wintering wildfowl continue to come to Chesapeake Bay. They arrive each season in numbers to quicken the heart of the amateur marksman, and of all those who are thrilled by the sight of a handsome flock of ducks or geese coursing proudly through the scudding clouds of a winter's afternoon.

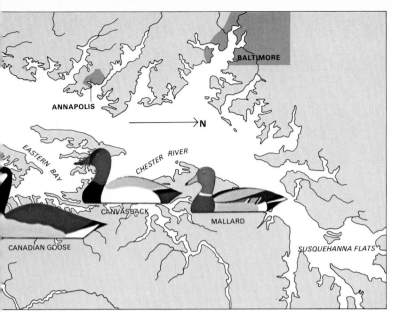

The six species of wildfowl that commonly winter on the Chesapeake in greatest numbers are shown on the map *(left)*, which takes in the upper two thirds of the bay, with the north at the right. Most of the migrant birds congregate on the Eastern Shore *(bottom).* Because that area is more rural than the western shore, they can feed better there on grains and seafoods and are less bothered by people and the pollution towns and cities create. The various species are pictured in the general areas in which they tend to congregate, although flocks of any of them may turn up elsewhere on the bay. Thus mallard ducks, which often gravitate toward the head of the bay for the fresh water and grains found in the marshes prevalent there, are shown near the right-hand edge of the map. Similarly, the white-winged scoters, deep-diving birds that feed on fish, are pictured where they are most at home, out in the bay's main channel.

7

Broadening
the Revolution

From his office high above the reconstructed center of Philadelphia, Edmund Bacon, one of the most imaginative, effective leaders of the Middle Atlantic renaissance, thought back upon his city's two-billion-dollar, 15-year rebuilding program and then addressed himself to the challenge of the future. "The concept has come through loud and clear," he said, "that we're dealing not so much with dream cities as with people and human problems." In Pittsburgh Ed Magee, retiring Director of the Allegheny Conference, was having many of the same thoughts—plus a few special qualms of his own: "The old crusading spirit has waned," he said, "and we're not sure how we can revive it. . . . The Conference will continue to be a meaningful force only so long as it focuses its attention on overriding problems. And," he added significantly, "the problems today may be different from those we originally attacked."

Lately these same realizations have begun to come through all across the three Middle Atlantic States. For despite the uplifting effect of the urban

Earphone-equipped youngsters from Oakleaf School in Whitehall, Pennsylvania, perform their own scientific experiments under the guidance of taped instructions. They are part of a University of Pittsburgh program to develop new educational techniques.

rebuilding programs and some substantial benefits from diversified light industry, dark blotches of poverty, obsolescence and unalleviated ignorance still stain the region's society. Just beyond the periphery of Philadelphia's revitalized central business district stand 80,000 units of urban housing that are euphemistically categorized as "substandard" (lay translation: slums). More than 375,000 families—80 per cent of them nonwhite—inhabit the slums of Philadelphia, and half of the young adults in these families drop out of school between the 10th and 12th grades and settle into a widening pool of unemployables.

Similar problems afflict Pittsburgh. There some 40 per cent of the families have incomes below $4,000 per year; Negro children in the nominally integrated ghetto schools show reading abilities of an average grade level of 5.6 in the sixth grade, while the norm in the favored white neighborhoods is 10.3; and some of the city's most critical natural resources have been handled little better than its human ones: although some progress has been made, both the Allegheny and Monongahela are still fouled with industrial wastes, their potential for recreation largely wasted. Baltimore is nursing a similar mixture of lingering physical and sociological frustrations. Its waterfront remains a drab, dangerous tangle of planless 19th Century industrial transport, while the city's inspired start toward peaceful integration has been slowed by the backlash defeat of successive open-housing laws.

Throughout the region, as the enthusiasm for the first wave of the renaissance passed by, it became all too evident that such deep stains as these cannot be permanently wiped out through any single expedient, whether it be knocking down old buildings or putting in the sort of modern research complexes that in the past 10 years have brought some 25,000 scientific-technical jobs to the Pittsburgh area alone. Said a Pittsburgh planner: "We need to bring together urban rebuilding, transportation, housing, recreation, open space and education into one program of total community development." He might well have added the need for a modern, coherent system of government to replace the bickering hodgepodge of outmoded county, municipal and state administrative units that have been partly responsible for holding back the continued progress of renewal.

Few taller orders of a purely peaceful nature have ever been laid before a society. But if the orders are not in large measure fulfilled, there is a real danger that the early gains of the renaissance may be thrown away. And no one is more aware of that unhappy possibility than the men who were instrumental in making those gains. "With all due respect to what we're doing here," admitted a Maryland redevelopment expert, whose first concentration has been on the purely physical aspects of renewal, "we're not really getting to the heart of the problem: human renewal."

This concept of the primacy of human problems —and of the breadth and depth of a truly effective program of renewal—applies not only to the major cities, where the region's remaining troubles are most intensively focused, but also to the outlying countryside in which the problems, if perhaps less complex, are no less severe. It applies, for example, in the northern tier of Pennsylvania's counties (an area held back for decades by the lack of a major highway to stimulate economic growth), where not long ago half the students never got past the eighth grade. It has come through on Maryland's Eastern Shore, where the future for both black and white residents is so drab that only three of every 20 high-school graduates who leave the area for college ever return to the Eastern Shore to settle, and where limited training, together with limited capital, has kept business failures well above the national average.

"The people here [on the Eastern Shore] may want to bring in nice research and development plants," said one economic analyst, "but they have no good schools to offer the children of the scientists who would run the plants, and nothing for the wives to do. And in terms of trained personnel, there is no university for the research and development plants to feed off."

The residual human problems have become devastatingly clear among the industrial towns of the Allegheny ravines. In them, despite some earnest but far too narrow attempts to push ahead on the purely physical aspects of renewal, there continue to be few reliable ways for many of the people to make a living. Even after the bitter warning of four decades of intermittent depression, too many of these towns have clung to steel for their livelihood. "These mill towns were created in another day for another purpose," said an area businessman, "and the 20th Century is leaving them behind."

Clairton, 20 miles up the Monongahela Valley from Pittsburgh, has been relatively fortunate; U.S. Steel shut down some of its steelworks there, throwing 2,000 men out of work, but also brought in a new chemical operation that may offer fresh job opportunities. Worse off is Donora, farther up the river, where some 4,000 jobs evaporated over a period of time as the aging wire mills gradually went out of business, leaving a trucking firm with 85 workers the largest employer in town. As one possible solution, Donora has attempted—perhaps too late—to persuade light industry to locate in the town. But like Maryland's Eastern Shore, Donora lacks the educational facilities and the amenities that the leaders of light industry demand. "We have learned," said John K. Tabor, the Pennsylvania Secretary of Internal Affairs, in a latter-day reversal of Andrew Carnegie's old dictum, "that if you put all your eggs in one basket it can be a very serious situation."

Donora's Mayor, Albert P. Delsandro, in the best steel-country tradition, was even more blunt about the crisis facing the old industrial towns: "Frankly we're in one hell of a situation here," he said, as the word came in that the last of the big wire mills was to close. In nearby McKeesport, second-largest urban center in southwestern Pennsylvania, the situation was only a little better. Despite an ambitious $37 million downtown rebuilding project launched several years ago, retail business in McKeesport fell 35 per cent between 1952 and 1966, with few present signs of recovery. And in Clairton, where 13 downtown acres were bulldozed in a clearance project started in 1959, nothing had been done eight years later to rebuild the enclave of flattened rubble. This was due largely to the town's failure to win federal assistance, which comes now most readily not to quickie clearances but to programs that show an awareness of the full spectrum of renewal. "Federal projects will never rebuild towns that just aren't capable of helping themselves," says a former Chamber of Commerce head in one coal town, adding ominously, "Some towns should be allowed to become ghost towns—they did in the West."

It would be sad and even shocking if any of these communities, drab islands of obsolescence in the midst of the region's generally renewed prosperity, should have to accept such a harsh sentence. But a few towns in the Middle Atlantic States may be on their way to doing just that, their old economies so badly eroded that they may never be restored. Other communities, however, once every bit as sick as Donora and McKeesport, have managed to climb out of the abyss and become local leaders within the renaissance. Even in the late 1950s no one but a handful of passionate local boosters believed that the old coal camps of Scranton, Hazleton and Wilkes-Barre were headed anywhere but the scrap heap. Yet thanks to vigorous local initiative, coupled with an ever-widening view of the nature of renewal, they raised enough community money, later matched by state and federal funds, to build a diversified industrial complex that has meant some 60,000 new jobs. So successful have the anthracite towns become in rebuilding their economies that in 1967 the federal government canceled some loan assistance programs there on grounds that northeast Pennsylvania had become too prosperous to need "depressed area" aid any more.

The first new industries to come into these coal towns brought jobs that tended to be relatively low-paying—"manual stuff," snorted one Scranton politician. "But now," added a local booster in Wilkes-Barre, where renewal is moving into a second generation, "those companies wouldn't have a *prayer* of getting in here. We're going after the higher-pay, higher-skill stuff, the white-collar industries. . . . And now the sharp people from these businesses are coming in to help in community affairs."

"Industry and employment used to be our number-one problems," summed up a renewalist in Hazleton. "But that's about solved now. We feel we've gone about this right, to begin with, by getting the economic base up to where it ought to be."

With that much of the crisis behind, the key men in the outlying towns were taking a hard look at the progress thus far. And like their counterparts in the larger cities, they quickly saw the need to broaden the base of the renaissance so as to take in a larger share of society and ultimately to insure that the future would not be jeopardized by a failure to renew the people of the region along with its buildings and its economy. As they prepared to move ahead on this vital second phase of the renaissance, there was a remarkable agreement on where the next most urgent problems lay.

"The next logical step in our growth is toward education," said Representative Joseph McDade of Pennsylvania's 10th Congressional District. His words have been seconded by men like David Glenn, Baltimore's quietly effective Negro leader, by Richardson Dilworth in Philadelphia, by the powers in Pittsburgh and most particularly by Governor Raymond P. Shafer, who have come to realize the critical function of improved education in upgrading the region's human resources.

"Number one for Pennsylvania is education," Shafer told the state legislature in a major budget address after taking office in early 1967. Then he told them just how much No. 1 would cost. "Nine hundred and twenty-four million dollars, it dwarfs everything else in this budget," he said. "For Pennsylvania it is not so much an expense as it is . . . an essential investment in the future. Turn it down and Pennsylvania will die. Make it and we shall lead the Nation."

Most observers agreed that it was high time education dwarfed everything else in the budget, both in Pennsylvania and across the border in Maryland. For too many years public education in each of these states had been a starving stepchild of the legislatures. Just before World War II, Pennsylvania was spending a preposterously low $20.56 per pupil per year on elementary-secondary schooling. By 1962 that figure had risen to a more respectable $185.58, but in the same year the state ranked 48th in the nation in its per capita expenditures on higher education. Maryland's ranking, meanwhile, was hardly better at 39th in 1962.

Part of the reason for this dismal situation may have been the area's historical emphasis on private schooling. "We are a mature state," said one perceptive Pennsylvanian, "with a heavy entrenchment of the private sector." Pennsylvania indeed leads the country in this respect, with more than 100 private college-level institutions, among them some of the finest anywhere. The old Quaker college of Swarthmore, outside Philadelphia, has been described as the No. 1 college in the U.S. for its mother lode of National Merit award winners and Rhodes scholars and for its lofty standards of

Johns Hopkins *(above left)*, a bachelor Baltimore financier, railroad magnate and liquor dealer, was famed for his miserliness until in 1870 he left seven million dollars to found Johns Hopkins University and a free hospital for his city's needy. Although he gave no reasons for his sudden philanthropy, it has been said that he was influenced by one of his few friends, his cousin Elizabeth Hopkins.

Within a few years his hospital and the university's medical school had set a pattern of medical training that was to become standard throughout the U.S. Responsible for this rapid rise to greatness were four outstanding doctors—William Welsh, William Halstead, William Osler and Howard Kelly—shown above *(left to right)* in John Singer Sargent's painting *The Four Physicians*.

admission (an average of 2,000 applicants for every 260 acceptances). A place of distinction has been claimed for a number of the programs at Johns Hopkins in Baltimore, whose graduate school of medicine has long been a model for other institutions to follow.

One result of such excellence in private education has been that the Middle Atlantic leaders have tended to put their children—and their financial attention—into the private institutions. Thus, while the region's relatively small number of rich families became educationally richer, youngsters from the middle- and low-income groups were all too likely to wind up at an academic backwater like the University of Maryland, where scholarly standards sank so low that in 1954 the Middle States Association of Colleges and Secondary Schools provisionally suspended accreditation. The university has since made a substantial comeback under President Wilson Homer Elkins, who remarked as he set about an academic cleanup that "I hope to scatter a few books around campus so that the students will know what they are."

But the spirit of book scattering has not spread with sufficient force to the other institutions in Maryland's state system, at either the college or the secondary level. And therefore many young people are still not properly prepared to become productive members of a fast-changing society. Said one industrial executive whose company has been dredging Maryland in a more or less futile effort to find top young talent: "We in industry are faced each year with the appalling dilemma of hiring people who cannot read sufficiently well . . . of hiring junior executives who cannot write a grammatical letter . . . of screening hundreds of applicants to find those few who can spell, who follow directions and who show some evidence of discipline in their thought process."

Confronted by this crisis in its educational system, Maryland has not yet managed to come fully awake and in late 1966 was still paying its faculty salaries that averaged a full $1,000 below the national level. For Pennsylvania, however, there is impressive evidence that tolerance of mediocrity is ending, both for college training and for elementary-secondary schooling as well. During his four-year term as governor, from 1963 to 1967, William Scranton more than doubled appropriations for higher education to $134 million, and his successor, Governor Shafer, boldly asked for another boost to $220 million.

Part of these new funds were needed to help two large semiprivate institutions, the University of

Pittsburgh and Philadelphia's Temple University. In 1966 Pitt, financially exhausted after a 10-year orgy of expansion and internal spending, relinquished its private status for a "state-related" designation and in return got a state subsidy, $20 million the first year. Temple, deluged by increasing enrollments that jumped an average of 1,500 students a year in the two decades after World War II, gave up its own complete sovereignty for a similar amount. Shafer soon began to sound like a man who was putting at least one of his major problems behind him. "The number-one priority four years ago," he said in 1967, as he pressed ahead with the program Scranton had set in motion, "was providing enough facilities for higher education. And we've met that by acquiring Pitt and Temple and by doubling the enrollment of the fourteen state-owned or -aided higher-education institutions, and we're creating twelve community colleges." With that, he turned to other levels of the system.

"The one priority we have now," Shafer continued, "is graduate-school education. . . . We are not producing enough graduates . . . and these businesses and industries that require these good scientific brains that only a state with good graduate learning can provide, they won't come here unless we've got 'em. . . . We've got to have good education to keep the economy moving."

To sweeten the pot of graduate learning, Shafer proposed to offer $5,000 to various colleges and universities for each doctoral student whose credentials were acceptable to the recently created State Board of Education.

At the same time, Shafer moved to strengthen Pennsylvania's lower schools. "The subsidy to our elementary and secondary schools was up by more than one hundred million dollars in 1967, and I have set a goal of the state reimbursing the local schools fifty-fifty based on the average cost of pupil instruction." Such reimbursement would be a blessed relief to some school districts, where the state had rarely supplied as much as 25 per cent of the costs, and schools had found themselves trying to provide about $1,000 worth of pupil services each year from about $500 in resources.

While Shafer and his legislature were pouring new money into the state's educational system, various segments of that system were busy on specialized programs to improve the effectiveness of learning in their part of the region. Some of these programs were to feed off the new appropriations, others were started years ago on some extremely thin shoestrings. In either case, they were being watched by educators all over the Middle Atlantic region and in other states as well, where the quality of public instruction may have lagged as badly for want of money or progressive thinking.

One of the most exciting of these programs, both because of its past achievements and because of its implications for the future, has involved the development of classroom television at Pennsylvania State University, which pioneered in creating what many experts today have called the most effective television network in the country. During a typical term, some 12,000 students at the university's main campus in State College, Pennsylvania, see televised lectures piped from four main studios into 50 different classrooms. For example, an advanced psychology class sits in via television on a clinical interview with a seriously disturbed patient; a zoology professor dramatizes his lecture with a film clip showing the circulation of blood in the tiny capillaries of the tailfin of a goldfish; and a history professor can, if he wants, call up the blitzkrieg of Poland or the U.S. Dust Bowl of the 1930s.

Besides such clearly educational bonuses, television has stretched the university's educational dollar by bringing the televised presence of a single master teacher to as many as 1,000 students divided up into several separate, monitored classrooms. In addition, Penn State feeds its televised lectures to nine of the university's 20 satellite campuses scattered around the state. Though a number of old-line professors, still sensitive about the assumed benefits of the physical presence of a teacher in the classroom, claim that television can never produce an educational effect equal to that of an in-person lecture, Penn State has found no evidence that this is true. Tests carried out over a nine-year period showed no difference between a televised and an in-person lecture, even if the televised instructor did not take advantage of special audio-visual teaching aids. Furthermore, with the existing teacher shortage, television, in the words of one Penn State professor, represents at least a partial solution to the fact that "you can't [find] the better teacher even if you could pay him."

In Pittsburgh the local school system, collaborating with nearby universities, has set forth other enlightened concepts that have been copied elsewhere in the country—and that underscore education's role in renewing both the community and its people. "People put down roots where there is quality education," says Sidney P. Marland Jr., the city's Superintendent of Schools. "What we want to do is arrest the flight of the whites—to bring them back from the suburbs. . . . [The city] is the place for children to be living together and learning together for the good of the white as well as the Negro child." Under Marland about 20 per cent of Pittsburgh's high-school students have enrolled in a "Scholar's Program," a curriculum of intensive preparation for college. "This is part of our program for redressing the balance with the suburbs," says Marland, "and we're beginning to get some—not many, a few—people back."

For students with less aptitude for, or less interest in, college education, Superintendent Marland has launched a unique curriculum called OVT (Occupational-Vocational-Technical) within the city's regular high schools.

"The problem is that American schools have never—never—been relevant for the ten to twenty per cent of the kids at the bottom," said Marland, as he pressed ahead to try to make sure that Pittsburgh's schools became so. "Our Occupational track is for the very limited student," he continued, "who otherwise would be a dropout. This is things like waitress or gas-station attendant, and much of it is on-the-job training. Vocational would be a mechanic, more sophisticated than the Occupational track. And Technical is laboratory training, chemistry, metallurgical technology. The whole program is rolling now, serving about forty per cent of our youngsters. . . . We want to get to the point where half the students are in some kind of OVT. We want them to be ready with a marketable skill when they leave school."

The most ambitious of Marland's ideas was for his Great High Schools plan, by which he proposed to consolidate all high-school education in five brand-new 40-acre campuses distributed around the city. This bold move, for which an ultimate cost of upward of $100 million was projected, would not only provide high-school students with the most modern facilities designed on the flexible, informal pattern of a university campus but would also force complete and honest racial integration by replacing all the old neighborhood schools. Some observers have called it the "first massive effort to revolutionize urban education." The Great High Schools plan may in time fulfill that prediction. Marland was confident that it would: "These Great High Schools must be seen as a genuine and realistic solution to these new dimensions of expectation," he said, "and we must have the time to make them real as centers of social and economic restoration, and relevant vocational preparation, as well as centers for academic . . . opportunity."

Philadelphia's school-board president in the late 1960s, Richardson Dilworth, who as district attorney and later mayor provided much dynamic force for the city's first wave of renewal, tried to start his own local schools on the same upward path. Dilworth began with an ambitious construction plan for 71 new schools and attempted to press ahead on a scattering of academic enrichment and special-help programs, especially for children in the ghetto areas. By the end of 1967, however, even the blunt, energetic former Mayor had not been able to break completely through the long-standing wall of public inertia that the city erected around its public-education system. Therefore much of the Dilworth program remained in the blueprint phase. Philadelphia's most significant educational progress, in fact, was being generated from outside the public system and, in one case, altogether outside the conventional framework of formal education.

On the western bank of the Schuylkill River five public and private institutions, headed by the University of Pennsylvania, formed an education-centered organization called the West Philadelphia Corporation, which has begun a many-pronged advance on renewal. For example, university professors have shaped imaginative course material for most of the 9,100 elementary-secondary school children in the immediate area. Moving ahead on other fronts, the corporation has succeeded in getting some 2,000 acres certified for rebuilding and renovation under its guidance, and in making a start on a $50 million University City Science Center that will cooperate with industry in developing new products and new businesses for the area. This science center will in time employ some 5,000 people whose work is expected to generate as many as 60,000 jobs in light industry.

At the other end of town, on the edge of a festering Negro slum called the Jungle, a big, broad-shouldered Baptist minister named Leon H. Sullivan has started Opportunities Industrialization Center, a job-training and basic education program rooted in the healthy, bootstrap concept of self-help. Raising as much money as he could through local donations—and getting the rest by selling the white community on the benefits of a better-trained, better-motivated Negro population —Sullivan established the first center in an abandoned municipal jailhouse in 1964. Within three years the program had spread to six new centers around the city and was preparing some 4,000 underprivileged Philadelphians annually for good jobs. So successful has he been that the federal government in 1966 and 1967 gave Sullivan $5.1 million for similar centers in eight other cities, while privately supported programs got underway in some 16 more. By the end of 1967 Sullivan was

	PENNSYLVANIA	MARYLAND	DELAWARE	UNITED STATES
Per cent of population of elementary and high-school age (5-17) in 1966	24.8 (2,868,000 students)	26.7 (965,000 students)	27.3 (140,000 students)	25.9 (50,814,000 students)
Per cent of students (5-17) in public elementary and high school (1966)	76.9	83.8	84.0	86.5
Average number of students per classroom teacher in public schools	24.6	24.5	22.6	24.6
Average expenditure for public schools per student (1966-1967)	$562	$559	$591	$529
Per cent of population enrolled in institutions of higher learning (1965)	2.4 (273,795 students)	2.7 (96,430 students)	2.4 (12,334 students)	2.8 (5,526,325 students)

Education in the Middle Atlantic States follows similar patterns, as revealed by the above table. In each state approximately one fourth of the population is of school age *(first horizontal row of figures)*. But in Pennsylvania the percentage of students enrolled in public schools is low *(second row)*, indicating a large proportion of the state's students are in private or parochial schools. Teachers in all three states have about the same pupil load *(third row)* and all are close to the national average. In terms of annual expenditures per public-school pupil *(fourth row)* all three states rank fairly well, Delaware being seventh in the nation, Pennsylvania 12th and Maryland 15th. (Sums spent by other states range from a high of $840 in New York to a low of $291 in Mississippi.) A nearly equal percentage of the population in each state *(fifth row)* is enrolled in school beyond the high-school level; surprisingly, for such long-settled states, all three fall below the national average and below other old states like Vermont and Massachusetts.

branching out from pure job education into neighborhood investment corporations to finance a shopping center in the midst of the Negro community and into the underwriting of banks and other businesses whose profits could be turned back into the training program in a self-renewing cycle. And he was paying particular attention to pressure from Philadelphia Negroes for equal housing opportunity: using funds from his investment pools, he started building an apartment complex in North Philadelphia for lower-middle-income tenants. "When they refuse to rent to us now," said Sullivan, in reference to some of the city's stubbornly discriminatory real-estate agents, "they'll find us buying the building."

By turning his attention to the housing situation, Sullivan was facing a problem that goes beyond race prejudice. Even if there were no segregated neighborhoods, and even if every Philadelphian could afford decent living quarters, there simply would not be enough well-built houses or apartment units to go around. It is another of the frustrating ironies of the Middle Atlantic States that this region, which has shown such vigorous leadership in rebuilding large portions of its cities and giving new life to its economy, is still at an impasse on urban housing. In fact, some of the most spectacular of the early renewal projects, while they helped to revive center-city business activity, actually worsened the low-income housing crush by pushing thousands of families out of slums slated for clearance and into other slums that were themselves already overcrowded.

So far the Middle Atlantic cities, like other municipalities around the country, have found no sure answer to their housing problem, partly because of lingering prejudice, partly from lack of coherent housing programs and partly through shortage of funds. John Mauro, Pittsburgh's City Planning Director, admitted that housing was secondary for years in the renaissance because "our first battle was to keep this town alive economically. . . . It's true we haven't made as much progress in housing as we should have . . . but we had to save jobs before we could divert full attention to the problem of relocating families." In addition, he pointed out that until the passage of the 1965 Federal Housing Act, "We never had any real support at the federal level to assist the city, and without federal aid we couldn't build anything."

Since then, however, the federal government, like many of the planners within the region, has seen a need to shift some of the emphasis of renewal away from remodeling midtown commercial districts to

157

the less spectacular but just as urgent business of human renewal and neighborhood reclamation. In some cases the shift caught a few of the region's redevelopers with their plans down. Edmund Bacon, for example, found himself at least temporarily cut off from federal funds for a huge midtown transportation office and shopping center called Market East, in which Philadelphia's two suburban commuter rail lines would be linked together in close proximity to municipal subway and bus lines. "I am in sympathy with the federal government's emphasis on the poorer areas," he said, adding, "but in a broader sense you have to worry about things like Market East, for they keep the economy alive."

Bacon was confident, however, that Market East ultimately would receive federal financing. Meanwhile, with federal money more available for projects like neighborhood housing, some promising steps were made in that area. Philadelphia, authorized in 1967 to receive a grant of $70 million over three years to rehabilitate vacant houses, set a five-year goal of creating 45,000 low-income housing units. Some of the units were to be brand-new public projects, others would be renovated structures in existing but run-down neighborhoods. Renovation is favored by many urban experts since it allows the people to remain in familiar surroundings while improving the nature of those surroundings. Pittsburgh, also combining renovation and new construction, had 4,900 low- and middle-income dwelling units either just completed or in the works in 1968. Baltimore, meanwhile, was sliding back into increasing de facto segregation from its good early gains in neighborhood renovation, while it waited for Governor Spiro Agnew's administration to produce a state-wide open-housing law and thus enable the city to pump new life into its own housing program.

While the Middle Atlantic leaders, by focusing some of their energies on the underlying human problems of housing and education, have created a broader definition of renewal, they have by no means stopped building and planning major new commercial projects in their central cities. Ed Bacon's continuing concern for his Market East plan was just one example. Another was the Pennsylvania Railroad's plan to finance a 148-acre office and residential park that will extend the physical area of Pittsburgh's original renaissance northward along the Allegheny River. At the same time, the full concept of renewal has been extended still further to include other aspects of the society.

In an effort to stimulate the economy into moving ever faster, Pennsylvania is embarked on an ambitious 10-year highway-building program that is expected to cost some $10 billion. When finished it will provide the smaller cities and rural districts with a degree of mobility never before enjoyed by either the people or their goods. The new prosperity of the anthracite towns, based on light industry, is already riding upward on the first completed stretches of the four-lane system, which permits the fast, flexible trucking service that the diversified companies must have to keep profitable delivery schedules. Pittsburgh and the old mill towns in its area looked impatiently toward the completion of the western part of the network, both as a selling point for prospective new industry and as a better means for moving the steel that has remained too tightly bound to rail lines.

Other parts of the transportation system are being developed and extended at the same time. Philadelphia is upgrading its antiquated ocean-port facilities, adding from 15 to 21 new general-cargo berths in an attempt to capture trade that has gone to other terminals. The same city began preliminary work in 1967 on a $50 million automated air-freight facility that one city official said "may ultimately generate more revenue than passenger service . . . [and] is destined to produce more jobs and higher industrial payrolls and profits for the entire Delaware Valley."

In land transportation The Budd Company of Philadelphia was producing 150-mile-per-hour self-propelled rail-passenger cars for the Pennsylvania's projected high-speed train service between New York and Washington, scheduled to start in 1968. The federally supported experiment will, its sponsors hope, pull traffic off highways and also restore some lost rail-passenger revenues. In a more localized effort to cut down on the highway crush, both the Pennsylvania and the Reading Railroads got subsidies from the state and from the city of Philadelphia that allowed the two roads to begin modernizing their commuter service. And finally Pittsburgh, in an effort to relieve its urban street congestion—as well as to attract the plants of makers of transport equipment—began to concentrate on new ideas for intra-urban transportation systems. The first fruit of this concentration, brought forth with the help of the Westinghouse Electric Corporation, was a completely automated experimental minitrain, a rubber-tired chain of small cars that runs by computer control on a concrete track, stopping, starting and meeting split-second schedules without the need of a single trainman.

Some of these projects will become long-term solutions to one or another phase of the region's need

A landmark in public education was established in the 1950s by Maryland's Washington County School Board when it pioneered the partial use of closed-circuit television in its classrooms. The photograph above, taken in 1956, the first year of the test, shows a class of 11th graders in Hagerstown South High listening to a history lecture that is being simultaneously transmitted to seven other high schools. The success of the technique, which economizes on teachers' classtime and gives them more hours for individual student contact, has made the Washington County experience a model for school systems throughout the country.

for increased mobility. Others may be of only temporary importance—lessons upon which ultimate solutions will eventually be built. For as the region keeps reaching out farther and farther to find workable answers to its many problems, it also continues to find other, more subtle dilemmas lying beneath the first layer of solutions. Superhighways stimulate intercity commerce, but ultimately they may dump so many vehicles into town that traffic begins to strangle, and new transit systems must be designed to relieve the press of vehicles on the streets. To be truly effective, a transit system, in turn, should serve both the inner city and the surrounding suburbs. But once a city tries to cross its municipal borders with any kind of cooperative project for the whole metropolitan area, it is likely to run into heavy fire from the encircling towns and even counties, which are perfectly happy to feed off any services the city will provide but want no share of the tax levies needed to underwrite those services —and are horrified by the thought of giving up any of their autonomy to the big, bad city.

This problem of suburban and exurban hostility toward the city—"the cold and sower temper of the back counties"—exists all over the nation. But nowhere is it more urgent than in the Middle Atlantic region, where the basic patterns of settlement and of government were laid down long ago in colonial or early Federal times, when, in the words of Joseph S. Clark Jr. (who in 1956 had been elected a U.S. Senator from Pennsylvania), no "far-reaching legal or political authority was required to do whatever needed to be done to preserve law and order and perform relatively simple governmental functions of a purely local nature." Today the multiplicity of tiny villages, towns and county governmental units established in the 18th Century still exists. These were overlaid by a second layer of towns that sprang up during the boom years of coal and steel. In the midst of them grew the cities, with no jurisdiction or taxing powers beyond their old municipal borders—and almost no friends.

Pittsburgh is perhaps the prime example. The city, which is wholly within the borders of Allegheny County, has only limited powers to govern itself and is only one of a staggering total of 129 governmental units in that county. "Here you have a . . . city like Pittsburgh," says John Mauro despairingly, "fighting a battle every year to support itself, while one hundred and twenty-eight municipalities suck on it, all pulling in different directions."

Not long ago Pittsburgh suffered through a classic demonstration of what happens when its neighbors all pull in different directions. The city's political and business leaders tried to bring everyone together to start a long-needed cleanup of the Allegheny, Monongahela and Ohio Rivers. At first progress was almost impossible; among the 129 different local governments, dozens of communities defended their own special interests in the rivers and prophesied that any cooperative system would prove inordinately expensive. Fortunately, Pittsburgh, after much wrangling, was able to enroll enough of the area's communities to make a start on the increasingly successful project, but even today some communities have not joined.

Philadelphia stands in the same awkward position vis-à-vis its many suburbs. For example, school-board chairman Dilworth has said he would like to create a metropolitan school board that would include Philadelphia and parts, if not all, of the surrounding counties. But, says Dilworth, suburbanites view this with horror. "As things stand now," said the former Mayor, "the public schools [in the city] are becoming blacker and blacker and the suburban schools and the private schools and parochial schools within the city are becoming whiter and whiter. And what could be more divisive or undemocratic in our society than this?" In transportation, however, Dilworth did manage while he was still mayor to help join the city with several suburban counties to form what became known as the Southeastern Pennsylvania Transportation Authority (SEPTA), which now supervises the revived rail commuter lines and is negotiating to buy up public mass transit lines.

The state governments have until recently been of very little help to the cities in working out their metropolitan problems, for the legislatures were heavily loaded with rural delegates. "The rural people, in Pennsylvania at least," says Joseph Clark, sounding again one of the ancient songs of the Middle Atlantic, "are very allergic to the problem of taxes and couldn't care less about the problems of the city." The rural-oriented state government at Annapolis had been abysmally slow in granting Baltimore the right to float bond issues on its own, and consequently as late as the winter of 1967-1968 the city fathers were still trotting up to the capital for permission to raise money.

But the states are now beginning to show signs of mending their ways. In 1967 both Maryland and Pennsylvania called constitutional conventions to recast their obsolescent frames of government. Pennsylvania has divided the state into 13 areas, encouraging them to develop their own regional plans. Of these, one of the most quickly effective so far in helping break down old hostilities has been the Southwestern Pennsylvania Regional Planning Commission, embracing Pittsburgh and its six surrounding counties. Pittsburgh businessmen, in fact, are becoming so optimistic about the possible benefits that may come out of their cooperative commission that Adolph Schmidt, a high officer in the Mellon empire, observed: "If I had to make a personal judgment I'd have to say that at the regional and state levels, we're far ahead of the whole United States."

Ahead of the whole United States. Perhaps. Perhaps not. But Schmidt's enthusiasm for his area's plans and its probable future is typical of a 20-year change in the basic mood, in the economy and in the emotional climate of the whole Middle Atlantic region. In 1946 very few people anywhere in these states would have described their communities as being ahead of the whole United States. Yet today, despite lingering enclaves of poverty and backward thinking, there is a current of pride and optimism flowing through the region. Thanks to the vigor of the first wave of the renaissance, Pittsburgh is confident that it will never sink to the grimy depths to which its 19th Century coal-and-steel mentality once carried it. Rather the city speaks pridefully of the start of a second renaissance—of the coming of new industries, of the growing strength of its universities, of the excellence in the school system— and of continuing to move ahead. The leaders in Baltimore, once perhaps the slowest-acting of all major Eastern cities, say with conviction, "We're moving." And indeed Baltimore was moving at last to rebuild the land along the inner harbor, moving for a fair-housing law, moving to do something "not only about the physical part of the city," in the words of businessman Walter Sondheim Jr., "but also the social part." In Philadelphia the Brahmins in the suburbs, once blandly aloof from the city's despair, are involving themselves more and more in the continuing problems of the urban core, as the second wave of renewal gets underway: "I'm only one of dozens of men getting a great exposure to city problems," said Gustave Amsterdam, Chairman of the Philadelphia Redevelopment Authority. "It's a delight to see them inspire one another." And in the revitalized coal town of Hazleton, where the early seeds of renewal were sown so long ago, the town's former Chamber of Commerce president, Victor Diehm, said proudly, "It was our efforts that started this whole thing going, that started us on the way to the point where now we can't find *people* to fill all the jobs we have. We feel we have definitely done what we started out to do."

A devoted instructor, Mrs. Emma R. Green has taught French for 25 years in Wilmington High School.

A region's staunch and stable people

The Middle Atlantic States were settled by sturdy, hard-working folk. Weathering bloody labor strife, many of them doing dangerous work in the region's great mills and mines, they made these states pre-eminent. And they have been joined by equally determined newcomers who are helping to push this long-settled region again into the forefront of American achievement.

Photographs by Steinbicker/Houghton

COMMERCIAL FISHERMAN

Robert Leslie Frampton has fished the waters of Chesapeake Bay and the Choptank River for almost 60 years. Like his father before him, he sets out from Maryland's Tilghman Island every morning to catch crabs or, in the winter, rockfish. The weather is his greatest adversary. During cold winters he must battle ice and fierce winds; when the waters freeze he may be stranded ashore for as long as a month.

IMPOVERISHED MOTHER

Mrs. Ruth Marshall, shown with two of her four sons at right, lives in a slum section of Vienna, Maryland. Deserted by her husband, she is forced to depend entirely on welfare checks to sustain her family. The small, ramshackle house they live in has neither electricity nor inside plumbing and has been condemned as unfit for habitation. Such miserable conditions continue to be far too common in the Middle Atlantic region.

REFINERY REPAIRMAN

Clad in goggles and helmet, burly David "Red" Barlow, an expert oil refinery
worker, takes a break in front of the massive chemical towers of the Sun Oil Company's
installation in Marcus Hook, Pennsylvania. A member of the plant's maintenance
crew for more than 20 years, Barlow is a specialist in the rough work of repairing the
heavy equipment, such as the huge boilers, used by the oil industry. Since Sun Oil operates 24
hours a day, seven days a week, Barlow must frequently work the long night shifts.

LOCAL POLITICIAN

Moulton Lewis Charles Frantz has lived all his life in the same house in
Allentown, Pennsylvania, where he was born in 1904. Active in politics since 1925,
he has been the chairman of the Lehigh County Republican Committee since 1953,
responsible for raising funds and coordinating campaigns for candidates on the
local, state and national levels. During his long career he has been assistant to Congressman
Willard S. Curtin, clerk of courts for Lehigh County, tax clerk and chief deputy sheriff.

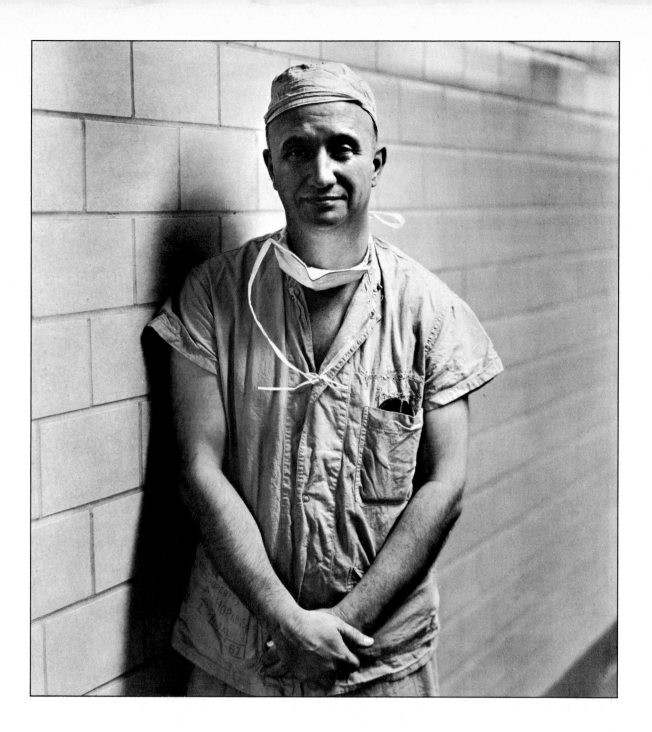

ANESTHESIOLOGIST

Dr. Donald W. Benson, who moved to the Middle Atlantic States in 1956, heads
the anesthesiology department at Johns Hopkins University in Baltimore. "The
Hopkins," as Baltimoreans call it, has one of the nation's most respected medical schools. Dr.
Benson works a grueling 12-hour day, much of it in the operating room. Besides teaching
and practicing anesthesiology, he has done valuable research work.

PROMINENT PHILADELPHIANS

C. Jared Ingersoll, standing at left with his wife, Agnes, is the head of one of
Philadelphia's oldest families. One of his forebears was a signer of the U.S.
Constitution; he himself has been a director of U.S. Steel and the Pennsylvania Railroad. He
has also headed the Greater Philadelphia Movement, the group spearheading the city's
renewal. Mrs. Ingersoll has made their 18th Century house into a Philadelphia landmark.

MIGRANT WORKER

Glen Douglas, shown holding a bunch of freshly cut gladioli, ekes out a hard
living as a migrant worker. Laboring in Florida in the winter, he comes north to
Wittman, Maryland, with his family in June and gets a job unloading trucks at a tomato-
canning factory; his wife also works there skinning tomatoes. In mid-August they
both move on to work at the gladiola farm, where they stay until November.

UNION LEADERS

The five men at left are all officials of the tough United Steelworkers Union. The
first four, Joseph Hovansik, James Engler, John Tegyi and Nick Kiak, help run the
union around Bethlehem, Pennsylvania; the local Bethlehem works is seen behind
them. At right is William Moran, the union's chief in 21 counties of Pennsylvania and all of
New Jersey. Once a coal miner, he has worked his way up to his present position.

RESEARCH CHEMIST

Claibourne D. Smith works as an organic research chemist at one of the oldest
(founded 1802) and most successful U.S. firms, I. E. du Pont de Nemours & Company.
Born in Memphis, Tennessee, Smith joined Du Pont's Central Research Department in
Wilmington after receiving his doctorate from the University of Oregon in 1964.
His work takes him into the forefront of the company's search for new synthetic substances.

HEADMASTER

Ludlow H. Baldwin *(right),* a Baltimorean, is the headmaster of that longtime
Baltimore institution, the Gilman School for boys, founded in 1897. A graduate of Johns
Hopkins and the Harvard Law School, Baldwin joined the Gilman faculty in 1943 because he
felt that in education he could make the most meaningful contribution to his native
city. Gilman has graduated many of the leaders of Baltimore business and civic life.

MIDSHIPMEN

Midshipman First Class Joseph F. Lucey *(above, left)* and Midshipman Fourth Class
Keith Bersticker stand in front of Bancroft Hall, the midshipmen's dormitory at the U.S.
Naval Academy in Annapolis, Maryland. Founded in 1845, the academy has long graduated
the men who have commanded the great ships of the U.S. Navy. Its handsome
buildings, which date from 1899, give the academy an air of both elegance and permanency.

COAL MINERS

Members of a rugged breed, miners John Fusco and Ed Polewski stand by the
elevator-shaft entrance of a mine *(right)* in southwestern Pennsylvania. Both men have
lived in this coal-mining area all their lives and have worked in the pits for almost 30 years.
Each day an elevator plummets them 400 feet into the earth, where they perform the
rough job of operating a machine that cuts coal much as a chain saw cuts wood.

Suggested tours

On this and the following pages seven maps show sections of the Middle Atlantic States that are of interest to the tourist. No attempt has been made to show every road and town. Instead, scenic routes, parks, historic sites and other special features are emphasized. A text accompanies each map. Opening dates and hours, especially for tours of businesses, should be confirmed locally, since they may vary. The seven areas covered are numbered on the small map below to correspond with the descriptive text.

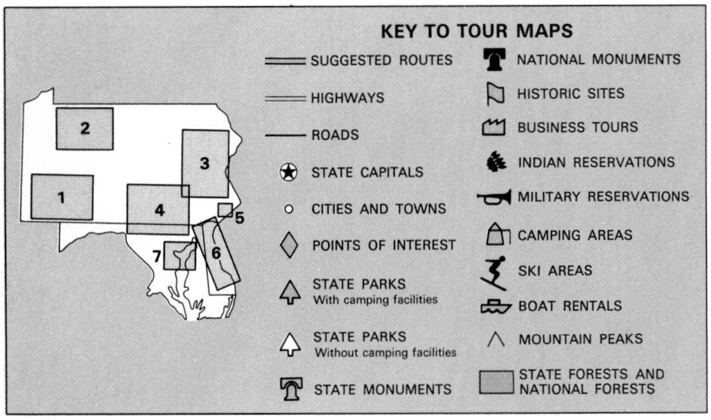
KEY TO TOUR MAPS
1
2
3
4
5
6
7
SUGGESTED ROUTES
HIGHWAYS
ROADS
STATE CAPITALS
CITIES AND TOWNS
POINTS OF INTEREST
STATE PARKS
With camping facilities
STATE PARKS
Without camping facilities
STATE MONUMENTS
NATIONAL MONUMENTS
HISTORIC SITES
BUSINESS TOURS
INDIAN RESERVATIONS
MILITARY RESERVATIONS
CAMPING AREAS
SKI AREAS
BOAT RENTALS
MOUNTAIN PEAKS
STATE FORESTS AND
NATIONAL FORESTS

1. Western Pennsylvania

The metropolis that dominates western Pennsylvania, Pittsburgh, provides a starting point for a trip through a historic section of the Keystone State.

Pittsburgh itself can boast of many interesting sights, such as its "Golden Triangle" downtown area, where the Monongahela and Allegheny Rivers meet to form the Ohio, and the Carnegie Institute. A gift from steel magnate Andrew Carnegie, the institute has exhibits in natural history and a noted collection of modern paintings.

To the east of Pittsburgh, south of Route 22, is the Bushy Run Battlefield. Here the Ottawa Indians were defeated by the British in a 1763 battle that was instrumental in securing western Pennsylvania. Fort Ligonier, built in 1758 and now restored to its original condition, lies southeast of Bushy Run along Route 30.

Route 30 continues east into the heart of the skiing and camping country that lies near Laurel Mountain. To the southwest, the National Road, begun in 1815, was America's first "highway." It is now U.S. 40. Along this route are Fort Necessity National Battlefield at Farmington; Searights Toll House near Uniontown, where tolls for the National Road were collected; and the David Bradford House at Washington, which has been refurnished in the style of the late 18th and early 19th Centuries.

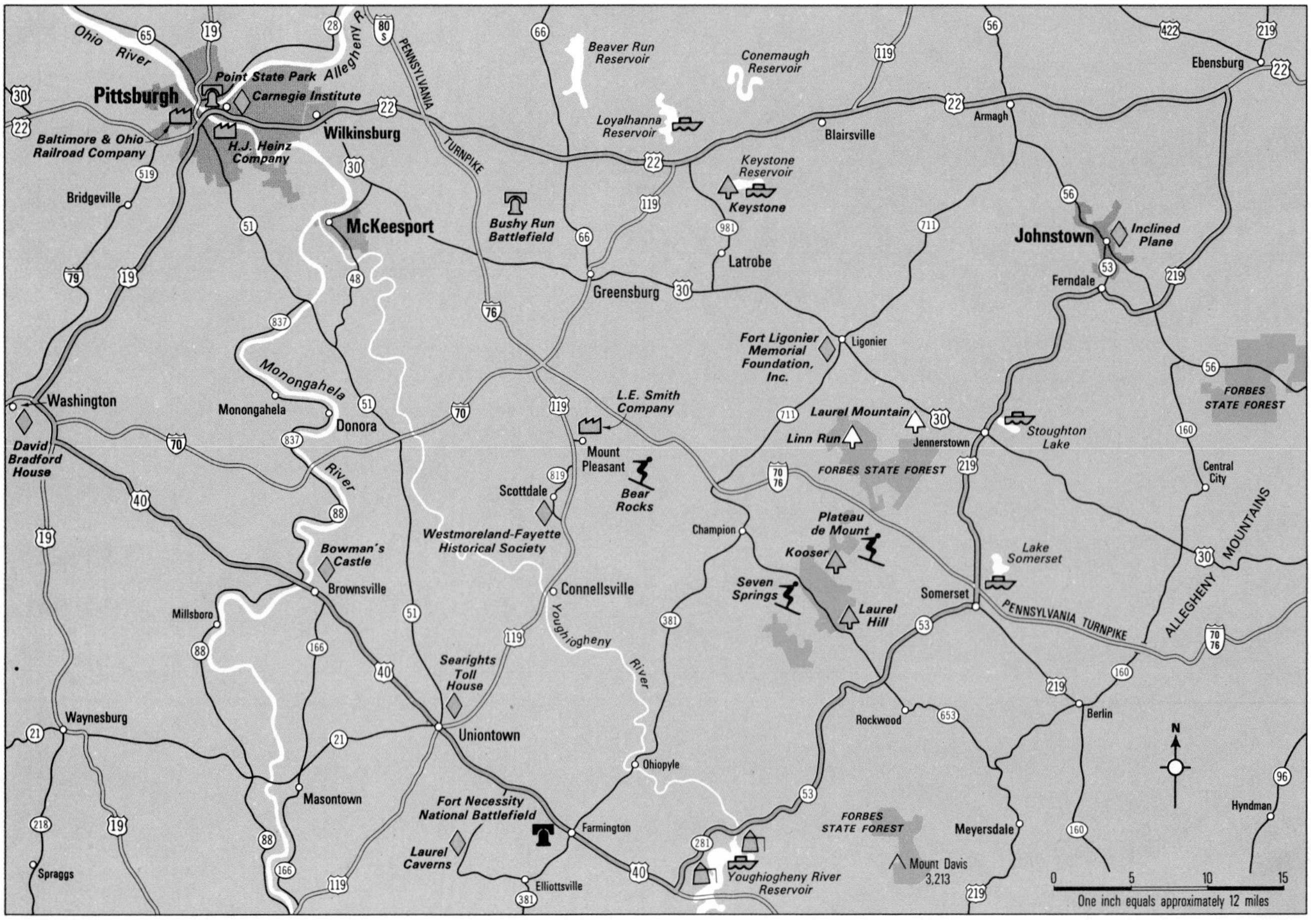
Ohio River
Pittsburgh
Point State Park
Allegheny R.
Carnegie Institute
Baltimore & Ohio Railroad Company
H.J. Heinz Company
Wilkinsburg
Bridgeville
McKeesport
PENNSYLVANIA TURNPIKE
Bushy Run Battlefield
Beaver Run Reservoir
Loyalhanna Reservoir
Conemaugh Reservoir
Keystone Reservoir
Keystone
Blairsville
Armagh
Ebensburg
Latrobe
Greensburg
Johnstown
Inclined Plane
Ferndale
Fort Ligonier Memorial Foundation, Inc.
Ligonier
Washington
David Bradford House
Monongahela
Monongahela River
Donora
L.E. Smith Company
Mount Pleasant
Bear Rocks
Laurel Mountain
Linn Run
Jennerstown
Stoughton Lake
FORBES STATE FOREST
Central City
Scottdale
Westmoreland-Fayette Historical Society
Champion
Plateau de Mount
Kooser
Seven Springs
Laurel Hill
Lake Somerset
Somerset
ALLEGHENY MOUNTAINS
PENNSYLVANIA TURNPIKE
Bowman's Castle
Brownsville
Millsboro
Connellsville
Youghiogheny River
Searights Toll House
Uniontown
Waynesburg
Masontown
Rockwood
Berlin
Ohiopyle
Fort Necessity National Battlefield
Farmington
Laurel Caverns
Elliottsville
Youghiogheny River Reservoir
FORBES STATE FOREST
Mount Davis 3,213
Meyersdale
Hyndman
Spraggs
N
0 5 10 15
One inch equals approximately 12 miles

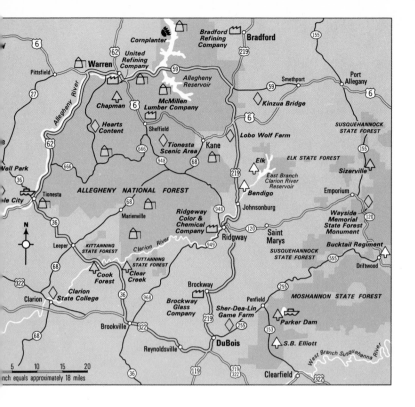

2. Northwestern Pennsylvania

Historically, northwestern Pennsylvania is noted as the birthplace of the U.S. oil industry; today this area is popular with campers and hunters alike because of its many thousands of acres of carefully preserved wilderness.

Drake Well Park, near Titusville, on Route 27, marks the spot where oil was first extracted in quantity in the United States. There, on August 28, 1859, a crude well driven by Edwin Drake and William Smith produced several barrels of what has been called "black gold." A replica of the original well house and a museum housing memorabilia from the days of the oil rush that followed are highlights of the park.

Soon after the discovery of oil at Titusville, the area was swarming with wells and boomtowns. One of these ephemeral towns is Pithole City, now marked with plaques. The country's first oil-carrying pipeline was built here in 1865, at the height of the town's prosperity.

East of Pithole City is countryside so picturesque it has been set aside as national and state forestland. These tracts are easily reachable by car along any of the map's suggested routes. Excellent camping facilities are sprinkled throughout the forests, and this section of Pennsylvania abounds with wild game, particularly deer, turkey and bear, and with fish, especially trout and bass.

3. Eastern Pennsylvania

This section of Pennsylvania, which borders New Jersey, was the frontier of colonial America during the early 18th Century, a fact that is reflected by the nature of the area's many historical sites.

From Scranton, Route 611 leads southeast past excellent camping and skiing facilities to the Delaware Water Gap, a spectacular 1,200-foot-deep gorge that the Delaware River has carved through Kittatinny Mountain. Additional recreation areas lie west of the gap along Route 80. Bethlehem, south along Route 191, is the site of the Annie S. Kemerer Museum, which offers a fine collection of 18th and 19th Century American furniture, glass and china. Nearby Bell House, built in 1745, housed one of the first girls' boarding schools in the country. At Lost River Caverns, near Hellertown, visitors may take guided tours through five underground chambers that feature crystal formations. Farther south, the Mercer Museum, in Doylestown, has on display a collection of preindustrial-era tools and artifacts as well as exhibits of Pennsylvania Dutch folk art. Graeme Park, south on Route 611 from Doylestown, features buildings that have been restored to show how wealthy 18th Century Pennsylvanians lived.

Route 422 runs west past the old ironmaking town of Hopewell Village, which has been restored to mirror the prosperous 1820-1840 period, and the Daniel Boone Homestead, which incorporates the frontiersman's boyhood home. Roadside America, on Route 22 west of Hamburg, is a famous miniature village where small-scale exhibits portray aspects of American history.

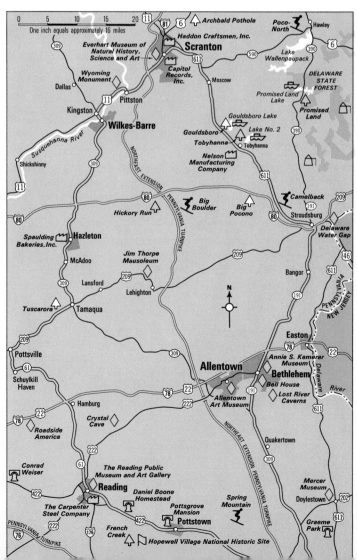

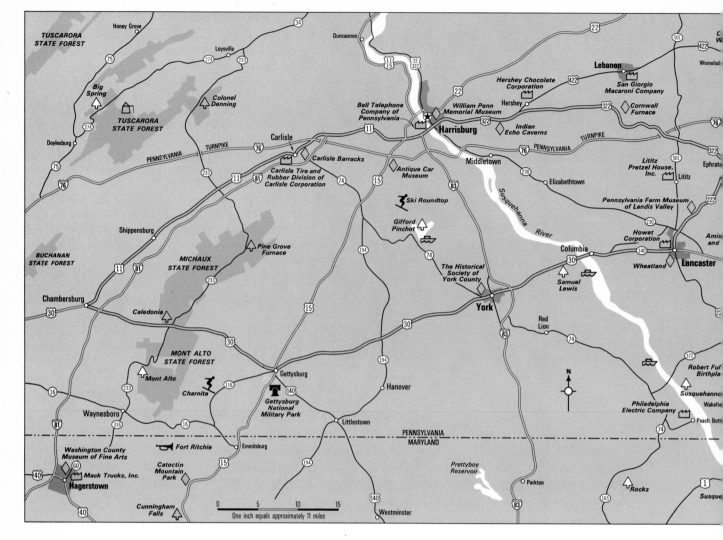

4. Central Pennsylvania and western Maryland

The eastern part of this section, around Lancaster, Ephrata and Lebanon, Pennsylvania, is best known as the Pennsylvania Dutch country *(pages 113-125)*. There, black-hatted and bearded Amish farmers and their soberly dressed families can be seen riding in horse-drawn buggies—their religion prohibits automobiles—along quiet country roads. At Ephrata is the Ephrata Cloister, an 18th Century German Protestant settlement restored to show how austerely the most devout of the Pennsylvania Dutch immigrants once lived. The nearby Pennsylvania Farm Museum includes more than 250,000 pieces of early farm equipment and rural craftwork.

North and west of Ephrata, on Route 322, lies Cornwall Furnace, one of the few early iron furnaces that remain intact. Due west of this fascinating survival of a past era is Hershey, home of the well-known Hershey Chocolate Corporation, which conducts tours of its facilities. Twelve miles west of Hershey, on Route 322, is Harrisburg (population 391,000), the capital of Pennsylvania. In its new William Penn Memorial Museum, which includes a planetarium and an art gallery, the exhibits

range from folk arts and crafts to science and technology.

West of Harrisburg, on Route 11, at Carlisle, are the Carlisle Barracks, second-oldest Army post in the country, where stands a Hessian guardhouse from the Revolutionary War. For outdoors enthusiasts, Big Spring and Colonel Denning State Parks in the Tuscarora State Forest west of Carlisle, as well as parks in the Michaux and Mont Alto State Forests to the south, offer excellent hiking and camping facilities. For history buffs and general tourists alike, no trip through this section is complete without a stop at Gettysburg National Military Park, site of one of the decisive battles of the Civil War. Within the 25-square-mile park more than 1,400 monuments and markers commemorate the bloody three-day battle. Guided tours of the park are available, and a park museum displays objects gleaned from the battlefield plus a map tracing the course of the fighting. Just over the state line, in Hagerstown, Maryland, the Washington County Museum of Fine Arts houses a large collection of European and Oriental paintings. There, too, Mack Trucks, Inc., conducts tours through its manufacturing plant.

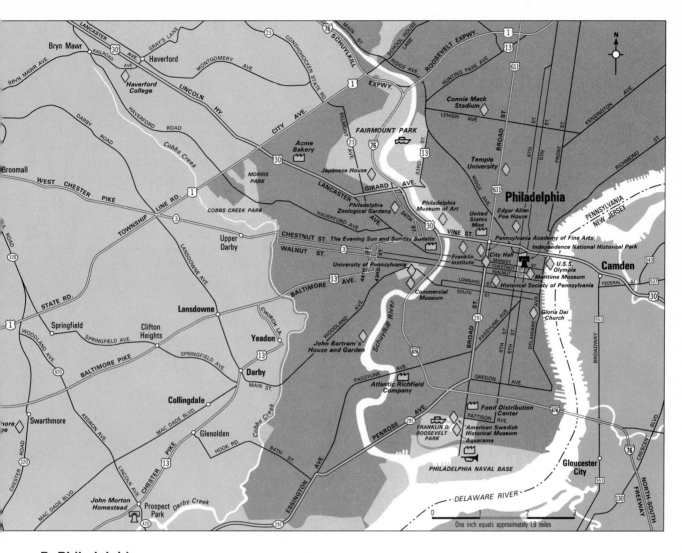

5. Philadelphia

The largest city in the Middle Atlantic States, Philadelphia is a modern metropolis with a noble tradition. As befits its age and importance in U.S. history, the city has many fine homes, public buildings and museums. Perched above the Schuylkill River (whose banks are lined by the often elegant boathouses of the city's rowing clubs) is the mammoth Philadelphia Museum of Art, one of the nation's premier galleries. The collection ranges from superb portraits done by native Philadelphian Thomas Eakins to *The Large Glass* and *Nude Descending a Staircase*, trail-blazing works by Marcel Duchamp. At the Franklin Institute the visitor can view exhibits—many of them fascinating working models and push-button displays—illustrating the fundamentals of science and the history of man's scientific achievement. Just north of the institute lies the U.S. Mint, where the visitor can see how coins are made today and how they were made as far back as 1773. Also to be seen in this part of Philadelphia are the city's highly successful slum-clearance and restoration projects.

On North 7th Street, near the mint, is the Edgar Allan Poe House, where the celebrated author lived from 1842 to 1844 and where he wrote "The Raven." South of this historic residence lies Independence Hall, where the Second Continental Congress adopted the Declaration of Independence. In the hall's stair well hangs the Liberty Bell, symbol of the nation's freedom.

East of Independence Hall, at the foot of Chestnut Street, is moored the U.S.S. *Olympia*, Commodore Dewey's flagship during the Battle of Manila Bay in 1898. Visitors can tour this last survivor of the Spanish-American War. And at the Historical Society of Pennsylvania, on Locust Street, the personal effects of such famous Americans as George Washington, Benjamin Franklin, Thomas Jefferson and William Penn are displayed. West of the Historical Society, across the Schuylkill, lies the main campus of the University of Pennsylvania. An Ivy League school with an excellent scholastic reputation, the university had its beginnings in a seminary founded by Franklin and others in 1740. West of the city lie several other fine institutions of higher learning, including Swarthmore, Bryn Mawr and Haverford Colleges.

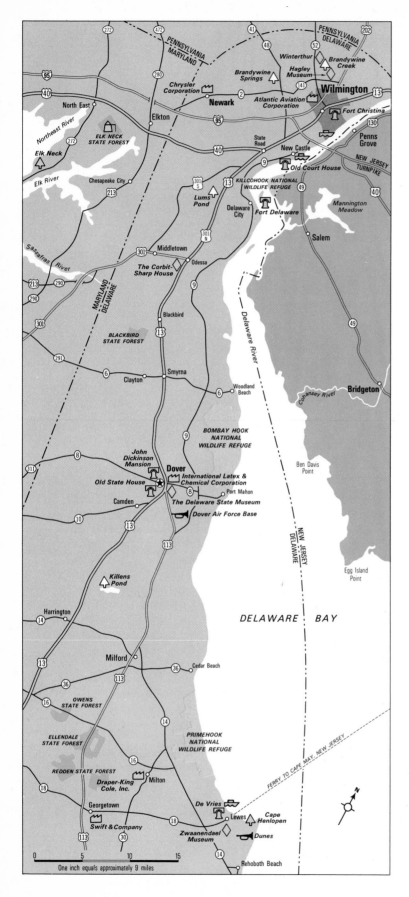

6. Delaware

Many travelers see only the densely populated northern tip of Delaware around Wilmington, but the rest of the state, from the shores of Delaware Bay to the interior farmland, offers many sites of scenic and historic interest. In Wilmington (population 93,336) a monument marks the site of Fort Christina, the first permanent settlement in Delaware, established by a group of Swedes and Dutch led by the Dutch colonial administrator Peter Minuit. A few miles north, on Route 141, is the Hagley Museum, where a well-presented history of American industry is housed in a 19th Century textile mill on Brandywine Creek. Just north, on Route 52, is the noted Henry Francis du Pont Winterthur Museum, a mansion housing a superb collection of antique home furnishings.

At New Castle, a well-preserved colonial village south of Wilmington, the Old Court House, dating from the 1730s, houses many historical relics of the early settlers. Farther to the south, on an island near Delaware City, stands Fort Delaware, built just before the Civil War and used as a prison for captured Confederate soldiers. At Odessa, on U.S. Route 13, is the 18th Century Corbit-Sharp House, now a museum and one of the finest colonial homes in the state. Dover (population 14,210), Delaware's capital, still has its old town green, laid out in 1717. On the east side of the green is the Old State House (1772) that continues to serve for state business. A few blocks away is The Delaware State Museum, with exhibits showing early life in the state plus artifacts of the Delaware Indians. Tours, arranged in advance, are available at the International Latex & Chemical Corporation. Near Georgetown, at the bottom of this map, Swift & Company offers group tours of its chicken-processing plant, one of the largest in an area where broiler raising is the major industry. East of Georgetown, at Lewes, is the Zwaanendael Museum, a reproduction of part of the town hall at Hoorn, Netherlands. A nearby monument honors the Dutch colonizer David Pietersen de Vries on the presumed site of the first Dutch fort.

7. The Baltimore area

Baltimore, the third-largest city of the Middle Atlantic States region, is a metropolis whose roots extend back into the colonial era. It was founded in 1729 on a site where the Patapsco River makes a natural harbor; the Patapsco also flows into Chesapeake Bay. Because ships could thus move easily from Baltimore to the sea, the city was, almost from the first, an important port.

Today Baltimore is a modern and vibrant urban center, but one that proudly shows its history. Fort McHenry, on the Patapsco, has exhibits and a film that re-create a key battle of the War of 1812. It was during a British bombardment of this fort that Francis Scott Key wrote the poem that provides the words of the U.S. national anthem. Flag House was the home of Mary Pickersgill, who sewed the U.S. flag that Key saw still flying by "dawn's early light." What is considered by many the world's

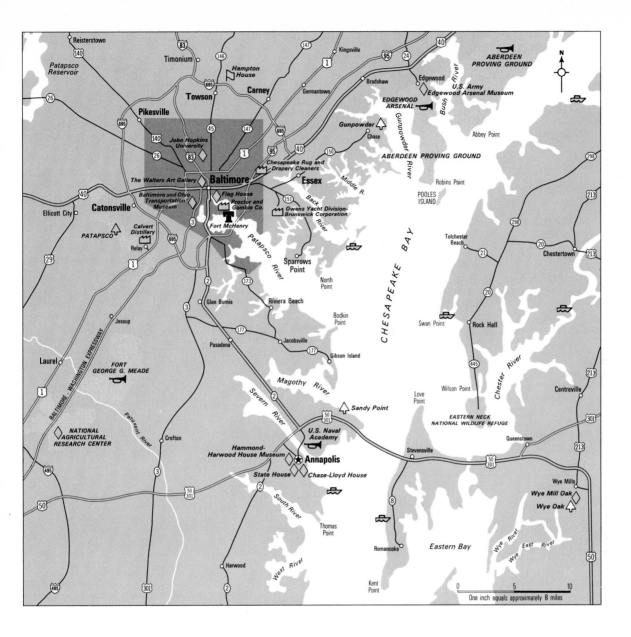

Reisterstown
Timonium
Hampton House
Carney
Kingsville
ABERDEEN PROVING GROUND
Patapsco Reservoir
Germantown
Bradshaw
Edgewood
U.S. Army Edgewood Arsenal Museum
Towson
EDGEWOOD ARSENAL
Pikesville
Gunpowder
Chase
John Hopkins University
ABERDEEN PROVING GROUND
Robins Point
Abbey Point
Chesapeake Rug and Drapery Cleaners
The Walters Art Gallery
Baltimore
Essex
Middle R.
POOLES ISLAND
Catonsville
Baltimore and Ohio Transportation Museum
Flag House
Proctor and Gamble Co.
Back River
Owens Yacht Division-Brunswick Corporation
Tolchester Beach
Ellicott City
Fort McHenry
CHESAPEAKE BAY
Chestertown
Calvert Distillery
PATAPSCO
Sparrows Point
North Point
Relay
Patapsco River
Swan Point
Rock Hall
Glen Burnie
Riviera Beach
Bodkin Point
Jessup
Jacobsville
Gibson Island
Wilson Point
Centreville
Laurel
FORT GEORGE G. MEADE
Pasadena
Magothy River
Love Point
Crofton
NATIONAL AGRICULTURAL RESEARCH CENTER
Severn River
Sandy Point
EASTERN NECK NATIONAL WILDLIFE REFUGE
Queenstown
U.S. Naval Academy
Hammond-Harwood House Museum
Annapolis
Stevensville
State House
Chase-Lloyd House
Wye Mills
Wye Mill Oak
Wye Oak
Thomas Point
South River
Romancoke
Eastern Bay
Wye River
West River
Harwood
Kent Point

One inch equals approximately 8 miles

finest collection of old locomotives is housed at the Baltimore and Ohio Railroad Transportation Museum.

Also of special interest in Baltimore is The Walters Art Gallery at Charles and Centre Streets. This collection, begun in the mid-19th Century, is considered one of the most comprehensive in all of America, specializing in the art and architecture of major civilizations.

North of Baltimore, near Towson, is Hampton House, a Georgian mansion built in 1783 which houses collections reflecting the styles and tastes of the last 150 years. Route 40, which runs through Baltimore and then northeast, passes Edgewood Arsenal, a U.S. Army base with a military museum.

To the south of Baltimore, Route 2 leads to Annapolis. This city, on the western shore of Chesapeake Bay, was founded in 1649 and is Maryland's state capital. A local historical society conducts tours of the city's landmarks, which include its old but still busy waterfront and its State House. For more than six months in 1783 and 1784 the State House was the Capitol of the United States; it was here that Washington resigned his commission as general of the new nation's Army. The building also boasts the oldest existing American flag, as well as the biggest wooden dome in the country. Nearby is the U.S. Naval Academy, which may be visited by the public.

Route 50 leads east from Annapolis, crossing Chesapeake Bay to the Eastern Shore, a land of creeks and coves that is popular as a recreation area. One of the Eastern Shore's many old villages is Wye Mills, where the state tree—the 450-year-old Wye Oak—stands, along with a water mill built in the late 17th Century, a chapel that dates back to 1721 and a colonial schoolhouse.

Museums and galleries

Delaware

Dover
The Delaware State Museum, 316 S. Governors Ave. State history, crafts, industries and Indian artifacts. Tues-Sat 11-5; Sun 2-5.

Lewes
Zwaanendael Museum, Savannah Rd. and Kings Hwy. Colonial items pertaining to state and county history; Indian artifacts. Tues-Sat 10-5:30; Sun, hols 12:30-5:30.

New Castle
Dutch House, E. Third St. Historic house; c.1690 period furnishings. Mar-Nov: daily 11-4.

New Castle Historical Society, 2 E. Fourth St. Historic Amstel House, colonial furnishings. Mon, Tues, Thurs-Sat 11-4.

Wilmington
Fort Delaware Society, Pea Patch Island. Fort Delaware Museum; Civil War artifacts. May 29-Sept 12: Sat, Sun, hols 12-7.

Hagley Museum, Barley Mill Rd. and Brandywine Creek. Brandywine industry of 19th Century; restoration of early Du Pont powderworks. Tues-Sat 9:30-4:30; Sun 1-5.

The Historical Society of Delaware, 6th and Market Sts. Delaware historical documents and artifacts; Old Town Hall. Mon 1-9; Tues-Fri 10-5.

The Wilmington Society of Fine Arts, Delaware Art Center, 2301 Kentmere Pkwy. Nineteenth Century English and American paintings. Mon-Sat 10-5; Sun 2-6.

Winterthur
The Henry Francis du Pont Winterthur Museum. American decorative arts and interior design from colonial times to present. Ten South Wing rooms Tues-Sat 9:30-4:30; tours of Winterthur Gardens and 16 period rooms as announced Apr-June.

Maryland

Annapolis
Chase-Lloyd House, 22 Maryland Ave. Georgian mansion; antique furnishings. Mon-Fri 10-12, 2-4.

Hammond-Harwood House, 19 Maryland Ave. Eighteenth Century furniture and art works. Winter: Mon-Sat 10-4; Sun 2-4; balance of year: Mon-Sat 10-5; Sun 2-5.

Historic Annapolis, Inc., 18 Pinkney St. Guided tours of Annapolis given by group headquartered in the historic Slicer Shiplap House. May-Nov: Mon-Fri 10-4.

Maryland State House, State House Circle. Old Senate Chamber, old flags, portraits, documents. Mon-Fri 9-5; Sat 10-5; Sun 1-5.

U.S. Naval Academy Museum, U.S. Naval Academy. Art and artifacts dealing with maritime history. Mon-Sat 9-5; Sun 11-5.

Baltimore
The Baltimore Museum of Art, Wyman Park Dr. French 19th and 20th Century paintings; colonial rooms. Tues-Sat 11-5; Sun 2-6; winter only: Tues eves 8-10.

Baltimore and Ohio Transportation Museum, Pratt and Poppleton Sts. Collection of railroad and other transportation relics. July 2-Sept 14: Wed-Sun 10-4.

Enoch Pratt Free Library, 400 Cathedral St. Prints of old Baltimore; war posters; memorabilia of H. L. Mencken. Mon-Fri 9-9; Sat 9-5:30.

Fort McHenry National Monument and Historic Shrine, foot of Fort Ave. Exhibits demonstrating the history of the fort and of Maryland in the War of 1812. Summer: daily 8 a.m.-8:30 p.m.; balance of year: daily 9-5.

Maryland Academy of Sciences, 400 Cathedral St. Archeology, astronomy, geology, mineralogy and paleontology; planetarium. Oct-May: Mon-Sat 9-4:45; June-Sept: Mon-Sat 9-4:30.

Maryland Historical Society, 210 W. Monument St. Maryland history; period furniture; maps and prints; Chesapeake Bay maritime collection. Tues-Sat 11-4; Sun 1-5.

The Peale Museum, 225 N. Holliday St. History of Baltimore; relics of painters Rembrandt and Rubens Peale. Tues-Sat 10:30-4:30; Sun 1:30-5:30.

The Star-Spangled Banner Flag House, 844 E. Pratt St. Federal period relics; documents relating to Francis Scott Key and Mary Pickersgill. Tues-Sat 10-4; Sun 2-4:30.

U.S. Frigate *Constellation*, foot of Pratt St. Historic U.S. Navy vessel with exhibits devoted to naval history. June-Aug: Mon-Sat 9-5; Sun 12-5; Sept-May: Mon-Sat 10-4; Sun 12-5.

The Walters Art Gallery, Charles and Centre Sts. Painting, sculpture and decorative art from early Egypt through 19th Century. Sept-June: Mon 1:30-5, 7:30-10; Tues-Sat 11-5; Sun, hols 2-5; July: Tues-Sat 11-4; Sun 2-5; Aug: Mon-Sat 11-4; Sun 2-5.

Boonsboro
Washington Monument State Park, Old U.S. Rte. 40. Collection of firearms, Indian relics, Civil War mementos. Daily 9-6.

Easton
The Historical Society of Talbot County, 29 S. Washington St. Models of 18th and 19th Century sailing vessels; colonial artifacts. Tues, Fri 10-4.

Edgewood Arsenal
U.S. Army Edgewood Arsenal Museum, Building 1958. History of chemical-biological-radiological warfare dating from 1890. Mon-Fri 8-4:30 and by appointment.

Great Falls
Chesapeake and Ohio Canal Museum, MacArthur Blvd. on C&O Canal. Historic house made into a museum with exhibits pertaining to canal's history. June-Labor Day: daily 10-6; Labor Day-May: weekends.

Hagerstown
Washington County Museum of Fine Arts, City Park. American, European and Oriental art. Tues-Sat 9-5; Sun, hols 1-6.

Sharpsburg
Antietam National Battlefield Site museum, State Rte. 65. Civil War relics, photographs, documents; papers of General Robert E. Lee. Winter: daily 8:30-5; summer: Sat, Sun, hols 9-6.

Towson
Hampton National Historic Site, 535 Hampton Lane. Historic house; period furnishings and paintings. Tues-Sat 11-5; Sun, hols 1-5.

Union Mills
Shriver Homestead. Original household and agricultural items; mill museum. June 10-Sept 10: Mon-Sat, hols 10-5; Sun 1-5.

Pennsylvania

Allentown
Allentown Art Museum, Fifth and Court Sts. S. H. Kress collection of Italian Renaissance art; European painting; 20th Century American painting. Mon-Sat 10-5; Sun 2-5. Closed Aug.

Ambridge
Old Economy, 14th and Church Sts. Village built by Harmony Society; original furnishings; prints. Winter: Mon-Sat 9-4:30; Sun 1-4:30; summer: Mon-Sat, 8:30-5; Sun 12-5.

Bethlehem
Annie S. Kemerer Museum, Moravian College campus. Eighteenth and 19th Century American glass, furniture and china; 19th Century landscape paintings; headquarters for tours of historic houses. Mon-Fri 9-5.

Lehigh University Art Museum, Lehigh University campus. Paintings; Chinese porcelain and prints; engravings and lithographs. Mon-Fri 9-5; Sat 9-12; Sun 2-5.

Birdsboro
Daniel Boone Homestead, U.S. Rte. 422. Historic house; period furnishings and farm tools; blacksmith shop. Winter: Mon-Sat 9-4:30; Sun 1-4:30; summer: Mon-Sat 8:30-5; Sun 1-5.

Boalsburg
Boal Mansion and Museum and Columbus Chapel, State Rte. 322. Spanish chapel once owned by a branch of Christopher Columbus' family; contains old paintings and ancient church furnishings. May-Oct: daily 10-6.

Carlisle
Hessian Guardhouse Museum, Carlisle Barracks. War relics, rifles, pictures, 1777 powder magazine. May-Nov: Sun 1-5.

Chadds Ford
Brandywine Battlefield Park, U.S. Rte. 1. Site of Brandywine battle of 1777 with Washington's and Lafayette's headquarters. Oct 16-Apr: Sat, Sun 10-5; May-Oct 15: Tues-Sun 10-5.

Chester
Delaware County Historical Society, 410-412 Market St. Historic items; Old Court House building (oldest building in the

U.S. in continuous use). Mon-Fri 1-4; Sat 9-12. Closed Aug.

Cornwall
Cornwall Furnace, Old Furnace Bldg. Blast furnace for Revolutionary War; tools and equipment used in early ironmaking. Winter: Mon-Sat 9-4:30, Sun 1-4:30; summer: Mon-Sat 8:30-5; Sun 1-5.

Elverson
Hopewell Village National Historic Site, off U.S. Rte. 22. Restoration of ironmaking village. Labor Day-July 4th: daily 9:30-5:30; July 4th-Labor Day: Mon-Fri 9:30-5:30; Sat, Sun, hols 9:30-7:30.

Ephrata
Ephrata Cloister. Remaining buildings of early religious community. Winter: Mon-Sat 9-4:30; Sun 1-4:30; summer: Mon-Sat 8:30-5; Sun 1-5.

Erie
Erie Public Museum, 356 W. Sixth St. Art and history museum; pioneer artifacts; planetarium. Tues-Sat 10-5; Sun 2-5.

Gettysburg
Gettysburg National Military Park Visitor Center. Civil War artifacts; audio-visual exhibits; cyclorama of the battlefield. Oct-May: Mon-Fri 8-5; Sat, Sun 9-5; June-Sept: Mon-Fri 8-6; Sat, Sun 9-6.

Harrisburg
Fort Hunter Museum, 5300 N. Front St. Historic house; 1789 French and Indian War fort; 19th Century costumes and crafts. Tues-Sun 10-5.

William Penn Memorial Museum and Archives Bldg., Third and North Sts. Pennsylvania arts and crafts; military history; science museum and planetarium. Mon-Sat 9-4; Sun 1-5.

Jeannette
Bushy Run Battlefield Park, State Rte. 993. Arboretum planting denotes fort and battle sites; Indian artifacts; military items. Daily during daylight hours.

Lancaster
The Amish Farm and House, U.S. Rte. 40. Historic buildings, including Old Stone Barn from 1805. Dec-Feb: Sat, Sun 9-5; Oct, Nov, Mar, Apr: daily 8:30-5; May-Sept: daily 8:30-8.

Ligonier
Fort Ligonier Memorial Foundation, U.S. Rte. 30. Restoration of 1758 French and Indian War fort. Nov-May: 10-4; June-Oct: 9-6.

Morrisville
Pennsbury Manor, off Bordentown Ferry Rd. Restored 1683 buildings built by William Penn. Winter: Mon-Sat 9-4:30; Sun 1-4:30; summer: Mon-Sat 8:30-5; Sun 1-5.

Philadelphia
The Academy of Natural Sciences of Philadelphia, 19th St. and The Parkway. Natural history fossils; habitat groups. June-Aug: Mon-Sat 10-4; Sun 1-5; Sept-May: Mon-Sat 10-5; Sun 1-5.

The Franklin Institute, 20th St. and The Parkway. Science museum with excellent exhibits; planetarium. Tues-Sat 10-5; Sun 12-5; planetarium only Wed, Fri eves 8-9:30.

Independence National Historical Park, 420 Chestnut St. Independence Hall; tours of historic buildings. Daily 8:45-5:45.

Pennsylvania Academy of the Fine Arts, Broad and Cherry Sts. Lectures, concerts; annual exhibitions of contemporary American art. Tues-Sat 10-5; Sun 1-5. Closed Aug.

Philadelphia Museum of Art, Benjamin Franklin Pkwy. at 26th St. American and international masters from all periods; tapestries; Far and Near Eastern art. Daily 9-5.

Pittsburgh
Carnegie Institute, Carnegie Museum, 4400 Forbes Ave. Natural history exhibits; transportation museum; dolls; stamps. Mon-Sat 10-5; Tues eves 5-9; Sun 2-5.

Carnegie Institute, Museum of Art, 4400 Forbes Ave. Excellent collection of American and European painting and sculpture. Mon-Sat 10-5; Sun 2-5; Oct-Mar: Tues eves 5-9.

Reading
The Reading Public Museum and Art Gallery, 500 Museum Rd. Early American art; science exhibits; natural history. June-Aug: Mon-Fri 9-4; Sun 2-5; Sept-May: Mon-Fri 9-5; Sat 9-12; Sun 2-5.

Valley Forge
Valley Forge Historical Society, Washington Memorial Museum. Revolutionary War memorabilia. Mon-Sat 9-5; Sun 1-5.

Yardley
Alexander Railroad Museum, Upper River Rd. Fine collection of toy trains, some more than 100 years old. Sat, Sun 2-5.

Local festivals and events

Delaware
Winterthur Museum Annual Garden Tour, Winterthur. Tour of extensive gardens surrounding the famous museum. Apr—June.

Old Dover Days, Dover. Tour of old homes and gardens. May.

Wilmington Garden Day, Wilmington. Tour of famous homes and gardens. Early May.

Miss Delaware Pageant, Rehoboth Beach. Beauty and talent contest, winner represents the state in the Miss America contest. Late June.

Operation Firecracker, Greater Wilmington Airport. One of the largest fireworks displays in the East. July 4.

Delaware State Fair, Harrington. State's largest fair. Late July—early Aug.

Surf Casting Contest, Rehoboth Beach. Selection of state champion surf caster. Aug.

Christmas in Odessa, Odessa. Tour of historic homes to view Christmas decorations of the past. Early Dec.

Maryland
Ratification Day, Annapolis. Anniversary of ratification of the Treaty of Paris and the end of the American Revolution; ceremonies in the State House. Jan 14.

Maryland House and Garden Pilgrimage, Baltimore. Tour of famous homes. First 10 days in May.

Maryland Clam Festival, Annapolis. Features boat parade, water show, clam-chowder cook off and crowning of a Clam Queen. Mid-Aug.

Maryland State Fair, Timonium. Agricultural and other exhibits at state's largest fair. End of Aug.

National Hard Crab Derby, Crisfield. Crab-cooking, crab-eating contests. Governor's Cup Race between live crabs. Sat before Labor Day.

Pennsylvania
Mummers' Parade, Philadelphia. Eight-hour parade featuring gorgeously costumed paraders, bands, beautiful floats. Jan 1.

State Farm Show, Harrisburg. One of the largest agricultural exhibits in the nation. Mid-Jan.

Poconos Winter Carnival, entire Poconos area. Snowmobile races, ski races, skating, tobogganing, iceboating. Late Jan.

Penn Relays, Philadelphia. One of the nation's largest track meets, held at University of Pennsylvania's Franklin Field. Last weekend in Apr.

Pittsburgh Folk Festival, Pittsburgh. Features handicrafts of 24 nationalities. May.

Bach Festival, Bethlehem. One of America's most important musical events, held at Lehigh University. Mid-May.

Three Rivers Arts Festival, Pittsburgh. Art shows, musical events, plays. June.

Elfreth Alley's Fete Day, Philadelphia. The residents of Elfreth Alley, a tiny old street, wear colonial costumes and open their pre-Revolutionary homes to the public. First Sat in June.

Pennsylvania Dutch Folk Festival, Kutztown. Folk dancing, community singing, oldtime games. Crafts and implements of yesteryear are exhibited. Food is served. First week in July.

Little League World Series, Williamsport. Aug.

Pennsylvania Horse Show, Harrisburg. One of the premier U.S. horse shows. Oct.

Army-Navy Football Game, Philadelphia. Nov.

Christmas in Bethlehem, Bethlehem. Holy observances are held in this town named for Holy City in Israel. Special music is provided by Moravian singers and elaborate decorations are displayed. Dec.

Wildlife of the Middle Atlantic States

A sampling of the natural life frequently found in the Middle Atlantic States is given on this and the following three pages. In each case both the common name and the scientific name of the plant or animal are given. The information supplied here is not intended to be comprehensive; for additional material on the fauna and flora of the Middle Atlantic region the reader should refer to the numerous specialized books on plants and wildlife. A number of useful and entertaining reference works that contain such information are listed on page 188.

Mammals

Star-nosed mole

Black bear

Mink

Eastern gray squirrel

Rooting out prey with its odd snout, *Condylura cristata* burrows through the soft ground of swamps in search of worms, beetles and even young snakes.

Ursus americanus, whose color may range to deep red, grows to a length of five and a half feet. Though a meat eater, it also feeds on berries and nuts.

Counting its bushy eight-inch tail, an adult male *Mustela vison* is nearly two feet long. Some 55 of the prized pelts are used in an average full-length coat.

Sciurus carolinensis is noted for the broad tail that makes up half of its 18-inch length. This tail serves as a balance and, in cold weather, as a blanket.

Deer mouse

Allegheny wood rat

Snowshoe hare

White-tailed deer

Also called the white-footed mouse, *Peromyscus maniculatus* is a commom mammal in the region. Yet few people have seen it, as it emerges only at night.

Not related to the black and brown rats of the cities, *Neotoma pennsylvanica* lives high in the mountains, away from man, where it feeds on seeds.

Lepus americanus is the region's only native hare, an 18-inch-long game animal that can jump as far as 10 feet. Its coat, brown in summer, turns white in winter.

Pennsylvania's state animal, *Odocoileus virginiana*, was a favorite with hunters long before the first white men arrived. A mature buck weighs 300 pounds.

Fish and reptiles

Mullet

Round pompano

Bluefish

Spotted weakfish

The mullet *(Mugil cephalus)*, one of the most wide ranging of all fish, is found as far north as Cape Cod, as far south as Brazil and throughout the Pacific.

Although it weighs just three pounds, *Trachinotus falcatus* is a prized food fish. Schools of pompano abound in Chesapeake Bay during late summer.

Pomatomus saltatrix, a hard-fighting game fish, travels erratically through the waters of the Middle Atlantic region. Some years it may not show up at all.

Cynoscion nebulosus, an important game and food fish, is covered with conspicuous black spots. It thrives in Chesapeake Bay during the warm weather.

Hardhead croaker

The mouth of *Micropogon undulatus* is adapted for scouring the ocean floor for shellfish and other food. The fish croaks by squeezing its air bladder.

Walleyed pike

Known in some areas as Susquehanna salmon, *Stizostedion vitreum* is noted for its large, glassy eyes. It is the largest of the pikes and is a valued food fish.

Largemouth bass

Micropterus salmoides was introduced into the Chesapeake Bay area some 80 years ago. Its fighting disposition has made it popular with anglers.

White crappie

Schools of *Pomoxis annularis* inhabit lakes and ponds, but often the young live in shallow river backwaters, where many are destroyed by autumn dry spells.

Yellow perch

Perca flavescens lives in large numbers in the ponds and lakes of the Northeast, feeding voraciously on minnows, worms and the young of other fish.

Northern brown snake

Formerly called DeKay's snake, the harmless *Storeria dekayi* thrives in any surroundings, from city park to swamp. It rarely grows longer than 16 inches.

Eastern hognose snake

Heterodon platyrhinos puts on a fierce show if disturbed, flattening its head and neck and hissing, but it is harmless and rolls over and plays dead when attacked.

Northern dusky salamander

Wide-ranging *Desmognathus fuscus*, a two-to-four-inch gray or brown salamander, is found throughout the region, from sea level to the highest hills.

Birds

Pintail duck

With its long, thin, pointed tail and slim neck, *Anas acuta* stands out from all other ducks. It has the widest breeding range of any North American duck.

Sparrow hawk

Smallest of the American falcons, *Falco sparverius* can drop swiftly from its treetop perch to attack small mammals. Falconers often train it to hunt on command.

Ruffed grouse

Bonasa umbellus, the state bird of Pennsylvania and a popular game bird, springs into the air with a startling whir of wings when flushed by dogs or hunters.

Wild turkey

Once driven from its woodland range by overshooting and forest razing, *Meleagris gallopavo* is staging a comeback with the help of wildlife management.

Sora rail

A marsh bird, *Porzana carolina* gorges on wild rice to store up fat for its fall migrations, which take it across open water to Bermuda and South America.

American coot

Also known as the mud hen, *Fulica americana* lives along lakes and rivers, sometimes taking over areas where ducks feed, much to the dismay of local hunters.

American oyster catcher

With a quick thrust of its long bill, *Haematopus palliatus* severs the shell-closing muscles of open oysters, then easily pulls out the tender meat inside.

Killdeer

Once nearly extinct, *Charadrius vociferus* is now protected by law. It feeds on destructive beetles, as well as ticks that annoy domestic animals.

Barn owl

Tyto alba, often found nesting in barns and steeples, silently hunts its prey of mice and rats by night, homing in on them with the aid of an acute sense of hearing.

Eastern belted kingfisher

Unlike most birds, the female *Megaceryle alcyon* is more colorful than the male. It prefers to live alone, fighting all kingfishers except its mate.

Barn swallow

Hirundo rustica erythrogaster is the only native U.S. swallow with a forked "swallowtail." When migrating, the bird follows rivers or coastlines.

House wren

The loud-singing *Troglodytes aedon* is better known for noise than for tunes. Preferring to nest in hollows, it seeks out birdhouses or holes in trees.

Golden-crowned kinglet

One of the smallest native U.S. birds, *Regulus satrapa* builds a nest of moss and lichens bound with spider webs, bark and roots and lined with feathers and fur.

Hooded warbler

Named for the black hood that encircles the face of the male, *Wilsonia citrina* breeds in cool ravines and hunts insects by darting about near the ground.

Baltimore oriole

The bright orange-and-black *Icterus galbula,* a familiar resident of shady elm trees, will build nests near homes if string or horsehair is left out for it to use.

Cardinal

The male *Richmondena cardinalis* is easy to identify by its flame-red color. During the winter, cardinals stop at feeding stations, nibbling on seeds.

Flowers and trees

Cattail

Typha latifolia grows in abundance around lakes and swamps, where it shelters nesting birds and provides food for geese and muskrats.

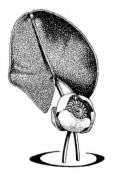

Yellow pond lily

Nuphar advena has foot-long leaves and colorful but odorless yellow flowers. It is often found floating in stagnant ponds, swamps and slow streams.

Virgin's bower

The white flowers that appear in summer on the trailing vine of *Clematis virginiana* are replaced in autumn by silky-haired fruits called "old man's beard."

Dwarf wild rose

Thriving on rocky slopes and in open forests, the *Rosa carolina* rarely grows taller than one or two feet. Birds and mammals feed on its fruit and seeds.

184

Hedge bindweed

Also known as wild morning glory, *Convolvulus sepium* sends out stems 10 feet long. It is hard to eliminate because its deep roots keep growing more stems.

Greek valerian

Clusters of bell-shaped blue (or white) flowers give *Polemonium reptans* the nickname bluebell. It is unrelated to the true valerians, a family of herbs.

Maryland golden aster

During the late summer and early autumn, *Chrysopsis mariana* turns the dry, sandy roadsides near the coast into an expanse of golden yellow.

Bouncing bet

By spreading quickly through gravelly wasteland, pink-blossomed *Saponaria officinalis* helps beautify otherwise dreary roadsides and embankments.

White pine

Although the stands of *Pinus strobus* have been reduced by overcutting and disease, this stately evergreen is still an important source of lumber.

Eastern hemlock

Tsuga canadensis creates a shade so dense that nothing will grow beneath it. The inner bark of the tree is rich in tannic acid, used for curing leather.

Bigtooth aspen

Named for the rounded teeth edging its leaves, *Populus grandidentata* quickly grows over burned-out areas. Its soft wood is used to make matches and pulp.

Black cherry

The largest native cherry, *Prunus serotina* grows to about 70 feet. Its reddish wood is used for fine furniture, and its fruit provides flavoring for syrups and extracts.

Beach plum

The round, purple fruit of *Prunus maritima*, a shrub that grows along beaches or in other sandy soil, is sweet when mature and is often used to make preserves.

Flowering dogwood

During the spring, the white *Cornus florida* blooms throughout forests in the shade of other trees. A cultivated pink variety is popular in gardens.

White ash

Fraxinus americana is a medium-sized tree, 70 to 100 feet tall, common in moist woods and along streams. Baseball bats are made from its hard wood.

American elder

Sambucus canadensis, a 6-to-10-foot shrub, is common in moist lowlands and near swamps. The dark, bitter berries are used for elderberry wine.

Statistical information

State nickname, date of admission, capital

Delaware: Diamond State; first of the original 13 states, admitted December 7, 1787; Dover.

Maryland: Called both Old Line State and Free State; seventh of the original 13 states, admitted April 28, 1788; Annapolis.

Pennsylvania: Keystone State; second of the original 13 states, admitted December 12, 1787; Harrisburg.

Population

By state (U.S. Census, 1966 preliminary estimate): Pennsylvania: 11,601,000.

Maryland: 3,611,000.

Delaware: 513,000.

By city (the region's eight largest metropolitan areas are listed below, followed by their population according to the January 1, 1968, estimate of the *Editor and Publisher Market Guide)*:

Philadelphia: 4,871,836.
Pittsburgh: 2,334,466.
Baltimore: 943,719.
Allentown: 531,823.
Harrisburg: 412,428.
Wilkes-Barre—Hazleton: 321,990.
York: 312,852.
Lancaster: 303,133.

Land areas

Pennsylvania: 45,333 square miles.
Maryland: 10,577 square miles.
Delaware: 2,057 square miles.

Principal rivers (total lengths in miles)

Ohio (Pennsylvania): 981.

Susquehanna (Pennsylvania, Maryland): 444.

Allegheny (Pennsylvania): 325.

Delaware (Delaware, Pennsylvania): 280.

Genesee (Pennsylvania): 144.

Schuylkill (Pennsylvania): 131.

Some Middle Atlantic superlatives

Pennsylvania is the country's largest producer of iron and steel, accounting for 24.4 per cent of the U.S. total and housing a third of the nation's steel mills.

Pennsylvania ranked first in the manufacturing of shoes in 1966, with 90,590,000 pairs.

Pennsylvania produces almost all of the nation's anthracite coal and ranked third in bituminous coal in 1966.

Pennsylvania ranks first in

Agricultural statistics (1964)

	Number of farms	Total acreage	Principal commodities
Delaware	4,401	717,013	Corn, soybeans, potatoes, hay.
Maryland	20,760	3,180,696	Corn, hay, tobacco, soybeans.
Pennsylvania	83,086	10,803,983	Hay, corn, potatoes, wheat.

Mineral production (1966)

	In thousands of dollars	Principal minerals in order of value
Delaware	1,980	Sand and gravel, stone, clays.
Maryland	74,161	Stone, sand and gravel, cement.
Pennsylvania	903,408	Coal, cement, stone, sand and gravel.

sausage products, scrapple, pretzels, cigar-filler tobacco and plantation-grown Christmas trees.

Pittsburgh is home to the world's largest manufacturers of aluminum, steel rolls, rolling-mill machinery, air brakes, plate and window glass, and safety equipment.

The first U.S. steam locomotive, Peter Cooper's *Tom Thumb*, was built in Baltimore, making its first run on the tracks of the Baltimore and Ohio Railroad in 1830.

Delaware leads the nation in chemical production.

Pronunciation glossary

Aliquippa (al uh QUIP pah). Borough on the Ohio River northwest of Pittsburgh; also major installation of Jones & Laughlin Steel Company.
Allegheny (AL uh GAY nee). Great steel center in western Pennsylvania; also a 500-mile-long mountain range extending from north-central Pennsylvania to southwest Virginia and a river in Pennsylvania and New York.
Amish (AH mish). Strict

Protestant sect, followers of the Swiss Mennonite Bishop, Jacob Amman, that settled in America.
Bryn Mawr (BRIN mar). Philadelphia suburb; seat of Bryn Mawr College.
Charleroi (SHAR le roy). Borough on the Monongahela River, southwest Pennsylvania.
Conshohocken (con sha HOCK en). Industrial borough on Schuylkill River, southeast Pennsylvania.

de Nemours (deh ne MOORS). Formal last name, taken from French town of Nemours, of original members of the du Pont family to settle in the U.S.
Duquesne (doo CANE). City in southwest Pennsylvania, site of major installation of U.S. Steel.
Eleuthère Irénée du Pont (AH looth AIR EAR a nay). Founder of the Du Pont Company.
Mauch Chunk (MAWK CHUNK). Anthracite mining borough, recently renamed for football great Jim Thorpe, on the Lehigh River in eastern Pennsylvania.

Monongahela (mo non ga HEE la). River in Pennsylvania and West Virginia; also manufacturing city in southwest Pennsylvania.
Schuylkill (SCHOOL kill). River and county in eastern Pennsylvania; pronounced SKOO kull by some Philadelphians.
Susquehanna (SUS que HAN ah). River and county in Pennsylvania.
Tilghman (TILL mun). Town and island in Maryland.
Wissahickon (wish a HICK un). Valley and creek in Philadelphia area.

Credits and acknowledgments

Maps for front and back end papers by Jeppesen & Company, Denver, Colorado. Maps on pages 174 through 179 © by The H. M. Gousha Company, San Jose, California. Map on page 57 by Lothar Roth.

The sources for the illustrations that appear in this book are shown below. Credits for the pictures from left to right are separated by commas, from top to bottom by dashes.
Cover—Robert Walch.
Front end papers—Drawings by Richard Boland.
Chapter 1: 8—Alois K. Strobl courtesy Philadelphia City Planning Commission. 14—Map

by Lowell Hess. 19 through 29—Richard Noble.
Chapter 2: 30, 31—Pennsylvania Historical and Museum Commission, Harrisburg (2). 34—Adapted from *The Plan for Center City Philadelphia*; Philadelphia City Planning Commission, 1963. 37—Jane Latta from Nancy Palmer. 38—The Bettmann Archive, drawings by Otto Van Eersel courtesy The New York Public Library (4). 43—Henry Groskinsky courtesy the Baltimore Museum of Art. 44—

Prints Division of The New York Public Library—courtesy The Henry Francis du Pont Winterthur Museum. 45—Courtesy The Henry Francis du Pont Winterthur Museum, Henry Groskinsky courtesy Mrs. Ferdinand C. Latrobe—Henry Groskinsky, courtesy Library of The Franklin Institute, Philadelphia. 46—Henry Groskinsky—Charles Phillips courtesy Metropolitan Museum of Art Library—Henry Groskinsky. 47—Courtesy The Henry Francis du Pont Winterthur

Museum—Henry Groskinsky. 48 —Courtesy The Historical Society of Pennsylvania—*Cabinet-Maker and Upholsterer's Drawing-Book,* by Thomas Sheraton, 1802. 49— Henry Groskinsky courtesy Metropolitan Museum of Art Library—Henry Groskinsky, courtesy Lewis Collection of the Smithsonian Institution; courtesy The Henry Francis du Pont Winterthur Museum. 50— Charles Phillips courtesy The Metropolitan Museum of Art, Bequest of Mrs. May Leask, 1916 —The Henry Francis du Pont Winterthur Museum. 51— Courtesy The Henry Francis du Pont Winterthur Museum (4). 52, 53—Courtesy Independence National Historic Park, Philadelphia; Commissioners of Fairmount Park courtesy Philadelphia Museum of Art, Pennsylvania Academy of The Fine Arts. Chapter 3: 54—Joseph Nettis. 58, 59—Drawings by Gaetano di Palma. 60, 61—Drawing by Otto Van Eersel. 63—Courtesy Warren J. Harder and Buchart-Horn. 67 —Carnegie Library, Pittsburgh— Culver Pictures, Inc. 68, 69—No credit, The Bettmann Archive, Carnegie Library, Pittsburgh—E. M. Newman from Wide World, The New York Public Library— Walker Evans for FORTUNE. 70, 71—Carnegie Library, Pittsburgh; Brown Brothers, Culver Pictures, Inc. (2), Brown Brothers—© The Frick Collection, New York (3). 72, 73—Fairchild Aerial Survey, Culver Pictures, Inc. (2), Brown Brothers (2)—Walt Sanders from Black Star, The Pierpont Morgan Library—Culver Pictures, Inc. 74—Emil J. Kloes from *The Pittsburgh Survey* courtesy Russell Sage Foundation, Culver Pictures, Inc. —Brown Brothers. 75—Pacific and Atlantic Photos, Inc.—The Bettmann Archive. 76—Culver Pictures, Inc., Brown Brothers— International News Photos. 77— Carnegie Library, Pittsburgh. Chapter 4: 78, 79—T. F. Healy Collection. 83 through 85— Culver Pictures, Inc. 87—Culver Pictures, Inc.—United Press International—*United Mine Workers Journal,* Wide World Photos. 91 through 101—Song excerpts from the Archive of American Folk Song, Library of Congress. 91—Brown Brothers. 92, 93—*The Pittsburgh Survey* courtesy Russell Sage Foundation —Ewing Galloway for FORTUNE. 94—Lewis W. Hine from *The*

Pittsburgh Survey courtesy Russell Sage Foundation. 95— Wyoming Historical and Geological Society, Wilkes-Barre, Pa.—Brown Brothers. 96—Lewis W. Hine from *The Pittsburgh Survey* courtesy Russell Sage Foundation. 97—*The Pittsburgh Survey* courtesy Russell Sage Foundation. 98—Wyoming Historical and Geological Society, Wilkes-Barre, Pa.—*The Pittsburgh Survey* courtesy Russell Sage Foundation. 99— *The Pittsburgh Survey* courtesy Russell Sage Foundation. 100, 101—Lewis W. Hine courtesy George Eastman House Collection. Chapter 5: 102, 103—Ray Kline from Associated Photographers, Pittsburgh. 106—Margaret Bourke-White. 107—Charles Rotkin for Photography for Industry. 109—Margaret Bourke-White. 111—Alois K. Strobl courtesy Philadelphia City Planning Commission, except for top left and bottom right Lawrence S. Williams, Inc. 113 through 125—Richard Noble. Chapter 6: 126—Cornell Capa for LIFE. 130, 131—E. I. du Pont de Nemours & Company, Wilmington. 134—No credit. 137—James Amos. 138, 139— The Bettmann Archive (2)— Robert Phillips. 140, 141 —Adapted by Matt Greene from *Boating* by permission Ziff-Davis Publishing Company, © 1965— David Q. Scott. 142—Brown Brothers—map by Gaetano di Palma. 143—The Bettmann Archive—David Q. Scott. 144, 145—Culver Pictures, Inc.(2)— M. E. Warren (2). 146, 147— Robert de Gast—The Mariners Museum, Newport News, Va., drawings by Matt Greene. 148, 149—Map by Gaetano di Palma —A. Aubrey Bodine. Chapter 7: 150—Leonard Schugar from Black Star for FORTUNE. 154—Culver Pictures, Inc. (2). 157—*Rankings of the States,* 1967; National Education Association, © 1967. 159— Peter Stackpole. 161 through 173—Steinbicker/Houghton. 182 through 185—Drawings by Rudolf Freund. Back end papers—Drawings by Richard Boland.

The editors of this book especially wish to thank Mary Cadwalader of Joppa, Maryland, for her assistance in its preparation. They also wish to acknowledge the help of the following persons and

institutions: American Iron and Steel Institute, New York City; Herbert B. Anstaett, Franklin and Marshall College, Lancaster; Frederic L. Ballard, Philadelphia; John J. Balles, Senior Vice President, Mellon National Bank & Trust Company, Pittsburgh; Whitfield J. Bell, American Philosophical Society, Philadelphia; William Boucher, Executive Director, Greater Baltimore Committee; Catherine Drinker Bowen, Haverford; Elbert T. Chance, University of Delaware, Newark; Senator Joseph S. Clark Jr., Pennsylvania; John Corcoran, Executive Vice President, Consolidation Coal Company, Pittsburgh; Victor C. Diehm, President, Station WAZL, Hazleton; Dudley P. Digges, *Baltimore Sun;* Richardson Dilworth, ex-Mayor, Philadelphia; Professor Rhoda M. Dorsey, Goucher College, Baltimore; Major General George M. Gelston, Adjutant General of Maryland, Baltimore; David L. Glenn, Director, Baltimore Community Relations Commission; John J. Grove, Assistant Director, Allegheny Conference on Community Development; Professor Samuel P. Hays, University of Pittsburgh; Jerold Hoffberger, Baltimore Orioles; Professor Edgar M. Hoover, University of Pittsburgh; Sidney Horenstein, Department of Fossil Invertebrates, American Museum of Natural History, New York City; Charles F. Hummel, Winterthur Museum, Delaware; Wilbur H. Hunter, Director, The Peale Museum, Baltimore; Rex W. Lauck, Assistant Editor, *United Mine Workers Journal,* Washington, D.C.; Robert C. McCormack, Special Assistant to Governor Raymond P. Shafer, Harrisburg; Representative Joseph M. McDade, Pennsylvania; Theodore R. McKeldin, ex-Governor, Maryland; Edward Magee, former Executive Director, Allegheny Conference on Community Development, Pittsburgh; Professor Hugo V. Mailey, Wilkes College, Wilkes-Barre; Sidney Marland, Superintendent of Schools, Pittsburgh; Martin L. Millspaugh, Charles Center-Inner Harbor Management, Inc., Baltimore; Mr. and Mrs. Claude Oldt, Sinking Spring, Pennsylvania; George F. O'Neil, Pinkerton's, Inc., New York City; Frederic A. Potts, Chairman of the Board, The Philadelphia National

Bank; R. Stewart Rauch Jr., President, Philadelphia Saving Fund Society; Norman Robertson, Vice President, Mellon National Bank & Trust Company, Pittsburgh; Allan C. Rusten, Associate Executive Director, Greater Wilmington Development Council; Adolph Schmidt, Vice President and Governor, T. Mellon & Sons, Pittsburgh; David Q. Scott, U.S. Naval Institute, Annapolis; William Scranton, ex-Governor, Pennsylvania; Governor Raymond P. Shafer, Pennsylvania; Walter Sondheim, Senior Vice President and Treasurer, Hochschild, Kohn & Company, Baltimore; W. Laird Stabler, State Representative, Delaware; William Stephens, President, Jones & Laughlin Steel Company, Aliquippa; Vernon D. Stotts, Maryland Waterfowl Biologist, Annapolis; the Reverend Leon Sullivan, Zion Baptist Church, Philadelphia; John K. Tabor, Secretary, Pennsylvania Department of Internal Affairs, Harrisburg; Lester Trott, Maryland Department of Economic Development; Mrs. G. A. Van Lennep Jr., Chesapeake Bay Maritime Museum, St. Michaels; William Willcox, Executive Vice President, Greater Philadelphia Movement; Edwin Wolf, Library Company of Philadelphia; Professor N. Gordon Wolman, Johns Hopkins University, Baltimore; Joseph Yenchko, Director, Industrial Development, CAN DO, Inc., Hazleton.

The editors would also like to thank members of the following organizations, educational institutions and companies. The Du Pont Company, Wilmington: Harold A. Brown Jr., John J. Burchenal, Theodore Cairns, Myron Emanuel, James A. Grady, Robert C. McCuen, G. Gordon Mitchell, Alexander Murphy, Henry Rothrock, Jurg A. Schneider and W. Rice Yahner. The Pennsylvania Railroad: Howard A. Gilbert, Cecil G. Muldoon, George R. Wallace. Philadelphia City Planning Commission: Edmund Bacon, Else Marks, Alois Strobl. The U.S. Steel Corporation: George Hess, J. Warren Shaver, Kenneth L. Vore. University of Pennsylvania: President Gaylord P. Harnwell; Professors Thomas C. Cochran, Wallace E. Davies, Donald Yoder.

Bibliography

* Available also in paperback.
† Available only in paperback.

General and historical reading

Allen, Frederick Lewis, *The Big Change.** Harper & Row, 1952.

Baltzell, Edward D., *Philadelphia Gentlemen.** Macmillan, 1958.

Bowen, Catherine Drinker, *Miracle at Philadelphia.* Little, Brown, 1966.

Bridenbaugh, Carl:
*Cities in Revolt: Urban Life in America 1743-1776.** Knopf, 1955.
*Cities in the Wilderness.** Knopf, 1955.

Bridenbaugh, Carl and Jessica, *Rebels and Gentlemen: Philadelphia in the Age of Franklin.** Reynal & Hitchcock, 1942.

Burnett, Edmund C., *The Continental Congress.*† Norton, 1964.

Dulles, Foster Rhea, *Labor in America.* Crowell, 1966.

Green, Constance Mcl., *The Rise of Urban America.** Harper & Row, 1965.

Jensen, Merrill, *The New Nation.** Knopf, 1950.

Morison, Samuel Eliot, and Henry Steele Commager, *The Growth of the American Republic,* Vol. 1 and 2. Oxford University Press, 1962.

Nettels, Curtis P., *The Roots of American Civilization.* Appleton-Century-Crofts, 1963.

Paullin, Charles O., *Atlas of the Historical Geography of the United States.* Carnegie Institution of Washington and American Geographical Society of New York, 1932.

Stevens, Sylvester K., *Pennsylvania: Birthplace of a Nation.** Random House, 1964.

Taft, Philip, *Organized Labor in American History.* Harper & Row, 1964.

Van Doren, Carl, *The Great Rehearsal.** Viking Press, 1948.

Special topics

Adamic, Louis, *Dynamite, the Story of Class Violence in America.* Peter Smith, 1959.

Alinsky, Saul, *John L. Lewis.* Putnam, 1949.

Allen, Frederick Lewis:
*The Great Pierpont Morgan.** Harper, 1949.
*The Lords of Creation.** Harper, 1935.

Beirne, Francis F., *The Amiable Baltimoreans.* Dutton, 1951.

Brewington, Marion V., *Chesapeake Bay; A Pictorial Maritime History.* Cornell Maritime Press, 1956.

Brody, David:
*Labor in Crisis: The Steel Strike of 1919.** Lippincott, 1965.
Steelworkers in America. Harvard University Press, 1960.

Brooks, Robert R. R., *As Steel Goes, ...* Yale University Press, 1940.

Brophy, John, *A Miner's Life: An Autobiography.* University of Wisconsin Press, 1964.

Carr, William H., *The Du Ponts of Delaware.* Dodd, Mead, 1964.

Chandler, Alfred D., Jr., *Strategy and Structure.** M.I.T. Press, 1962.

Coleman, McAlister, *Men and Coal.* Farrar and Rinehart, 1943.

Connett, Eugene V., *Duck Shooting Along the Atlantic Tidewater.* Morrow, 1947.

Davis, Horace B., *Labor and Steel.* International Publishers, 1933.

Dorian, Max, *The du Ponts: From Gunpowder to Nylon.* Little, Brown, 1962.

Dutton, William S., *Du Pont One Hundred and Forty Years.* Scribner, 1942.

Fisher, Douglas A.:
The Epic of Steel. Harper & Row, 1963.
Steel Serves the Nation 1901-1951: The Fifty Year Story of U.S. Steel. United States Steel Corporation, 1951.

Goodrich, Carter L., and others, *Canals and American Economic Development.* Columbia University Press, 1961.

Harvey, George, *Henry Clay Frick, the Man.* Scribner, 1928.

Hendrick, Burton J., *The Life of Andrew Carnegie.* 2 vols. Doubleday, 1932.

Holbrook, Stewart H., *Age of Moguls.** Doubleday, 1953.

Howland, Richard H., and Eleanor Patterson Spencer, *The Architecture of Baltimore.* Johns Hopkins Press, 1953.

Josephson, Matthew, *The Robber Barons.** Harcourt, Brace and World, 1934.

Kauffman, Henry J., *Pennsylvania Dutch American Folk Art.** Hobby House Press, 1964.

Klees, Frederic, *The Pennsylvania Dutch.* Macmillan, 1950.

Larkin, Oliver W., *Art and Life in America.* Holt, Rinehart and Winston, 1966.

Levinson, Edward, *Labor on the March.* Harper, 1938.

Lorant, Stefan, ed., *Pittsburgh: The Story of an American City.* Doubleday, 1964.

Lowe, Jeanne R., *Cities in a Race with Time.* Random House, 1967.

McGannon, Harold E., ed., *The Making, Shaping and Treating of Steel.* United States Steel Corporation, 1964.

Montgomery, Charles F., *American Furniture of the Federal Period.* Viking Press, 1966.

Morrison, Hugh, *Early American Architecture.* Oxford University Press, 1952.

O'Connor, Harvey:
Mellon's Millions. Day, 1933.
Steel-Dictator. Day, 1935.

Owens, Hamilton, *Baltimore on the Chesapeake.* Doubleday, Doran, 1941.

Pittsburgh Regional Planning Association, *Economic Study of the Pittsburgh Region.* 4 vols. University of Pittsburgh Press, 1963.

Reichley, James, *The Art of Government.*† The Fund for the Republic, 1959.

Schroeder, Gertrude G., *The Growth of the Major Steel Companies, 1900-1950.* Johns Hopkins Press, 1953.

Sheppard, Muriel E., *Cloud by Day.* University of North Carolina Press, 1947.

Sulzberger, C. L., *Sit Down with John L. Lewis.* Random House, 1938.

Tarbell, Ida M., *The Life of Elbert H. Gary.* D. Appleton, 1925.

Van Doren, Carl, *Benjamin Franklin; A Biography.** Viking Press, 1956.

Van Doren, Carl, ed., *Benjamin Franklin's Autobiographical Writings.* Viking Press, 1945.

Velie, Lester, *Labor U.S.A.* Harper, 1958.

Whitbeck, Ray Hughes, and V. C. Finch, *Economic Geography, a Regional Survey.* McGraw-Hill, 1941.

White, C. Langdon, and Edwin J. Foscue, *Regional Geography of Anglo-America.* Prentice-Hall, 1955.

Wilstach, Paul, *Tidewater Maryland.* Bobbs-Merrill, 1931.

Wyckoff, Jerome, *The Story of Geology.* Golden Press, 1960.

Natural setting and wildlife

Barker, Will, *Familiar Reptiles and Amphibians of America.* Harper & Row, 1964.

Doutt, J. Kenneth, *Mammals of Pennsylvania.* Pennsylvania Game Commission, 1967.

Fenneman, Nevin M., *Physiography of the Eastern United States.* McGraw-Hill, 1948.

Hylander, Clarence J., *Wild Flower Book.* Macmillan, 1954.

Kortright, Francis H., *The Ducks, Geese and Swans of North America.* Stackpole Books, 1953.

Luttringer, Leo A., Jr., *Pennsylvania Birdlife.* Pennsylvania Game Commission, 1966.

Matthews, F. Schuyler, *Field Book of American Trees and Shrubs.* Putnam, 1915.

Palmer, Ralph S., *The Mammal Guide.* Doubleday, 1954.

Peterson, Roger Tory, *A Field Guide to the Birds.* Houghton Mifflin, 1947.

Guidebooks

Delaware Writers' Project, *Delaware: A Guide to the First State.* Hastings House, 1955.

Fodor, Eugene, ed., *Fodor Shell Travel Guides U.S.A.; Mid-Atlantic.*† McKay, 1966.

Maryland Writers' Project, *Maryland: A Guide to the Old Line State.* Oxford University Press, 1940.

Mulkearn, Lois, and Edwin V. Pugh, *A Traveler's Guide to Historic Western Pennsylvania.* University of Pittsburgh Press, 1954.

Pennsylvania Writers' Project, *Pennsylvania: A Guide to the Keystone State.* Oxford University Press, 1940.

x

PRODUCTION STAFF FOR TIME INCORPORATED

John L. Hallenbeck (Vice President and Director of Production), Robert E. Foy and Caroline Ferri

Text photocomposed under the direction of Albert J. Dunn and Arthur J. Dunn

The Middle Atlantic States: the works of man

The total land area of the Middle Atlantic States is 57,967 square miles, less than 2 per cent of the U.S., but the region contains 8 per cent of the country's population. The land is so densely settled that more than two thirds is urban; only in north-central Pennsylvania does the population thin out to less than 130 people per square mile.

Economic activity in this region is diversified, ranging from locomotive manufacturing to chocolate making. Pennsylvania is the nation's largest iron and steel producer, accounting for one quarter of the total U.S. output. The state also mines most of the nation's anthracite coal. Maryland, in addition to manufacturing nuclear equipment and canning

25 per cent of the country's tomatoes, has a large fishing industry, selling an average of 14 million dollars' worth of seafood each year. Delaware's major industry is chemicals. Like Pennsylvania and Maryland, it is rich in farm products. Crisscrossing the area is a network of rivers and railroads, providing the states with efficient, inexpensive transportation.

Historical monuments, such as 225-year-old Independence Hall *(above)* in Philadelphia, where the Declaration of Independence was adopted and the Constitution drafted, are plentiful in the three Middle Atlantic States. A strategic area during the nation's struggle for independence, the region is a veritable museum in itself.